RUTH JACKSON, M.D.:
A LIFE ON THE LEADING EDGE

Patsy Mayes Jackson

BookSurge Publishing
2007

Ruth Jackson, M.D.: A Life on the
Leading Edge
Copyright 2006 by Patsy Mayes Jackson
All rights reserved

No part of this publication may be
copied in any manner or form, except
for brief portions for review purposes,
without expressed written permission
from the author.

Catalog in Publishing Data

Jackson, Patsy Mayes

    I.   Jackson, Ruth, M.D. II.
        Crthopedists—Texas—Biography
   III. Physicians—United States—20th
   Century IV. Medicine--Orthopedics

RD 728 J692   615.328 J

This book is dedicated to my husband, Paul Jackson, who from the beginning of our life together, encouraged me always to spread my wings and fly.

Foreword

A list of Board-certified female orthopaedic surgeons would claim that I was the 75th woman to gain Board certification in orthopaedic surgery. It makes it sound like I was a pioneer. But numbers don't tell the whole story. There was a lifetime, really two lifetimes, between the first woman to earn Board certification, Ruth Jackson, and myself. Ruth Jackson entered orthopaedic practice in 1932, and, despite her extraordinary clinical practice, landmark articles, and pioneering inventions, over 50 years passed before there were enough women in the field to form a society.

I'll never forget the first time I met Ruth Jackson. It was my last year of orthopaedic residency. I was attending the annual meeting of the American Academy of Orthopaedic Surgeons in order to try to figure out this profession I was struggling to join. As I wandered around, some blessed soul asked me if I was coming to the first-ever women's lunch. There was talk of forming a support group, she said.

I had not received the memo announcing this event. Should I go? I was somewhere between scared and giddy. What would these other women be like? Fierce competitors? Athletic giants? Geniuses? Potential friends? Luckily, I overcame my fears and went. And what a joyous surprise. About 40 well-dressed, articulate, orthopaedics-loving women were gathered together to talk about forming a support group. Everyone was friendly, positive, and gung ho. I had found my orthopaedic home.

But the real treat was Ruth Jackson herself. I remember her, addressing us in her trademark mink stole, waving her cane, and shaking her finger at us. She was about 80 at the time, but still far from retirement. In her own words, she said, "I'm not operating anymore, but I'm still busy enough to keep four girls busy in the office."

I was hooked then and there. Here was a woman who loved what she did so much that she was still doing it at age 80! And she was still willing to support and encourage the folks behind her! And despite the fact that she had practiced in an era when brawn was a critical component of the practice of orthopaedic surgery, at 4'10", she was even shorter than I, and much more petite.

Unfortunately, few of us present at that landmark meeting had the opportunity to know Ruth on a personal level. We were all fairly young, and she was, quite honestly, most intimidating. But all of us continue to celebrate her career and her perseverance, and we are grateful for her leadership.

Patsy Mayes Jackson, Ruth's niece, opens the first chapter of this book with a quote from Thoughts to Ponder: "Do not follow where the path may lead, go instead where there is no path and leave a trail." Ruth Jackson certainly had no path, and those of us who have followed have been challenged to live up to her extraordinary record of accomplishment. Ruth demonstrated that women, a group historically excluded from orthopaedics, could indeed not only participate but succeed. She demonstrated that skill, diagnostic ability, and ingenuity were more important than physical strength. Her book, *The Cervical Syndrome*, originally published in 1958, went on to four editions and is still available on the Web. By the life she led, and the things she achieved, Ruth left a trail that encouraged the women behind her to excel in orthopaedics.

It is important, moreover, not only to celebrate Ruth but the entire Jackson family. Ruth was the symbol and the pioneer, but it was Patsy Mayes Jackson who really made the Ruth Jackson Orthopaedic Society happen. In the early years, the RJOS consisted of an annual luncheon organized by a few dedicated souls. As the Society's second treasurer, I would roam about the AAOS annual meetings looking for women, confirming they were orthopaedic surgeons, and then begging them to pay dues. I was thrilled the year I signed up a record 40 members.

Patsy, who attended all these early meetings, quickly recognized that all of us were struggling to have careers and manage households, and that remedial help was desperately needed if the RJOS was to survive and thrive. She volunteered to take us on. Suddenly, we had a mailing list, a newsletter, and even a dues statement. Our paying membership soared to over 140 almost overnight! She knew us all by name, encouraged us, and acted as general listening post and den mother as we learned the ropes of building a fledgling organization. Make no mistake: Ruth gave us a rallying point, but Patsy was the Ruth Jackson Orthopaedic Society's fairy godmother.

A special thanks is due to Patsy's granddaughter, Lauren Rogers Hicks. In the early years, Lauren helped Patsy care for Ruth. More recently she has served as Patsy's traveling companion, and, of course, our cheerleader.

Much has been written about how isolating our society can be. Titles like "The Loneliness of the Long Distance Runner" and "Bowling Alone" conjure up images of separation and isolation that are frightening and depressing. Thanks in large part to Ruth, Patsy, and Lauren, I can say firmly that I have never felt that way in orthopaedics. Instead, I have felt as though I was part of an exciting and forward-thinking profession that cares deeply about improving musculoskeletal health for all Americans. Thanks in large part to Patsy's efforts, the Ruth Jackson Orthopaedic Society has survived and thrived, giving me several hundred friends and colleagues to care about. I may not know all the intimate details of their lives, but we have a most remarkable bond, thanks to the pioneering work of Ruth Jackson.

                Laura Lowe Tosi, M.D.
                Washington, D.C.

ACKNOWLEDGEMENTS

There are many people to thank for making this book possible. In addition to Jim Mathis, who allowed me journalistic freedom to write; the person who taught me all I know about journalism, Harry Quin, managing editor of the Daily Review and journalism professor at The University of Texas at Pan American, in Edinburg; Betty Harwell, English teacher at Edinburg High School and The University of Texas at Pan American, who set me back on the right path; were friends and mentors who didn't live to read this book.

All of those who so graciously allowed me to interview them on tape or gave me written accounts of their memories of their own lives and Ruth's: Sheri Lazalrere, Lucy Bentley*, Jeani Hill, Carole Gordon, M. D., Ed Hall, M.D., Leon Ware, M.D., Paul Goodfried, M.D., Theda Dowell, M.D., Tru Wilhelm, Ruth Smith, Penny Nichols Peterson, Mary Jo Todaro, Lucy Jones, friends and co-workers; Tommie Lee Fields, therapist, Mary Barr, receptionist; Walter Charette, business manager; Kieth (sic) Jackson, O.N. "Tip"

Jackson, Darrell Jackson, Barney Jackson, Pauline Bellcock Wasson, James Bellcock and Mabel Mundy Jackson, nephews, niece and sister-in-law, Harold Brehm, brother-in-law; to the staff at the Archives of the Special Collection on Women in Medicine, Drexel University College of Medicine in Philadelphia, Pennsylvania where some of Ruth's records and memorabilia are stored; and to those whose names, noted with a *, I had to change to comply with the recent Health in Information Privacy Protection Act.

Special thanks to Dr. Kathleen Hudson, author and English professor at Schreiner University in Kerrville, Texas for guiding me to Mindy Reed, Author's Assistant, who edited, and eased me through the hard parts of publishing and to lawyer and friend, Richard P. Hill.

Thanks also to Ann Washington, licensed professional counselor, former Director of Research/Evaluation at the McAllen Independent School District and member of the Valley By-Liners Club, for her advice; grandson-in-law, Jason Hicks, who designed the book cover; Olive Penry, and Dorothy Foreman, their input. And of course, my family: husband, Paul, daughters, Janis Jackson Rogers and her husband, the late Mike Rogers; Paulanna Jackson Watson and her husband, Steven; and grandchildren, Lauren Rogers Hicks, who went with Ruth and me to RJOS meetings; and Paul Rene Rogers, who helped stuff newsletters when he and Lauren were little; for all their unfailing support.

Last but definitely, not least, my other family, all the members, past and present, of the Ruth Jackson Orthopaedic Society, who kept me inspired, with special thanks to Laura Tosi, M.D., Helen Horstmann, M.D. Rosemarie Morwessel, M.D., Mary Ann Keenan M.D., Mary Lloyd Ireland, M.D., Diane Gilles, M.D., Alice Martinson, M.D., Peggy Naas, M.D., Janet Walker, M.D., Holly Duck, M.D., Diana Carr, M.D. and Suzanne Ray, M.D.

PREFACE

I met Ruth Jackson for the first time in 1948 when my fiancé, her nephew, Paul Jackson, Jr., took me to Dallas for the famous Cotton Bowl football weekend. He informed me that "my aunt, the doctor," (as everyone in the family called Ruth) had invited us to her home for cocktails. An instant rapport and my fascination with her struggle, sacrifice and triumph to become the first board certified Orthopaedic surgeon began that night.

After I retired from my job as Woman's Page Editor of the *Edinburg Daily Review*, I decided, in 1986, that I would write Ruth's biography for the members of the Jackson extended family. I spent many hours at her Turtle Creek home combing through her papers, pictures and taping interviews with friends, family members, her peers and staff: recording memories. Trips with her to the American Academy of Orthopaedic Surgeons Meetings from one coast to the other introduced me to members of the newly formed Ruth Jackson Orthopaedic Society. I have used the Latin spelling of "orthopaedic" in deference to the medical community.

The publisher of the *Edinburg Daily Review*, Jim Mathis told me "don't research forever; Write!", but neither of us counted on my becoming an active part of the Ruth Jackson Orthopaedic Society. My work helping keep computer records for them and publishing and writing their newsletter for several years added a few years and a different scope to the biography. The following chapters are comprised of personal interviews, letters and documents. This is not an academic treatise, but a factual testament to a remarkable woman. Each chapter begins with an affirmation from *Thoughts to Ponder*, a journal Ruth kept of her personal thoughts and observations.

"Do not follow where the path may lead, go instead where there is no path and leave a trail!"

INTRODUCTION

When Dr. Ruth Jackson of Dallas, the first woman to be Board Certified as an Orthopaedic surgeon, and Sara Horstmann of Philadelphia met in February 1986 at the 53rd annual meeting of the American Academy of Orthopaedic Surgeons, the significance of the meeting was apparent only to a few persons. Dr. Jackson, 83, was attending her 47th meeting.

It was the first for Sara, the three-week old daughter of Dr. Helen Horstmann, Chief of Pediatric Orthopaedic at the Medical College of Pennsylvania. This was in a stark contrast to the first six meetings Dr. Jackson had attended from 1937 to 1943 when she was the only female member. When the American Academy of Orthopaedic Surgery was formed in 1933, no practicing women orthopaedists were taken into the organization. Dr. Jackson's determination allowed her to overcome the obstacles set forth by family, the medical profession and society of the 1920s. In attaining her goal, a path in orthopaedic surgery was made for Sara's mother to follow. Realizing the social mores of the 1920s might prohibit combining marriage and children with a medical career, Dr. Jackson chose medicine and orthopaedic surgery instead of family life. Her patients have become her extended family.

Dr. Jackson was on the leading edge of the modern thrust of women in medicine. Her journey to become an orthopaedic surgeon paved, in a small way, the path for future generations of women orthopaedists. Her success was evident in 1983 when the Ruth Jackson Society, later renamed the Ruth Jackson Orthopaedic Society, was organized. Composed of women orthopaedists, the Ruth Jackson Society, of which Dr. Horstmann was treasurer the year she attended with her three-week-old daughter, was established as a networking organization to provide role models and help future medical students interested in orthopaedics attain their goals.

When Dr. Jackson passed her Board

exams at the fifth annual meeting of AAOS in Cleveland, Ohio in 1937, she was the only woman to take the exam. It would be six years before another woman was admitted to AAOS and another 30 years before the number of women orthopaedists would reach sixteen. By 1994 with approximately 19,000 members,[i] the largest organization of orthopaedic surgeons in the world had only 237 female members. Prior to her death, August 28, 1994, Dr. Jackson felt a deep satisfaction knowing that the largest group of 32 women orthopaedists had become board certified that year.

"Every successful partnership (marriage or others) is achieved by cooperation and desires. Indestructible, unquestionable belief in the end result in achievement. 'Adelante, siempre, adelante"'.

CHAPTER I

In Dallas, Texas during the early 1940s, when there were few women doctors and all doctors made house calls, there was a rumor flying through the halls of Baylor University Medical Center that one of the women physicians had been raped. After much speculation among the staff about whom it could have been, one doctor was heard to say, "Well, it wasn't Ruth Jackson. She would have killed him." Whether she would have is open to debate. That she could have was a given. A crack shot, Ruth, only 5'2", was an avid hunter and outdoors woman. Licensed to carry a pistol, Ruth had one in the glove compartment of her car until she had to quit driving in the 1980s. Then it was transferred permanently, to her bedside table at her home on Turtle Creek.

Ruth was accustomed to standing

up for herself; something she had been doing since she was a child. With a natural instinct for daring, and the determination to follow through with anything she did, Ruth Jackson took on the quest to become a doctor in an era when women were supposed to sit home and sip tea. She defied her father, who thought it unladylike; the University of Texas system, which discouraged women in any field it considered to be for "men only" and the medical hierarchy who thought women would make great nurses but not doctors.

Her father, William Riley Jackson, didn't approve of her choice of studies. When informed of her decision to study pre-med, he stated emphatically, "I think NOT." Enlisting the help of her mother, Belle, Ruth charmed and cajoled him until he gave in.

As far as conquering the Baylor Medical school system, she just kept attending class even though there were only three other female medical students to give her moral support. She persevered, even though the professor greeted the four the first day of

Ruth Jackson, M.D.: A Life on the Leading Edge

medical school by informing them that the women would have to make ten points more than the men to pass their courses.

Later in her resident programs and throughout her first years of practice, she concentrated on perfecting her work, earning the respect of her fellow physicians. Medicine was her goal. Medicine became her life.

But the "true grit" that helped her achieve her goals didn't begin there. It began in her early childhood on a farm in Iowa.

"It is work that gives flavor to life if you like it."

CHAPTER II

Some historians call the first thirteen years of the twentieth century, "the calm before the storm." The only known wars were minor conflicts in China and South Africa, far removed from the peaceful American Midwest. The population and scientific explosions which would be, in part, responsible for the demoralizing of established family at the turn of the century were just beginning. The women's movement, begun in the 19th century, would not make decided gains until the late 1920s. It was a time when ties to the family and the land were still strong. It was in this atmosphere that Mary Ruth Jackson was born on a farm near Jefferson, Greene County, Iowa, on December 13, 1902.

Her parents, Caroline Arabelle Babb and William Riley Jackson, started their married life July 22, 1886 with a team of horses, still owing for one, and the $50 given to them by the bride's father, Valentine Babb. Mr. Babb was the first Justice of the Peace in Greene County, Iowa having settled in a log cabin in what was then Washington Township June 22, 1850.[ii] Her father, W.R. had no formal education; however, he possessed an astute business sense. His family always said he was, "quite a horse trader." He soon parlayed his stake into extensive land holdings, owning land in Canada as well as his 500 acres in Iowa.

His wife was known to her family and friends as "Belle." Belle was a gentle, soft-spoken woman, with an inherent love of God and care for mankind. Family stories tell of being descended from a John Greene, a surgeon of Salisbury, England who sailed from Hampton, England in the ship *James*, April 5, 1635, to Boston to make his home in a land where he could worship God according to his own conscience.

Following in the tradition, Belle spent much of her time during her life in Iowa, helping the gypsies who camped on the Raccoon River near their home, delivering babies and ministering to the ill among them. Almost as tall as her husband, her large frame carried her weight well. Her reddish-brown hair was worn softly pulled back from her square shaped face. Her life was devoted to her family and her church. Love radiated from her gray-blue eyes and everyone loved her in return. Her daughter-in-law, Mabel Jackson, at the age of 95, spoke of her as, "a wonderful mother-in-law": a true accolade. "The grandchildren would vie for the chance to sit by her in church because she would put her arms around them," Mabel remembered. Engulfed in the embrace of their grandmother's arms, the boisterous grandchildren would sit quietly through the sermons at the Methodist churches they attended from Pleasant Hill and Scranton in Iowa to McAllen, Texas.

Belle's loving nature was tempered by a tremendous strength of character and an innate wisdom in practical and business matters. One of her grandsons said in later years, "Granddad never made a business decision without talking it over with Grandmother." The unique relationship between Belle and W.R. at a time when most women blindly followed their husband's wishes was probably possible because of Belle's ability to subtly guide and direct those around her. She demanded only three things from her family: "You don't smoke; you don't drink; and you always go to church."

Ruth inherited her father's maverick tendencies. In later years she smoked small black cigarillos, claiming she never inhaled; drank vodka, sometimes laced with aloe vera gel and attended church only at relatives' funerals.

From stories told by his sons, Harley and I.R. their father also didn't adhere to all of those policies when he and Belle were first married. A robust man used to working in the fields along side the harvesters, in his youth, W.R. liked to display his strength by hoisting a barrel of beer over his shoulder and drinking from the bung hole. They also remembered that he was not averse to slinging a whiskey jug over his shoulder once in a while. Stories abounded in the third generation about their grandfather's bare fisted exhibition fights at county fairs.

Although this picture of her father was totally alien to Ruth, upon reflection, she agreed that her older brothers and sisters had memories of her father as a young man. Ruth's memories were of an older father who had been reformed over the years by Belle's gentle persuasion. Her nephew, Darrell, stated emphatically that it took his grandmother quite a while to convert his grandfather to the way he was when Ruth was born. He remembered Ruth, lancing her father's many painful carbuncles. She would fix him a glass of fresh orange juice, which unknown to her mother, was liberally laced with whiskey before she lanced these nodes. He always enjoyed his orange juice, demanding many refills.

Belle's form of persuasion toward following the rules laid down in the Jackson household was foremost in one grandson's mind sixty years later. His account revealed that W.R., keeping to his "waste not, want not" regime had strict orders that no one was to pick a lemon from his Ponderosa lemon tree unless lemonade was going to be made. His grandson, Kieth pulled off one of the huge lemons in spite of the dire threats. He heard his Grandmother Jackson in the kitchen telling someone that she would not make lemonade from the lemon because he would then think that he could pull off a lemon whenever he wanted her to make lemonade. However, she couldn't stand the thought of wasting food, so the lemonade was made and so was her point because Kieth didn't get any.

As the Jacksons's land holdings grew, so did their family. The first four children were born between 1887 and 1893. The first born was Harley E. on March 2, 1887, followed by Winnie Ethel on August 20, 1888; Walter, September 26, 1891 and Irvin Riley, born January 2, 1893. Often referred to as the "second family", the first of the last three children was born eight years later. Another son was added to the family with the arrival of their fifth child, Paul Oliver on June 13, 1901. When Belle discovered that she was pregnant for the sixth time, she secretly longed for another girl.

"My mother had four boys and one girl," Ruth said, "She wanted another little girl so much. Before she died in 1948 she told me that she had prayed to God every night that I would be a girl. All of her children were delivered by a

horse and buggy doctor on the farm near Jefferson. When the doctor laid me in her arms and said 'this is a girl,' mother said, 'Thank you, God. This child I dedicate to you.'"

She was named after her aunt, Mary (known as Molly) and the Biblical Ruth. Her mother's pledge to God was to influence her daughter for the rest of her life. When Edythe was born September 3, 1904, the bond among the last three children soon became apparent. All three had bright red hair and were teased by the older children as being "the three little pigs." The gap between the "two families" was not a lack of affection, simply a mini-generation gap. By the time Ruth had the run of the farm with its horses, sheep, cattle and hogs, her older brothers and sister were married or in college.

Her niece, Pauline Bellcock Wasson, only ten years younger than Ruth, remembered her as "being quite a tomboy." She never played with Edythe's dolls, which were kept on the shelf on top of a built-out clothes closet in the room where Harley slept when he came home from law school. She preferred being outside playing with her older brothers. Her favorite attire for play was always topped by a soft floppy felt hat.

Her stance was a ramrod back, redhead cocked to one side, one eyebrow raised haughtily while her eyes flashed a dare to anyone within range. She could, and sometimes did, enjoy dressing up in her Sunday best dresses. She was the typical young lady when she walked down the aisle gowned in ruffles and frills as a ribbon carrier during her brother Walter's wedding to Mabel Mundy in 1912. Although Ruth was expected to help with the house work, she gravitated toward the farm chores allotted to her. Her love of horses was nurtured during these early years. Her father bought his horses in Nebraska and brought them by train to the farm in Iowa.

She was only two years old when her brothers began giving her horseback rides. They scooped her up in the saddle behind them and galloped through the fields. She was absolutely fearless on the back of a horse.

Once, she was riding behind her brother, Paul on "Old Babe" the single-footer, as he was rounding up the sheep to put them into the corral for the night. He put the spurs to her, causing the horse to lunge. Ruth flew into the air and landed with a "thump" on the hard-packed ground. "I jumped up and said, 'I'm all right.'" she recalled.

Even as a child she wouldn't give in to physical pain. She remembered when the doctor came to the house when she was only two to vaccinate the family for smallpox. She wasn't concerned about receiving her vaccination, but was fascinated with watching Paul and baby Edythe as they received theirs. Her curiosity in the medical procedure overcame her fear of pain. Evidence of her lifelong attitude toward pain was exemplified in the following incidents:

In 1986 she suffered from intense and constant pain in her hip and right leg for six months. She refused to stay home. Saying her patients needed her, she worked at her medical clinic five days a week. In January of 1987 to the amazement of everyone around her she boarded a plane, using a wheelchair and carrying a cane, to attend the 54th annual meeting of the AAOS in San

Francisco. After a strenuous week attending meetings, she flew home sans wheel chair, cane and pain.

In her fifties, Ruth fractured her wrist when she went outside to walk her huge German Shepherd. He pulled over to speak to a tree, she stumbled over the leash and fell, breaking her wrist. William Hall was living in her garage apartment. She called to him to come down. Before he got down to the sidewalk, she had reset her own wrist. Holding it very carefully in place, they went into the house and she told William to call Dr. Paul Goodfried to meet them at the clinic. Fortunately Dr. Goodfried was not playing golf that day and answered the phone saying he would meet them immediately.

Before she left she told William, as she walked past the bar..."Pour two jiggers of scotch, I'll open my mouth and you pour it into my mouth." He did, she swallowed it and that was the only pain medication she took. They went to the clinic and she told Dr. Goodfried how to take the x-rays, holding her own wrist in place the whole time. He developed them, and then he put the cast on. He recalled in an interview that she was telling him what to do the whole time.

"The only reason she didn't do it herself was because she didn't have an extra hand. Which she probably would have done if she could have.," Dr. Goodfried remembered.

Twelve year old Ruth's responsibility during harvesting season was to ride her horse to the fields carrying cans of water on either side of her saddle to all of the harvesters, most of whom were neighbors. By the next year, the tomboy was becoming a lady. She decided she was too old to ride the horse in the fields, so she hitched the horse to the buggy and sedately drove around with the ten gallon can of water sitting in the back of the buggy and she would dispense water to the harvesters.

But the tomboy was always beneath the surface. The mischievous imp in Ruth drove her to tease her younger sister, Edythe, unmercifully. "I was always teasing Edythe because she was the baby. I knew I wouldn't get a whipping and she would." Ruth said, "I would do things to make Edythe get a whipping."

Always dexterous with her hands, she made some stilts out of scraps around the house. As she walked on a wooden platform near the fence, Edythe, upon impulse, pushed her. Ruth went sprawling to the ground. Their mother, who happened to be looking out the kitchen window, saw this incident. In a rare display of anger, Belle rushed out to where the children had been playing and picked up the stilts. While Ruth and Edythe looked on in awe, their mother lifted the stilts over her head and without saying a word slammed them over the fence, breaking them into pieces.

One hot summer day Ruth and Edythe were on their way home from town after their music lessons. Ruth was driving the buggy with Edythe as her passenger. With one hand holding the reins Ruth grabbed Edythe's shoe with her free hand, throwing it out the back to the road below. She watched gleefully while the daintily dressed Edythe ran down the dry, dusty road to pick it up. Then, running furiously, she tried to catch up with the buggy again. As soon as a tearful Edythe climbed back into the buggy, Ruth repeated the indignity all over again. They arrived home with Ruth in high spirits and Edythe hot, dirty and exhausted. But Edythe never complained.

Her nephew, Kieth Jackson remembered Edythe, or "Babe" as the family called her, as being a real daughter of her mother. One who never raised her voice or said an unkind word about anybody. "Everybody had stories to tell on other members of the family," he stated, "but no one ever had anything bad to tell about Edythe".

Belle's admonition against smoking was not always effective. Ruth was always delighted when her big brother Harley would arrive home from vacation from law school in Ames, Iowa. His presence meant an exciting break from the rural routine. Ruth would sneak into his room and rummage through his trunk when the opportunity presented itself. There were always interesting discoveries to be made. Once, after securely closing the door so she could browse through this forbidden treasure undisturbed, she found a Meerschaum pipe tucked away in his trunk, which was an open invitation to a daring youngster such as Ruth. In those days kids would make grapevine, corn silks or roots of a grapevine. Ruth put some coffee grounds in the pipe, lighted it and sauntered down the stairs taking fast puffs on the pipe as she went. It wasn't long before she was very sick. Her mother found her weak and wan on the stairs, but she managed to hide the pipe before her mother saw it. "She never could understand why I got sick." Ruth said.

Belle's special feelings for Ruth were manifested in the protectiveness she displayed toward her. She never touched Ruth in anger. If Ruth did something wrong she had to sit down and tell her mother what she had done, then Belle explained to her why it was wrong and how she should have acted.

Ruth and Paul were both hot-tempered. Their nephew, Kieth compared them to two redheaded roosters going after it tooth to toe nail. "Ruth was as feisty as a little game bantam rooster," he recalled in later years. After a spat which resulted in Ruth's screaming at Paul, her mother calmly told her that there was one thing she must learn to do: control her temper. Ruth said she worked at it diligently after that, and eventually she learned to curb the all too frequent flashes of temper.

The lessons learned from her mother stayed with her. She took them with her into the operating room. She recalled only one time when she lost her temper in surgery, citing a life or death situation. She needed all the saline she could get. It wasn't coming fast enough. Shouting at the top of her voice she told them to "bring all the DAMNED saline in the hospital." Her orthopaedic resident at Parkland Hospital at that time, Dr. Margaret "Peg" Watkins was assisting her with the operation. Later Dr. Watkins quietly reminded her that she had not acted professionally by losing her temper in the operating room. She never did again.

While Ruth's mother never physically punished her, her father had no compunctions about raising his hand to Ruth. One of her favorite pastimes was getting on "Old Babe" bareback and surreptitiously following her older brother, I.R. and his fiancée, Fern, when they went on a date. Seeing the pair climb into the cutter or "one horse sleigh" one evening to go skating on the pond, Ruth debated whether to follow them. The debate with herself was settled quickly when the hired man dared her to follow them. Never one to turn down a dare, she told him to heist her up on "Old Babe."

Arriving at the iced-over pond, she slid off the horse and tied her to a tree, then made her unwelcome appearance known to the lovesick twosome. After enduring her company for awhile, I.R. finally suggested that since it was getting dark that she return home, with vague references to her safety.

"I knew why they wanted to get rid of me," she recalled knowingly, "But I took the hint." I.R. helped her mount "Old Babe" who set off at a sedate pace, carefully picking her way through the woods. The horse didn't shy at a covey of birds which flew up in front of her, but upon reaching the gravel road which led to the house "Babe" took off at a dead run. The horse had a double bit on her, two reins on each side. She tried everything she could to stop her. She kicked her in the sides, tried to turn her into a fence, but nothing would stop her. Hanging on for dear life she galloped into the barnyard.

"Old Babe" sensing a warm stall after her outing in the cold winter evening, made a sharp right turn as she ran for the barn, coming to a halt in front of a water tank. Ruth flew off the horse's left side and landed in the snow barely missing the water tank and an icy bath. When she recovered her breath, she looked up into the face of her irate father. Without a word he went to a nearby tree, cut off a branch and applied it to her backside. She never knew whether the anger covered sheer relief that she was unharmed or was over her wild ride home.

As she grew older, a motorcycle owned by one of the neighbor's hired hand became more of a lure than "Old Babe." When she returned from a hair-raising, but satisfyingly exciting motorcycle ride with the hired man, the first person she encountered was her father. This time, it was a razor strap and the words rang out loud and clear, "Never ride a motorcycle again." His advice was embedded in her mind as well as her backside.

Only once did Ruth remember being defended by her father. A plump child, she disliked having her chubbiness pointed out. Her older brothers loved to tease her, calling her "fatso." One day, her brother I.R. had piqued her to the point of tears with his jeers of "fatso." However, he made the error of saying it once too often within his father's hearing. Her Dad took out after I.R., caught him between the two houses and pulled him to the ground and gave him a sound thrashing, she remembered with satisfaction, "He never called me *fatso* again."

It was always Edythe who received the physical punishment from her mother. In most families it is the baby who is catered to and protected by the rest of the family, particularly the mother. Certainly Edythe projected the image of one who needed that protection more than Ruth. A picture taken of the three younger Jacksons, when Ruth and Edythe were about two and four, and Paul, almost six; shows Ruth, angry because she didn't want to stand in the middle. She stared at the world with a defiant look, hands stiffly at her side; her red hair parted and slicked down into two pony tails. Edythe, the soft, delicate child who would grow up to write beautiful poetry, gazes at the camera with wide round eyes, a bow caught in her red curls. Her arms are crossed and her hands are tightly clutched together as if fending off the world. She stands, as she would for the rest of her life, close to the sister whom she adored. Many of her poems were written about Ruth and some that weren't, were dedicated to her. She never seemed to resent Ruth's teasing, brushing it aside as a small penalty to be paid for the privilege of Ruth's attention.

Even as adults, the teasing didn't stop. Edythe was terrified of birds. One time, Ruth let her canary out of its cage to fly around when Edythe was in the room, knowing full well the extent of Edythe's phobia. Ruth's badgering of Edythe was the antithesis of her deep love for her younger sister.

There were few things that frightened Ruth. The only time Ruth ever spoke of being afraid was when as a young child she was deposited outside the entrance of the Methodist Church in

Scranton to join her father in the choir loft. She was supposed to put on a robe and go in to sing with the choir. She remembered a desperate feeling of being lost and frightened until someone came along who helped her with her robe, and then pushed her into the familiar church loft.

She was baptized in the Methodist Church in Scranton where her family spent much of its time. She even entertained the idea of becoming a foreign missionary to Brazil. Her reason for choosing Brazil was never clear to her. She might have gone through with this zealous calling, except, as she stated later, "For the angel on her shoulder guiding her in the right direction."

Ruth was a very precocious child. When she was two years old her mother had her on the stage at a church meeting "speaking a piece." This early training in elocution helped her throughout her life. She reveled in her public speaking ability. She started school at the age of four. She could read and write by the time she entered school. Her sister Winnie taught in the country school before she married. Ruth was her pupil in one of the early grades. According to Winnie's son, James Bellcock, his mother said she always had trouble making Ruth behave in school. A combination of Ruth's indomitable spirit and personality, and having a sister as a teacher probably caused the behavioral problems.

She attended the country school until she was fourteen. There was no high school in the rural area at that time. Even though she was eligible at the age of eleven, her parents would not allow her to attend high school in Scranton until her brother, Paul, who was 18 months older attended also.

It was a happy childhood for the younger children at the big house in Scranton. Free to roam the surrounding areas without the strict supervision to which their older siblings had been subjected, their imaginations ran rampart. The house, nestled near hills and forests on one side, was surrounded on three sides by open fields as far as the school house. A smaller house, where Walter and Mabel lived had been built nearby, with the ice house in between the two homes. The children were oblivious to the cold winters in

Iowa. The big windmill on the hill by the house provided the water piped into the house and the barn. The large kitchen, where everyone congregated, was equipped with a huge stove. Hot water was siphoned from the stove into the reservoir connecting the bathroom and kitchen so the luxury of instant hot baths was always available.

Belle spent some of these winter evenings quilting or crocheting, while W.R. entertained the family by playing his harmonica. Sometimes, to the delight of the younger children, he would break into a fast paced jig as he played, whirling and dancing around the room. Belle never chastised him for his impromptu dancing. Her reformation of this once fun-loving man did not in any way include repressing the essence of his spirit. After Belle died in 1948, Ruth was visiting her father when to her amazement and delight he picked up his harmonica, pulled her out of her chair and danced with her as he played a rollicking tune.

The cold Iowa winters also meant snow. The snow provided recreation for everyone in the form of ice skating on the pond or river. When the older boys went ice fishing, Ruth and Paul skated on the river, banging their poles along the ice to force the fish toward the holes cut out of the ice where Harley and I.R. waited with their baited fish hooks, their bodies and heads covered with blankets. The hired men would cut large chunks of ice out of the river in the winters, storing them in the ice house under layers of sawdust. The ice, which lasted most of the summer, provided the family with a summer delicacy, ice cream.

Summer was harvest time. This meant cooking for large groups of neighbors as well as the hired men. Ruth spent as much time out in the fields as she could, but her chores did not consume all of Ruth's time as there was always time for play. The apple trees around the house were wonderful for climbing. Without the battery-operated toys and games which would be available for children of future generations, Ruth sharpened her mechanical skills and her inventiveness by creating toys of her own. She loved to work with her hands, a childhood trait that would lead to her exceptional skills as an orthopaedic surgeon one day.

Hammers, drills and saws were used to turn an old broken down carriage into a moving force when "Old Babe" was hitched up behind it. She used the drill to make holes through the floor of the carriage, attaching wires to the axle to maneuver the wheels. Scrounging around the barnyard, she found two-by-four boards which she nailed to the sides and back of the carriage. The finished product provided many happy afternoons of fun for Ruth and anyone she would let ride with her as she steered the horse between the two houses, around the barn and by the ice house. She enlisted Paul's help with these projects, but Edythe always stayed indoors. The two of them made a bob-sled with one sled in front with handlebars attached to a swivel to guide it and another sled attached to the rear. Ruth carved the handles and they made the rails from the metal on carriage wheels. Their friends from Scranton came out to make the marvelous run from the top of the hill, around a curve, then down to the bottom of the steep hill. Paul rode the horse down, tied the sled rope to the saddle, dragged it back up the hill and off they would go again. She always said that if she hadn't become an orthopaedic surgeon she would have chosen to be an architect. She satisfied this urge by designing her Dallas orthopaedic clinic on Fairmont in 1945. Her inventive mind was always at work. Later in life she designed an automobile with many safety features, as well as the special pillow, known worldwide as the Cervipillo, for her patients with neck injuries.

While Belle was managing the house and raising the family, W.R. continued adding to his holdings. "My father was always ahead of his time compared to other farmers in those days," Ruth stated with pride. "He would buy undernourished livestock from other farmers, and then fatten them." He always accompanied the cattle whenever he shipped them to Chicago or Omaha to be sure they were properly auctioned. The other children taunted Ruth by claiming that her Dad had so much money because he took it away from their fathers. They didn't realize that their fathers had the same opportunity as W.R. did to care for their cattle properly and to prosper. Sometimes Paul would travel on the train with the cattle to supervise the loading and unloading for his father. Ruth, ever eager to drive the family's Model-T, drove him to the station. The Model T was tricky to operate. The "Tin Lizzie" had three pedals, clutch, reverse and brake. A lever with three positions, high gear, neutral and brake. To start the car, Ruth had to seize the crank with her right hand, slip her left forefinger through a loop of wire which controlled the choke, pull the loop of wire, which revolved the crank and as the engine started, leap onto the running board, lean in and move the spark and throttle to the left, hoping it would keep running. Many wrists were broken following this procedure. Although repairs could be made with baling wire, chewing gum and hairpins, these items could also cause problems. When Ruth drove home from the station, she tried to shift gears, only to find the car would shift only into first gear. [iii]

After a wild ride home, a careful examination by her father disclosed that her mother's bone hairpin had fallen into the gearshift and locked it into place.

Her father was by then an austere man with deep-set piercing eyes, squared jaw and a big bushy mustache. His stern attitude hid the deep love he felt for his family.

Most of his seven children would live near him for the rest of their lives and in various ways he would provide for them financially. W.R.'s generosity extended only to matters of importance. In most cases he was frugal and parsimonious. In order to see, Ruth had to sit close to the blackboard at the country school she attended. Her father still in his work clothes took her into Scranton to be examined in the family's doctor's office by a visiting ophthalmologist. The examination disclosed that Ruth was nearsighted and needed glasses. When her father hesitantly asked how much the bill was for the examination and glasses, the ophthalmologist looked at W.R. in his clean but well patched work clothes and asked sympathetically, "You don't have much money, do you?"

Fumbling around in his pocket, W.R. sidestepped the question by saying, "I think I have ten dollars in my pocket." Nodding his acceptance of the paltry sum the doctor and father closed the deal, both satisfied. W.R. had made a good bargain and the doctor because he had performed his good deed for the day. But this bargain hunting trait would soon cause an upheaval that affected the whole Jackson family.

"Desire must be transmitted into its physical equivalent."

CHAPTER III

In 1916 W.R. received an offer he couldn't refuse. Land in the Lower Rio Grande Valley in Texas was being touted as "Rich as the valley of the Nile," by the land promoters representing either themselves or one of the numerous land companies which thrived on the sweeping publicity campaigns waged during this period. No one mentioned that it was not a valley, but a delta.

Situated on the very tip of Texas, the Valley, composed of a flat strip of land approximately one hundred miles wide and one hundred and fifty long, stretched from the shores of the Gulf of Mexico on the east to the barren ranch land of Rio Grande City to the west, with Mexico as its southern border. Even after modern expressways crisscrossed the Rio Grande Valley, it took ten hours of driving to get out of the Valley east, west and north. But only fifteen minutes to the south took one into another country: Mexico.

The railroads were at last connecting this delta area with its irrigated farm land in the tip of Texas to the rest of the world. The land promoters took advantage of this means of transportation to bring prospective buyers to Texas. A land man at Jefferson, the county seat of Greene County, Iowa offered to take W.R. and Belle on a train trip to the Valley. The railroad car, which belonged to the Western Farm Land Company, made trips from Iowa to Pharr, Texas every first and third Tuesday of each month. [iv] The excursion, which cost only $40.00 per person, was too good a deal for W.R. to turn down. The land man, who was in fact a real estate agent, was sure that the combination of railroads, irrigation and fertile land with its wide range of crops, would be appealing to an enterprising man such as W.R. One of the selling points to a farmer was the fact that the temperate climate was conducive to growing crops year round. In addition to cotton, grain and a wide variety of vegetables, the citrus industry was beginning to burst upon the scene. Booming crops were produced in broomcorn and sugar cane in the land once called "the Wild Horse Desert."[v] No mention was made of the fact that Mexico bordering the Rio Grande Valley was in the throes of a revolution or that for the past two years the Mexican bandits, some claimed it was Pancho Villa's gangs, were terrorizing the area.[vi]

The promoters, who were often religious evangelists, went to great extremes to sell the eager pioneers. On one excursion in the earlier years, as the train traveled through land completely underwater due to a torrential downpour the night before, the quick thinking agent called for everyone to bow their heads in prayer. He prayed non-stop until the train was safely out of the flooded zone.[vii]

The sunshine as well as the promising future of the area convinced the elder Jacksons to buy 57 acres on the outskirts of McAllen on what is still known as Jackson Road. They also purchased 80 acres northwest of the McAllen property. They went back to Iowa, told the family what they had done and discussed their future plans. W. R. did not plan to sell the Iowa land and home on the farm. They were going to wait a year before they moved to Texas. They wanted to build a house on the 57 acres. They would sell everything on the Iowa farm, except the house, in a big sale. After living in Texas for at least three years, if they didn't like it they would move back to Iowa. Two of the older children would stay in Scranton for a while. His son, Walter and daughter-in-law, Mabel would stay on the Iowa home place. Also remaining in Iowa would be daughter, Winnie and her husband, Roy Bellcock. The rest of the family would follow their parents and their father's sister, Mattie and her husband, "Let" Roundy, of Marshalltown, Iowa, to the area referred to in the land promotion pamphlets as the "California of Texas." W.R. and Belle took Harley, their oldest son, and two carpenters back to McAllen to build the house.

Mabel Jackson lived in the Jackson family home on Jackson Road in McAllen, Texas until her death at 100, in 1990. The home with its landmark old red barn was demolished soon after her death by the bank which had bought their land. The Jacksons' Texas home was built to the specifications of the farm house in Iowa and included five large rooms and an entrance hall downstairs with four bedrooms and bath upstairs. Much of the lumber to be used in building the house on the country Texas road was shipped from Iowa. The house's big fireplace was a wise addition, even in this sun drenched country because the most severe blizzard in almost twenty years found its way to the Valley between January 10 and 12, 1918, plunging temperatures from seven to twelve degrees below freezing along the lower coast.

    In the spring of 1917, the house in Texas was completed. The sale was held in Iowa. In March the younger generation of the Jackson family began their 1300-mile trek to Texas and the Promised Land. The three younger children had no idea of what lay ahead of them.

"We find in the crucible of experience only the gold that we have poured into it."

CHAPTER IV

With their entourage, five of the Jacksons left the rolling prairies of Iowa in two King model cars. One was a brand new open top touring car with wide running boards. Rotating between the cars were I.R., his three year old son, Barney; fourteen year old Ruth; Paul, who was fifteen and Edythe, twelve. They traveled through the plains of three states without incident, spending the first night in a small town in Missouri. When they arrived in Oklahoma, which had been a state for just ten years, they had their first serious trouble on the unpaved roads. Then one of those infamous Oklahoma dust storms hit. A cloud of the red powdery substance soon filled the carburetor on the older car causing a halt to the caravan. It was impossible to get the car repaired, so I.R. decided to leave the car in Oklahoma.

I.R., Barney and the three

children were to travel together in the other King car to Texas. Being the trader that he was, W.R. later managed to a good bargain for the useless car.

The Jacksons had entrusted the three younger children to twenty-four year old I.R.'s care, confident that he would see them safely to McAllen. This was not exactly what happened. With their departure from Oklahoma, the adventure began in earnest.

There was no big bridge spanning the Red River joining Oklahoma and Texas. They had to camp on the river bank until they could ford the river. Aptly named, during the stormy spring months, the Red River could become a tumultuous torrent of bronze red water from the churning of the red earth forming the river bed. The delay was a lark for Ruth, who always enjoyed camping out. For Edythe, the prim and proper young lady, it was unbearable, while the fastidious Paul endured the wait. One can only imagine I.R.'s feelings in this situation, saddled as he was with the three teenagers as well as a three year old. Fortunately for all, it wasn't too long before the river calmed to a trickle once again as it often did and they were able to cross uneventfully. Once across the river the group was at last in Texas. They spent the night in a hotel near the border where Ruth had her first experience with a Texas cowboy. The girls were sitting in the lobby of the hotel when a gangling cowboy sat down beside her.

He didn't heed the red hair and flashing brown eyes when he put his arm around her to give her a hug. He was just one of the men, who to his dismay, would discover Ruth's strength and determination. The incident passed without bloodshed and the next two stops were Waco and San Antonio.

Each night at the hotels, Barney, I.R. and Paul shared one room while Edythe and Ruth roomed together. After dinner, Ruth pulled out the forbidden playing cards she had sneaked in her bag to play solitaire. Card playing ranked right up there with smoking and drinking. Her mother never knew she had taken the cards with her. Ruth couldn't even remember where she acquired the cards for the trip, but she had been bitten by the bug for good. Her habit continued throughout her life. As soon as she arrived home from her clinic in the evenings, she would pick up the deck of cards she kept on the table by her favorite chair in her living room on Turtle Creek Drive and shuffle for a game of solitaire. She claimed she couldn't sit without keeping her hands busy.

From San Antonio it was still a 225 mile trip on to McAllen, and I.R. had enough. Three year old Barney was sick, probably whooping cough and I.R., who had been kicked in the chest by a mule several years before, complained of renewed chest pains.

Later Ruth would say, "Whenever I.R. didn't want to do anything he would use his accident as an excuse to get out of doing whatever he didn't want to do."

Once again the Jackson family parted company. I.R decided that he would take Barney to McAllen by train and the younger trio could drive the car to McAllen by themselves. Paul, with the girls in tow, drove I.R. and Barney to the railroad station, waved a blithe farewell to his brother and nephew then started the journey to McAllen. The gods were kind by not allowing a glimpse into the future. Young, confident and unafraid, these three children didn't realize just what they were undertaking by making this trip alone. They had no map. Some of the roads at that time were just cow trails. Bandits were still raiding the ranches throughout that desert area. Spring in South Texas can bring extremes of boiling hot sun or freezing blowing rains, neither of which is conducive to riding in an open touring car. They could not get the top up on the car so the three red haired, fair skinned novice pioneers were exposed to the weather the whole trip. They traveled through country scattered with mesquite brush, littered with rattlesnakes and creeping with tarantulas. The drive, which takes only five hours via modern expressways, took the youngsters three days.

The first day was fairly easy. They arrived in Alice, the town named for the daughter of Captain Richard King, near the Kingsville headquarters for the famous King Ranch, and spent an uneventful night. Between Alice and Hebbronville were 50 miles of desolate ranch country. Most of the big ranches had cattle guards at the entrance. When they drove upon a big gate unexpectedly, Paul couldn't slow the car because of the sandy road; he hit the gate and blew out a tire. After changing the tire he drove into Hebbronville, where they left the car at the first garage they saw. Hebbronville consisted of a couple of garages which also sold groceries and one hotel. In reality, it was just a village used as a gathering place for the ranch families scattered throughout the vast area. The hotel was a bonus for the trio. They felt quite at home when they learned that the woman who ran the hotel was from Iowa. They enjoyed a good night's sleep as well as home cooked food in addition to the motherly concern of their new Iowa friend.

But trouble was to plague them once more. Before they left the city limits the next morning, they blew out another tire. Fortunately, it happened in front of the only other garage on the edge of town. They were lucky in another respect because the owner, probably curious as to why three very young teenagers were traveling alone, had the good sense to ask them where they were going. When they told him, he was appalled. "You kids can't get there if you have never been through the ranches. You have to have a guide. There is a man here who will guide you through the ranches to Mission for $15.00," he advised.

They put their heads together for a family discussion and probably made the best decision of their life: to hire the guide.

"Thank God we did," Ruth recalled later," He knew where the water tanks were when our radiator went dry, where the high points in the sand were so we didn't get stuck, where the cattle guards were to the vast ranches and where we could get gasoline." She shuddered as she remembers the huge black buzzards swooping overhead as they greedily followed the youngsters in their open car.

"I always said there was a guardian angel sitting up there telling us all just what we should do," Ruth stated emphatically.

When they finally arrived in Mission they gratefully paid the young guide and left him on a street corner in the downtown area. She often wondered how he managed to return the hundred miles to Hebbronville. Unaware of the frantic search underway by their parents, who had preceded them to Texas, they slowly drove the ten miles to McAllen on their own, taking in the sights of this land which was to be their new home. They drove through acres of citrus orchards between Mission and McAllen.

It was their first sight of these trees with the fragrant blossoms which would produce not only delicious citrus fruit but also would provide the means for their family's livelihood for many years to come. New to them also were the palm trees. The green jagged edges of the palm fronds reaching toward the sky were so different from the soft wavy apple trees around their Iowa home. Puffs of white clouds drifted in from the nearby Gulf of Mexico and scattered across the blue sky. The irrigation ditches where the water flowed sluggishly to the fields of broomcorn and recently planted vegetable crops intrigued them. No waiting for the heavens to open its water-filled clouds before a crop could germinate. It was all new and exciting and they were completely unaware of the stir their prolonged absence had caused. "I'll never forget the look on my mother's face when we drove into the driveway," Ruth remembers. "She and my father had been frantically calling on the telephone to officials in every town between San Antonio and McAllen searching for us to no avail." Her parents almost disowned I.R. for leaving them to travel on their own.

Belle's fears for the safety of her three teenagers were justified for several reasons. Not only was Mexico a few miles south of the Jacksons's home, in a state of revolution, but President Woodrow Wilson had just called the United States Congress into an extra session over the sinking of U.S. ships by German submarines. By April 6, 1917, he had signed a resolution declaring a state of war between the U.S. and Germany. Because of the Mexican bandit raids across the Rio Grande into Texas, American troops had been stationed along the border since early in 1916, which caused McAllen's small community to boom overnight. Following a raid by Mexican bandits at the Las Norias flag station in the lower Valley, it was revealed that some of the bandits had been found wearing German military decorations and carrying German weapons. This reinforced the suspicions that Germany was strongly involved in supporting the banditry as a means of keeping America's attention away from the state of war in Europe that had been underway since 1914. The depth of Germany's interest in the area was revealed later in testimony, much in front of the Falls Congressional Committee in Washington D.C.

    The famous Mexican revolutionary, Carranza, recruited many Germans who held commissions in his army. The Mexican Minister of Telegraph, Mario Mendez, was paid by the German government to send coded messages, his money routed first through Carranza. [viii] Uppermost in Belle's mind was the news of the Zimmerman Telegram, just released by President Wilson, which was directed from Dr. Alfred Zimmerman, secretary of foreign affairs for Germany, to Von Bernstorff, German ambassador to the U.S. in Washington. It stated that Mexico would be expected to join in the war effort against the

U. S. with her reward being allowed to reconquer Texas, New Mexico and Arizona. [ix]

The guardian angels seemed to be watching over South Texas as well as the three youngest Jacksons during this period. The show of force by the American troops along the border turned Mexico away from any idea of joining with Germany and the area became more settled as it began to prosper along with its growth.

Many of the settlers were sold a "pig in a poke," buying land sight unseen, which turned out to be worthless. W.R., knowledgeable about land, had chosen his parcels of land well. The land around the house on what would be and still is called Jackson Road, was planted in grapefruit, tangerine and orange orchards with about 25 acres of farmland left open near the house. The 1000 acres of land he later bought near Sullivan City in the northwest part of the Rio Grande Valley was planted in grain and broomcorn.

According to Mabel Jackson, whose husband, Walter farmed the Sullivan City farm for about a year, the only cotton crop planted failed because there was no irrigation in the area. Mabel and Walter were supposed to live on the ranch when they moved to the Valley in 1927. W.R. offered to build them a house on the ranch, but after seeing the desolate area they declined. Actually the farm was near Sam Fordyce, a town which became a ghost town after the completion of the railroad into Starr County about this time. It was reincarnated during the 1970s when it was used as a film site for the movie based on the novel "She Came to the Valley" written by a native of nearby Mission, Texas., Dr. Cleo Dawson.

"There wasn't even a cow's trail for a car to go down," Mabel spoke in later years of the desolate countryside. "We went up there and took a picnic lunch once while Walter worked and we had to keep moving around the trunk of a tree because there wasn't any other shade."

Temperatures could reach well over one-hundred degrees in the summers and with Walter's eight children, the living conditions in the area seemed intolerable. Ruth's memories of Sullivan City are more pleasant. To her, the remoteness and desolation were exciting and stimulating, providing adventures, not back breaking work.

"We traveled the sixty miles with my father to the ranch once when he went up to feed the cattle. Accompanied by mother and several of my parent's friends, we all took shotguns along to hunt. I had my first gun, a 16-gauge shotgun purchased at Sears and Roebuck. My father took me along with the other hunters walking down the corn rows. He told us that we had to be very careful. But when we saw White Wing doves flying, he told us all to fire at the same time. Three of us fired together at his command and we killed twenty-one birds with three shots. My mother and her friend cleaned the doves and we had a dinner party out there." Her love of hunting began that day. She would return to the Valley annually to hunt White Wing doves for many years.

The Sullivan City property may not have proved as profitable for farming as the McAllen land, but W.R.'s luck held with the discovery of oil on his property. The first attempts to drill for oil in the Valley were made in this area, named the Sam Fordyce field in

Starr County in 1919. Although his first attempts were unsuccessful, Otto Woods, a wildcat oil well driller, came back to the site in 1934 upon the advice of a man who claimed to be able to prophesy the future. On September 19 of that year his prophecy was proved correct when a column of oil shot over one hundred feet into the air before drillers could shut off the valve.

Production peaked later at 4,800 barrels a day. ^{x}The early land promoters' advertising responded to why a person should invest in land in the Rio Grande Valley with, 'that land does not die or run away.... Banks may fail; governments may be overthrown; successful products or methods of manufacture today worth millions may be made valueless by new discoveries tomorrow, but land is always land," proved to be correct.^{xi} Underneath the land was oil and gas.

W.R. sold the Sullivan City land but retained three-fourths of the mineral rights. With three shallow wells flowing, Ruth's one-seventh interest in the leases provided her with an income over the years until the oil companies started drilling slant wells in adjoining Hidalgo County causing their shallow wells to dry up. Whether it was luck, good timing or foresight that brought W.R. to the Rio Grande Valley during the broomcorn boom, the rise of the citrus industry and the burgeoning oil industry along with the benefits of the newly completed railway and irrigation networks, is immaterial. Ruth, Paul and Edythe were the beneficiaries of the monetary rewards which provided them with a relatively carefree existence during their school years. This enabled them to live a good life in their new environment, as one where "all over the country, broomcorn farmers were buying new farm homes, new cars and living of country gentlemen."[xii]

As the young are prone to do, they quickly settled into their new life style. The Jacksons's home was located on the dividing line of the McAllen and Pharr- San Juan-Alamo school districts. Paul, Ruth and Edythe enrolled in the PSJA high school when they arrived that spring, but two conditions caused them to relocate in the fall. Paul, who seemed to have been born sophisticated and debonair, had a temper. As his nephew, Kieth Jackson stated "I don't think the temper part is a bit 'un-Jackson like anymore than the red hair." Temper and pride were Jackson characteristics shared by many in a family of distinctly individual characters. It was a combination of these two characteristics which caused Paul's problems with the high school principal.

During class one day there was, in Ruth's words, a ruckus in the classroom. The teacher saw, or felt, the spitball that was thrown and accused Paul of the act. When he tried to make Paul pick it up, he refused. Denying that he was the culprit, he steadfastly and repeatedly refused to obey the teacher's command. One thing led to another, which led Paul directly to the principal's office. As was W.R.'s habit, he arrived that afternoon to drive Paul home from school only to be met by an irate principal and an unrepentant son.

During the drive home, Paul's explanation of the situation seemed to satisfy his father to the point that he announced that Paul and Ruth would not have to return to the PSJA high school the following year. W.R.'s decision illustrates his pride in his family's reputation because transferring to the McAllen schools meant paying tuition for the two youngsters. As penurious as W.R. was, this was a big concession.

During this fracas, Ruth was at home suffering from the effects of typhoid fever. She had come home from school one afternoon complaining of a terrible backache, headache and running a high fever. Her father had the doctor, a retired physician who lived across the street from them, come examine her. After diagnosing it as typhoid fever, he put her on a program of quinine and bed rest for four weeks. Her prolonged absence from school caused her to lose her credits for her freshman year when she was ill.

In the fall of 1918, Ruth and Paul were attending school in McAllen's brand new high school. Ruth worked in the administration office polishing her secretarial skills as well as helping to pay their tuition. Ruth and Paul soon surrounded themselves with a host of new friends sporting such nicknames as ""Kat," "Skinny," "Brother" and "Roxie. With her usual zest, she enrolled in ballet classes, studied "expression" as it was called then and participated in all available sports activities. Her fondest memory is playing "Snow White" in the school play.

Maintaining a very high average throughout high school, she was relegated to third place instead of first because of the absence of her grades for her freshman year. The position of class poet as third place was created for her. She often laughed about being noted as the class poet, but throughout her life, she would jot down her philosophical thoughts as they came to her. She loved poetry, often quoting long poems from memory to friends during conversations. It irked her when she couldn't remember a complete poem. One evening at the age of 83, after unsuccessfully trying to remember the ending to "Dangerous Dan McGru" she retired for the evening. She aroused the whole household when in the middle of the night she turned on every light in the large two story house looking for the book with her partially remembered poem. The only ones who didn't hear the ending of the poem were the police since she had forgotten to disconnect the burglar alarm before descending to the first floor of her home.

Although in a speech made at her fifty year class reunion in 1970, she praises the McAllen school system and faculty spearheaded by superintendent, E. R. Bentley and principal, P. E. Phipps, as being "instrumental in giving us inspiration in our formative years," she often lamented the fact that the school provided no Latin or German. This lack of foreign language deterred her admittance to several medical colleges in later years.[xiii]

Her last weeks at McAllen High School were filled with many social events. The round of parties included a banquet served by the ladies of the Presbyterian Church, which featured ice cream in the school colors of purple and gold; a theater party, a Charades party, swimming at Lake Campacuas with a campfire dinner topped off with a stop at Captain Palmer's house in Mercedes for eggnog. The grand finale was the Junior/Senior Banquet, with her escort, George Osborne.

The social restrictions must have

relaxed a little by May of 1920. Before then, in 1917, the McAllen School Board had decided that teachers could not attend public entertainment or dances on school nights and had to get permission from the school board to go out of town. Two years later most of the female teachers lived in a dormitory built for their use, known as the Faculty Club, where they were not allowed to have men or children as visitors. The only restriction on Ruth's activities still included one: no dancing! The lure was there for the teenager and one night she succumbed. She was going to spend the night with one of her classmates and the two had planned to attend a social by a respectable men's organization that centered around the "forbidden fruit."

Ruth always told her mother the truth, so she told her that she was going to attend the dance. As always in protecting Ruth, Belle neglected to mention this fact to W.R. If it was a sin, it was of "omission." When Ruth wasn't home at eleven o'clock, W.R.'s concern grew. When Belle confessed that Ruth was attending a dance, he drove to the party and stormed in. Ruth was on the dance floor with a young man when her father burst into the room. He marched over to her, grabbed her by the arm and took her home. She didn't even get to spend the night with her friend. But that evening, she learned to dance and literally waltzed what there was left of the night away. Her brother, Paul, aided and abetted the pseudo criminal by occasionally taking her with him to dances when their parents were visiting in Iowa, once again leaving them under the supposedly watchful eyes of their older siblings. She would talk him into dragging her along in exchange for keeping his wardrobe in the perfect shape he demanded. Their parents returned to Scranton every summer from 1917 until 1927 when Walter's family moved to McAllen.

Ruth didn't attend many dances during that period of time, but always loved to dance. At the 1986 American Academy of Orthopaedic Surgeons annual meeting in New Orleans, while attending the reception for the president of the Foot and Ankle Society, at the age of 83, she requested that the band play "The Yellow Rose of Texas." She whirled around the dance floor, solo, as the orchestra played her request much to the delight of those attending. Two years later she proved that the fifty-year age span between her grand-nephew, Donald Jackson was mere illusion when they cleared the dance floor at her grand-niece, Cindy Jackson's Dallas wedding.

When the class of twenty, which included Ruth and her brother, Paul, attended the high school commencement exercises, Ruth was gowned in organdy ruffles and frills. She was always proud of the fact that she stitched that dress together by herself saying how much simpler it would have been if women had worn mini skirts then. The dresses were worn to the ankle while the boys suit coats were pulled in at the waistline as if they were bras and girdles. Their tight pants reached well above their ankles. Long hair for women and short hair with pompadours was in vogue for men. She added to this observation that at least the sexes were distinguishable then.[xiv]

Good-natured and fun loving, Ruth attracted the boys like the citrus blooms attract the bees. Before she completed high school one of her beaus asked her father for her hand in marriage. Much to her chagrin, her father was ready to give it, thinking Ruth was agreeable to the union. When the National Guardsmen from various regions in the country first arrived in McAllen in 1916 they were unacceptable as companions for the young ladies. With the arrival of the New York 7th Regiment, nicknamed the "silk stocking "or "millionaire" regiment because of the presence of such men as Cornelius Vanderbilt, the restrictions were relaxed.[xv] It was one of the guardsmen, Homer, who tried to ensnare the elusive Ruth.

It was the daughter, not the father, who quickly pointed out she was too young to marry. For years she kept the pink sapphire ring her unlucky suitor gave her. Eventually, she used the setting for her medical ring, giving the gemstone to her sister, Edythe.

At the same time she was being romantically pursued by soldiers, she was corresponding with Earl Hudson, who had been left pining away for Ruth in Scranton, Iowa. In order to attend school while her parents were in Texas making arrangements for their move, Ruth had stayed with the local pharmacist's family. The night before she left for her new home, Ruth and Earl attended a roller skating party. When Earl took her home, he held her hand, looking at the ring he had just placed upon her finger. He said, "Well, I guess you know what this means don't you?" To Earl it was an engagement ring. To Ruth it was simply a friendship ring. She wasn't closing the door on the relationship since the Jacksons spent some time each summer staying with Mabel and Walter in Iowa and their friendship could be renewed and kept alive on an annual basis. Whether it was a bid for sympathy or a premonition on his part as to Ruth's future vocation, his letter of September 16, 1918 tells of an upcoming tonsillectomy and his wish for Ruth's "understanding" presence. Addressed to "My 'Little' Ruth," he wrote, "Think of your dear old friend back in Iowa for I am going to have my tonsils removed this week. I wish you could be with me for I am sure I am afraid of nothing while you are near. You could not let anyone hurt me."

Even then he sensed her extraordinary protective attitude and empathy for the ill. Almost as an after thought, in the last paragraph of his letter he mentions that his brother, Roscoe, had been wounded in the shoulder by German shrapnel while serving a tour of duty in France. Earl, who later joined the service, survived the battles but died in the 1918-19 flu epidemic.

The war didn't affect the Jackson family personally. Although the Selective Service Act authorized May 18, 1917 requiring registration and drafting of all men between the ages 21 and 30, even though eligible, her brothers were probably exempt due to their work in agriculture. By 1918 the biggest war threat to those living in the Rio Grande Valley was appearing on the screen at McAllen's Columbia Theater, where for 50 cents Ruth and her friends could see "The Kaiser, The Beast of Berlin." [xvi]

Ruth remembered receiving a letter from an unknown soldier who wrote to her informing her of the death of his comrade in a battle in France. In going through his friend's pockets after he was killed the young soldier found Ruth's picture with her name and address. She does not know who the unfortunate young man was nor where he got her picture.

Later she would add to her string of conquests, becoming engaged to "Governor" Bobby Stevens of Mission, Texas, an A&M student whom she met traveling home on the train from the University of Texas. That engagement would be one of the first that she was to break, all because of her desire to become a doctor.

"He who floats with the current not guiding himself according to higher principles, ideals and convictions is a mere article of the world's furniture, a thing moved rather than a moving and living being-an echo not a voice."

CHAPTER V

The seeds of Ruth's desire to become a doctor probably were implanted from early childhood as she observed her mother's ministering to the ill. However, they would not bloom until she was in her third year at the University of Texas at Austin. A growth of this subconscious desire probably began to stir during her adolescence and impending womanhood because she always kept a part of herself aloof from the permanent entanglements which marriage and children would bring. Time after time she would be on the brink of a lasting relationship, only to pull back from the commitment. She would refuse to marry the only true love of her life, Don Keyes, an intern she met at the University of Iowa; afraid she would be influenced to give up medicine to become a housewife. Her two brief marriages, after she had become established as a doctor, were for completely different reasons. The first to Dan McClung in 1939 as she herself admits, because he reminded her of her first and only real love. Ruth tried to clone a pliable Danny into another Don, making him grow a mustache such as Don wore; buying clothes like Don had worn, even making him change his after-shave lotion.

The second, a platonic marriage was for business reasons to keep her from losing her homestead after a disastrous business venture in the early '70s. In Texas, a homestead owned by a male was exempt from seizure under bankruptcy laws. A single woman homeowner could have her home taken away from her. At one point in her life Ruth tried to convey her philosophy about love in a letter to an ardent suitor whom she was rejecting with the following words, "...Whether I do or whether I don't find that love and companionship doesn't matter a great deal to me. ... My life has been built around one ideal-and that is 'service to others.' The joy that I find in doing things for other people is a joy that no one can touch. It is real and

Ruth Jackson, M.D.: A Life on the Leading Edge

lasting-it is not affected by petty arguments and misunderstandings. And if that is all the happiness I am to receive from this existence then I am content. It is very gratifying because I know that no one can touch it. My efforts may not always be appreciated but my satisfaction comes from the doing. So you see, my dear, that no one person can mean my happiness or my unhappiness."

Love was one subject not uppermost in Ruth's mind as she prepared to attend the University of Texas in Austin in the fall of 1920. Neither was the fight, which had been ongoing by the Women's Movement during this period of time. Fifty-one years after the amendment was first broached and through the tireless efforts of Susan B. Anthony, at 4:00 a.m. on August 26, 1920, the 19th Amendment to the Constitution, giving women suffrage, was enacted. Although Ruth would become a member of the American Women's Medical Association for a few years she was never involved in the Women's Rights movements pertaining to physicians.

When asked her opinion of the

Women's Right's Movement, she would explain: "Only because I believed that women physicians should stand on their own two feet and accomplish much for the oncoming physicians by doing a 'jam-up' job in their chosen profession."

    Perhaps Ruth's interest in the movement would have been sparked even at the age of seven if she had heard Grover Cleveland's statements written in the *Ladies Home Journal* in 1910 after suffragists had brought 500,000 names to their representatives petitioning Congress for the vote. "Sensible and responsible women do not want to vote," he wrote, "The relative positions to be assumed by man and woman in the working out of our civilization were assigned long ago by a higher intelligence." His attitude was mild considering the future treatment of the militant women in the movement in 1914. Women picketing the White House in 1914 were hauled off to jail, stripped naked and thrown into dirty cells with syphilitic prostitutes. One woman, protesting an injustice was put on bread and water for 17 days in solitary confinement.

South Texas was far removed from these activities which took place mostly in the Eastern states. No nightly barrage of television news nor access to socially oriented radio programs and newspapers such as women in later years would have to stimulate their activist inclinations was available to steer Ruth to these paths. Even with Ruth's independent spirit, her first attempt at studying medicine was easily dismissed from her mind due to her obedience to her father.

She had always heard her mother say that she wanted to be a doctor, so while thumbing through the catalog in preparation for the entrance exams at the University of Texas, she decided to take a premed course. She had talked with a neighbor who was studying social services and decided that since "Papa" didn't want her to go into medicine she would major in economics and sociology and minor in psychology and business administrations. Wise choices for her, since in later years she would be involved in many business ventures: some good; some disastrous.

The decision made, Ruth enrolled at the University of Texas, September

23, 1920. She elected to take the basic courses with emphasis in science. Her first semester she took English, American history, civics, Spanish and algebra. Her scientific leanings were evident with her enrollment in Chemistry and Zoology. Physical training appealed to her since she made her only "A" of the first semester in that subject.[xvii] But she had not given up entirely her childhood desire of becoming a foreign missionary. Therefore, she included in her curriculum two years of Bible study with Dr. Ernest Webb, a Yale graduate and head of the University of Texas' Bible Department. "By the time I finished the two years of Bible study, I had changed my mind," she said. She explained her reasons were the result of her biology and embryology classes. "There are two distinct accounts of the creation in Genesis," she states," One is that God looked upon the earth, wanted to have someone to take care of the earth so he created Adam and Eve. Equally! The other was that He created Adam and because he didn't have a help-mate, He took a rib from Adam, created Eve and pronounced them man and wife."

Then the scientist takes over as she adds, "So, if He took a rib out of Adam to make Eve, all men should have eleven ribs on one side instead of twelve. When you study embryology you know that they all start out the same!"

Just two years later, the famous Scopes trial was fought in court in 1925, the clash of ideas between Darwin's Theory of Evolution and religions brought the Scopes trial to the national forefront. It is ironic that William Jennings Bryan, the prosecutor of John T. Scopes, the teacher in the public school system in Dayton, Tennessee who was arrested for teaching Darwin's theory of evolution, had established a home in Mission, just a few miles from the Jacksons' McAllen residence. Growing up in the cultural atmosphere generated by this great fundamentalist thinker and orator, might have helped form Ruth's inquiring mind.

Her first two years at the University, Ruth lived in a boarding house provided for students in the Austin community. She shared a room with two other girls. The room was for studying since all the girls on her floor slept dormitory style on a large enclosed porch. Her sophomore year she was able to rent a room which she shared with one other girl. As soon as possible Ruth moved into a room by herself, citing an obnoxious roommate as the cause.

Meals were often eaten at the boardinghouses, which were the only places available for young ladies to reside during her first two years. She still found time for an active social life, occasionally dating Moses Kenebel, a geology student. Their paths crossed in later years after taking diverse trails. He, to marry and go to work for a major oil company traveling throughout the world while Ruth forged ahead with her medical profession in Dallas.

She remembers receiving a call from Moses, who had seen her picture when it appeared as one of the "Twelve Outstanding Women in Texas" in the 1948 edition of the *Holiday* magazine. He told her that, sensing that she would be practicing in a big city, he always looked for her listing in the phone directory in every city he visited over the years. He took her out to dinner

and she reciprocated by taking him to visit her lake home at her Kaufman farm.
"On the way to the farm Moses pointed out the live oak trees along the way. He said that wherever there are live oak trees growing naturally, you'll find oil," she said, adding that he had the ability to find oil by just flying over the countryside.

Her junior year, Ruth and Edythe, a freshman, lived at the new Scottish Rites dormitory, referred to by her brother-in-law, as the "Waldorf Astoria of the University." It was here that Ruth met her friend Kathryn Buckner, whose father was a Methodist minister at the time. Kathryn, a premed student, and Ruth would form a friendship which lasted for many years. The social prestige of Scottish Rites dormitory was reflected in the rules and regulations. Hats and gloves were required for church, teas and receptions. Any young man calling on his date at Scottish Rites dormitory had better know her name for he would be met by a matron with a tablet and pencil in hand along with a stern look of disapproval if he didn't meet her standards. Ruth and Edythe had to wait in their room until someone called from the phone in the hall downstairs announcing that their dates had arrived. Proper dress at mealtime included breakfast and excluded arriving at the table in one's nightgown. One young lady appeared each morning in a light raincoat over her sheer nightgown, until one sunshiny morning a bit of lace peeped out from under the tailored coat. Her lazy mornings were over for her with that appearance.

This strict supervision was not much of a deterrent to Ruth, who managed to stay out of too much trouble during her stay. The church was still a big influence in her life at that time. Many of the social functions Ruth attended were connected with the Epworth League, a Methodist organization for young people. At one of these functions she met Ruby Daniel, whose life she would influence. Ruth sang in the University Methodist Church choir at Austin. Later as a medical student at Baylor University Medical school she took private voice lessons from Celeste Morton, the choir director, but at the banquet when Baylor University Medical Center honored her in 1986, Ruth admitted she was tone deaf, and couldn't carry a tune. "I could tell when somebody else was off-key, but I can't tell when I am, so I was very careful when I was in the choir to just open my mouth and let the other people do the singing," she recalled. When her sister, Edythe joined Ruth at the University in 1922 she resumed her protective role.

    Once again Edythe shielded Ruth from the wrath of their father. Ruth's inclination was to be free with her money. Always fashion conscious, Ruth was quick to do away with her long tight skirts, high patent leather shoes and black or tan stockings to become a modern "Flapper." Her wardrobe soon consisted of the stylish gowns with hemlines nine inches above the ground and climbing; sleeveless evening gowns and the abandonment of her corset. Edythe would pay some of Ruth's bills so it would look as if they spent the same amount of money, according to Edythe's husband, Harold Brehm. Ruth's idea of protecting Edythe was to try to pick her boyfriends. Edythe's protestations were met with a firm announcement from Ruth that "I just want the best for you." Translated that meant, "Only with my approval will his qualities pass muster!"

Away from the eagle eye of her stern father, Ruth's exuberant personality spread its wings and flew. She even dared to "bob" her long red hair. As short haired women were associated with radicalism, her reception upon arrival during vacation time was volatile. Her father told her in no uncertain terms that "only prostitutes wear short hair." The storm must have been of short duration because she eventually convinced her mother to go to a "hair dressing" parlor and bob her hair also. She was eager to embrace all the rudiments of the revolution in manners and morals brought on by prohibition, the automobile, the movies and the popularity of the radio. If her father had objected to the traditional tea dances, he would have been appalled by the new form of dancing disgustedly described by the Hobart College Herald as" a syncopated embrace, dancing glued together, body to body, cheek to cheek."

By her senior year Kathryn Buckner and Virginia Singleton had joined Ruth as roommates. Even though the two sisters took part in the social activities they didn't neglect their studies at the university. They enjoyed their vacations at home in the Valley, by this time only a day's drive from Austin. Ruth's nephew, Darrell, was always delighted when his Aunt Ruth came home from the University of Texas. His parents had moved from Scranton to McAllen where his father, an attorney, had a successful practice. He even delved into politics, serving as mayor of Scranton at one time. Lured by the thought of year round sunshine and the offer of W.R. to set him up in the insurance business and provide them with a home on McColl Road, they joined the Jackson clan in Texas.

Darrell adored his Aunt Ruth. As a two year old he would follow her wherever she went. The affection was obviously mutual because Ruth used to take Darrell with her when she went out on dates. Darrell would climb up in the back of the car often falling asleep there during the outings. "I was a little pest when we lived in the Valley. If it hadn't been for me she would have been the First Lady of Texas since I went on dates with her and "Governor" Stevens," he often teased. Ruth would point out that "Governor" was just a nickname for Bobby Stevens so he didn't wreak too much havoc by his presence. This bond between them lasted a lifetime, cemented even stronger when Darrell lived with Ruth for a time during his formative years.

When Ruth returned to school her junior year in the fall of 1923, another major change was to occur that would affect the rest of her life. "My sociology class had assignments to work with charities," she reflected on this turn of events, "I was sent out to a black family's home in East Austin to see how many groceries they needed for the week."

It probably never occurred to Ruth not to fulfill her assignment in East Austin just because the women students were warned never to go into the area of East Sixth Street. This was the area in the 1920s where the dregs of humanity congregated, filling the flop houses, working in the brothels and roaming the streets. Since Mrs. Lawhon, the fourth floor matron, would have been unhappy if any of the SRD girls went downtown on a streetcar without a hat, Ruth probably donned a stylish chapeau, hopped the streetcar from Guadalupe Street to complete her assignment. Alighting from the streetcar on Sixth Street with her chin thrust foreword and her famous raised eyebrow; she emanated a dare to anyone to just try to molest her.

    Even as a young girl, Ruth had no compunctions about entering the area. She called on a small, dilapidated home of this self-reliant workman who was forced to take charity because he needed medical attention. This was the time of segregation in the South. Jobs were scarce enough for anyone with black skin. For one who was incapacitated, finding one was impossible. She saw the crowded conditions of the family, their lack of the basic necessities of life, taking in the paint peeled rooms bare of furniture. But her eyes kept going to the father. Propped up in bed in the living room which was permeated with the smell of wintergreen ointment, the only medication he could afford, he quietly suffered the pain from a sore and swollen knee. This upset her. This touched something deep inside her which was to change the path of her life forever. "It took me about two minutes to find out how many groceries they needed. The whole thing left me cold," she remembers. "So when I went back to turn in my report to the United Charities I gave myself a good talking to," she had to do this every once in a while she explained, "and I said to myself-'Ruth Jackson, this is not for you. Anybody could do this. What you really want to do is find out what's wrong with that man's knee and put him back to work so he can take care of his own family!" Her first act when she arrived at the dormitory was to pour over the University catalog. Collecting all the available material concerning qualifications for entering medical school, she discovered that one of the qualifications included two years of German, French or Latin. She had had a few brief months of German, concentrating her foreign language to two years of Spanish, thinking it would help if she decided to become a foreign missionary. She realized, due to her solid scientific background, that if she entered summer school for two summer sessions she could finish premed work and still have enough advanced classes in economics, sociology and psychology to graduate.

Her only obstacle was getting around the foreign language problem. Her first real challenge was at hand. She wrote a long letter to her mother explaining her decision and outlining her plans. "I know exactly what happened when that letter arrived," she says emphatically, "My father blew his stack. I can just hear my mother saying to him as she patted him on the arm. 'Now Daddy, now Daddy, if that's what Ruth wants to do that is what she is going to do.'"

Once again, the steel hand in the velvet glove soothed its unsuspecting victim into submission. Belle and Ruth had their way.

"If we are to act with effect we must count for something with our fellow men."

CHAPTER VI

To understand what problems Ruth would encounter in her quest for her medical degree it is necessary to be cognizant of the attitudes and obstacles put forth by society and the medical profession prior to and during the 1930s and early '40s. Women had been admitted to the American Medical Association in 1915 after a long, arduous struggle. At a meeting of the American Medical Association in Washington in 1868, the question of admitting women doctors came up for the first time. Recognition of all regularly educated and well-qualified physicians was advocated, but when a resolution endorsing qualified women doctors was made, it was discussed at length and then indefinitely postponed. At the 1872 meeting of the Association in Philadelphia, another resolution was presented. It read, "While we admit the right of women to acquire medical education and to practice medicine and surgery in all their departments, we deem the public association of the sexes in our medical schools and at the mixed clinics of our hospitals, as impracticable, unnecessary, and derogatory to the instincts of true modesty in either sex."[xviii]

One woman physician who entered medical school in the 1920s was told by a fellow student "You are not a man, you are not a woman. You are an unsexed thing, studying medicine out of morbid curiosity."[xix] Another woman in training overheard a classmate saying, "I don't want my wife to know anything I don't teach her." [xx]These remarks as well as the one attributed to Sir William Osler, Canadian physician and renowned medical historian and teacher, who stated that there were three classes of human beings, men, women, and women physicians, were mild compared to the ostracism practiced since the inception of the first medical school at the University of Pennsylvania in 1767.[xxi] Although women had traveled as far as Europe to receive training in midwifery, the first medical school in the United States would bar women from receiving a medical degree.

The first institution to enable women to acquire medical knowledge was the Boston Female Medical College founded in 1848 by three Boston physicians. In the spring of 1850 the Female Medical College of Pennsylvania was chartered.

Harvard's first attempt to become co-educational in 1850 under Oliver Wendell Holmes resulted in disaster. One woman and three black students were accepted causing a student riot, due mostly to the inclusion of the blacks. Miss Harriet Hunt, its only woman applicant had to withdraw and it would be almost another hundred years, 1945 before Harvard at last accepted women in the Harvard Medical School.[xxii]

The battle at the Female Medical College of Pennsylvania brought cries from county societies as well as the State Medical Society on the basis that "women were unfit for medicine" and that "some of the professors are irregular practitioners." [xxiii] The leaders, headed by Ann Preston, a former graduate and great advocate of woman's rights, fought the battle against women's exclusion until the beginning of the Civil War when the college was closed. It reopened as the Woman's Medical College of Pennsylvania with Ann Preston as its Dean at the end of the War. Next called the Medical College of Pennsylvania, it opened its doors to male medical students for the first time in history in 1969. On July 1, 2002, it became known as the Drexel University College of Medicine. In 1857, Dr. Elizabeth Blackwell, the first woman physician in the U.S., established the New York Infirmary for Women and Children to train women to receive practical training.

    The first medical school to adopt a policy of co-education was the Central Medical College of New York at Syracuse, an eclectic institution, in 1849-50. The eclectic school was based on the principle of embracing the widest possible range of views and stressing the use of indigenous plant remedies. Although the National Eclectic Medical Association had formally approved co-education in medicine by a resolution in 1855, it did not accept women for membership until 1870. The women physicians who graduated from these colleges, Marie Lakrewaska, and the Blackwell sisters'

Woman's Medical College of the New York Infirmary treated mostly women and children, or were in salaried position of hospitals, clinics and universities. Between 1850 and 1895, there were 19 medical colleges for women.

By 1900, eleven had been disbanded and in 1910 only two remained, The Woman's Medical College of Pennsylvania and a homeopathic institution in New York.[xxiv] The 7,387 American women doctors registered in 1900 were due largely to the fact that Switzerland and Germany had admitted women to medical schools as early as 1870. Many American women seized this advantage to train for their profession, and some universities were becoming more liberal in the administration's attitudes toward admitting women.[xxv] According to Carol Lopate in her book *Women in Medicine* during the first half of the 20th century the entrance way into medicine had been smoothed but the discrimination that existed against them at higher levels still remained. From the year Ruth was born in 1902 until 1926 the number of female medical students had declined from 1,280 to 992 out of a total of 18,840.

Ruth Jackson, M.D.: A Life on the Leading Edge

The number of women physicians reached a peak of six percent of the national total in 1910, not reaching that level again until 1950. It took another 20 years before the 1970s would see a break through in the number of women attending medical school.[xxvi] The fluctuating mores during the centuries had contributed to the attitudes toward women physicians.

During the pioneer times, a woman worked along side her husband in all aspects of work, including in the field, and usually was the one who ministered to the sick. With industrialization and the movement toward urban living, the slogan "A woman's place is in the home" was born. The Victorian attitude with its stern sexual morality forced women to hide behind their corsets and stays. The few women physicians were sought after by upper class women who did not want to submit to examination by a male physician.

Wars provided women physicians with some opportunities. One woman who was the first graduate of a well-known medical school was told during World War I that she would be admitted to medical school only because of the military situation and the shortage of men. If things changed and enough men applied she would be "thrown out." [xxvii]

Although many women physicians did volunteer during World War I, they were banned from enlisting in the military service. The American Medical Women's Association in conjunction with the Suffrage Association and the American Red Cross worked together to send women doctors overseas. Women contract surgeons were employed during World War I without commissions, but with the salary of a First Lieutenant. [xxviii]

Through diligent efforts on the part of the American Medical Women's Association a petition was sent to Washington at the beginning of World War II requesting that women physicians be allowed to serve their country. The bill signed by President Franklin Roosevelt in 1943 stated, "That hereafter during the present war, and six months thereafter...shall be enacted a measure to provide for the appointment of female physicians and surgeons in the medical corps of the army and navy." This did not keep those

Ruth Jackson, M.D.: A Life on the Leading Edge

who were commissioned from being barred from the Medical Reserve Corps after the war, supposedly a privilege for all who served.

World War II allowed women physicians to step into positions vacated by male physicians who were called into the service. These same women physicians were often put out to pasture like milk cows after the men returned from active duty.

Ruth was eager to volunteer during World War II. She sought the advice of the Academy's Armed Service Committee. Many physicians and surgeons from the Dallas area had volunteered as members of the 56th Evacuation Hospital receiving their commissions in the U.S. Army in February, 1941.

Dr. Henry M. Winans, a specialist in internal medicine at Baylor University Hospital and professor of medicine at the medical college, was commissioned a lieutenant colonel and given the responsibility of organizing the hospital unit, in collaboration with Dr. G. M. Hilliard, administrator of Baylor University Hospital. As a result of the Japanese attack on Pearl Harbor, the 56th Evacuation Hospital's organization was accelerated with 29 of the unit's officers composed of staff members at Baylor University Hospital, faculty members of the Baylor College of Medicine or medical college alumni. Two were from the College of Dentistry. None were women. There was a nursing complement commanded by Margaret Rea which included 31 nurses.[xxix]

Ruth was discouraged from volunteering for the service by the Academy's Armed Service Committee as well as a colleague who warned her, "You'll end up delivering babies or treating the soldier's wives because they won't let you practice orthopaedics. You'll be needed more here at Parkland Memorial Hospital where you are the Chief of Orthopaedic Surgery," he advised. His advice was well heeded.

Due to the shortage of doctors during the war, Ruth often had to resort to performing the plastic surgery on her own patients. She had to do all her own skin grafts. "I even 'pinned back' the ears of two young boys with unusually protruding ears," she recalled. It was just part of her orthopaedic training that she found necessary to do at times.

After World War II, which forced separations and losses in many families, the media emphasized the importance of marriage and motherhood. This period was called "The Great Withdrawal" by Jess Bernard due to the fact that the percentage of women Ph.D.'s dropped drastically.[xxx]

It had never been Ruth's nature to withdraw from any projected goal; only to forge ahead. It probably never occurred to her that anyone would or could deny her the opportunity to study medicine. With this attitude, after receiving her Bachelor of Arts degree from the University of Texas in June, 1924 she applied to several medical schools. Most medical schools at that time required a student to have studied two years of German, French or Latin.

With only a few months of German to her credit she was concerned that her two years of Spanish would not qualify her for admission. Also at this time the emphasis for admission to medical school was on the scientific disciplines centering on comparative vertebrate anatomy, general biology, physics and chemistry.[xxxi] All Ruth needed was a solid science background, which she had, and a recommendation from one instructor; providing she could work out her problem with her foreign language. Her embryology instructor at the University of Texas solved her problem by writing a glowing recommendation for her which resulted in her being accepted at four medical schools: Tulane in New Orleans; the University of Texas at Galveston; one in St. Louis, Missouri and Baylor College of Medicine in Dallas.

To Ruth's advantage was the fact that the door to women in medicine had been pushed open a crack after Abraham Flexner's famous report that was published by the Carnegie Foundation in 1910. After being hired by the foundation to survey medical education in the United States, Mr. Flexner personally visited every medical school in the United States, evaluating the schools on the basis of their requirements for admission, the caliber of their faculty and the quality of their laboratories and physical facilities.

His report included the following

statement: "Woman has so apparent a function in certain medical specialties and seemingly so assured a place in general medicine under some obvious limitations that the struggle for wider educational opportunities for the sex was predestined to an early success in medicine." He further stated that "as the opportunities of women have increased, not decreased...their enrollment should have augmented, if there is any strong demand for women physicians or any strong ungratified desire on the part of women to enter the profession one or the other of these conditions is lacking-perhaps both." Still only 20% of those matriculating graduated from medical school at the time the report was published. [xxxii]

Ruth did not have to take a Medical College Admission test such as students take today, have her grade point average scrutinized, have multiple recommendations, nor be interviewed by an admissions committee. Both male and female applicants today must be interviewed by the Medical School's Admissions Committee.[xxxiii] This committee is charged with considering many factors in its decision to accept a student into medical school. Several factors go beyond statistical and mathematical determinants, but according to one of the guidelines proposed by the opinions of five New York State Supreme Court Justices solicited by the AAMC several years ago; these are used to "humanize" the process.

A woman can anticipate being asked her views on combining marriage, children and a medical career. Elizabeth Morgan, M.D. relates the story of one of three of her interviews at Harvard Medical School in her book, *"The Making of a Woman Surgeon."* After stating that she was wasting his time that she would be married before she left college he ended the interview by saying, "You're going to be married, my dear, and you will never make a doctor. How absurd can you be?" Her cab driver, taking her back to Cambridge had different advice. He asked her if she was in college and what her major was. When she replied biology he told her she should become a doctor. "That is exactly what I want to be," she told him. He jerked his head around and glared. "You gotta specialize. That is what you have to do. It's not just medical school. Afterwards, you gotta specialize. We need more women doctors."[xxxiv]

Although Ruth did not encounter problems such as Dr. Morgan coped with in her struggle to enter medical school, in a subtle way they shared the same problem. While Dr. Morgan's problem concerning career versus marriage and family was with other's opinions, Ruth's was within herself. In an interview published in *Texas Woman Magazine* [xxxv] in June 1979, she rails against women who receive their medical degree, marry and never practice medicine, by stating emphatically, "If you're going to be a doctor, then be a doctor! If you're going to be a housewife, then be a housewife. There's no reason you can't do both, but abandoning medicine after pre-empting a student who wanted that slot-this has created prejudice."

Upon notification of her acceptance at four medical schools she had to make a decision where she wanted to study. Conferring with her parents, who wanted her as close to home as possible, Ruth decided that it would be best if she accepted the appointment at Baylor College of Medicine which at that time was still located in Dallas. She was never to regret her choice. She arrived at Baylor College of Medicine during a period of expansion bolstered by the desire of the Baylor Board of Trustees at Waco to build a medical center that would equal any in the United States.

According to Laura Henderson "this period saw the evolution of the *Baylor-in-Dallas* concept, as the Texas Baptist Memorial Sanitarium, the Baylor College of Medicine, the School of Nursing, the School of Pharmacy and the School of Dentistry were all placed under the authority of the Board of Trustees of the parent university at Waco."[xxxvi]

In November 1920 at the recommendation of the Baylor Board of Trustees, the Baptist General Convention of Texas had voted to consolidate Texas Baptist Memorial Sanitarium and the College of Medicine under one governing body: The Board of Trustees of Baylor University. [xxxvii] The Baylor trustees designated Texas Baptist Memorial Sanitarium as the official teaching hospital for the medical school and limited practice in the sanitarium to medical school faculty and members of the sanitarium staff with pledges to make additions "as necessary for carrying out in every detail the making of a really great and first-class College of Medicine and Hospital."

The sanitarium was officially renamed Baylor Hospital in 1921, which by the time Ruth arrived would be in the process of becoming the largest hospital in the Southwest and the second largest in the South. It received the highest ratings of excellence by both the American College of Surgeons and the American Hospital Association. It was here that she would not only study medicine, but would return to become affiliated with her real love, what would become the Baylor University Medical Center, for the rest of her life.

It was as if Baylor Hospital, Dallas and Ruth began to bloom and grow all at the same time. Dallas is, in the words of the late historian Herbert Gambrell, "an example of a city that man has made, with a little help from nature and practically none from Providence." And man was busy at work in the early 1920s making it a bustling city with its Magnolia Building flying the world famous "red horse." The first major paved road in Dallas County opened as the Belt Line Road. The expansion of Southern Methodist University and the nineteen story Medical Arts Building being built by the former dean of the Baylor College of Medicine, Dr. Edward H. Cary. It was here that Ruth would establish her first office when she began her practice several years later.

She arrived in Dallas for her first session of medical school in the fall of 1924. She enrolled in the twenty-fifth session at Baylor College of Medicine on October 24, 1924 joining two hundred and forty-three students on campus. One hundred and twelve of these were in Ruth's freshman class.[xxxviii]

Kathryn Buckner, whose father was a Methodist minister, later a Bishop, and Ruth met at the University of Texas in Ruth's junior year. They were to room together throughout medical school, at the Scottish Rites dorm. Even though Kathryn had been a premed student before Ruth decided to change her major, Ruth said she wasn't influenced by Kathryn's professional choice. The two girls were joined by two other females in the freshman class numbering one-hundred and twelve. Their first taste of the bitter pill to be swallowed if they, as mere females, wanted to continue their medical education was dosed out to them by the doctor speaking to the freshman class at orientation.

"Now you know, you girls...we don't want you here. You have to make ten points higher in your grades to make the same grades the boys do." he announced in front of the whole group. If his purpose had been to frighten them away, it had the opposite effect on the five foot two dynamo named Ruth Jackson.

"Well, that was a challenge," she stated emphatically, "It made you knuckle down to business if you really wanted to do it. It's true I had to do it. I probably would have been second in my class if I hadn't tried to change some of the obstacles put before the women students." In a 1987 interview Ruth stated that she had recently discovered that when she entered medical school the women were required to have four years of premed while the men had to have only two years.

One of the unfair practices, not allowing the women students into the men's urology department, was her first target. It seemed doubly unfair to Ruth since the men were allowed to attend the women patients in the obstetrics-gynecology department. The students were supposed to go to the outpatient clinic at Baylor to examine patients and take histories. In fairness to the faculty, by 1924 even though the additions to Parkland Hospital had been completed in 1923, all the facilities were not available for clinical teachings.

The increases in enrollment produced a problem in the conduct of the laboratory courses because of limited space in the student laboratories, with some of the freshman courses being taught in two sections. Adjustments also had to be made for some of the sophomore classes. The pressure on the faculty to teach under these conditions could have been one of the reasons why women were discriminated against. They were not allowed to attend the clinic for men, where most of the male patients who had gonorrhea or syphilis were treated in those days. Feeling that part of her education was being neglected because of this oversight, Ruth registered a complaint. "I told the doctor who was teaching the course that if we (the women) were going to be doctors we needed to know not only about women, but men too. I strongly emphasized that we should not be barred from attending whatever department the men were in," she said.

The doctor was not impressed with her argument and in spite of her good marks on exams and excellent work taking patients' histories, gave her a barely passing grade. In addition, the women were still not allowed into the men's department. She took satisfaction in the fact that out of the original 112 members of her freshman class, only fifty-eight finished medical school and all four women medical students were among the graduates.[xxxix]

There were times when she had to fight to keep in school. Semantics played a part in Ruth's embarrassment and potential failing grade during an oral exam in Dr. William W. Looney's anatomy class. Dr. Looney asked her to describe the "bed of a stomach." To Ruth a bed was something to lie upon. She had never thought of the stomach as lying on a bed. "I told him that I did not know that a stomach had a bed," she said, "but of course what he wanted me to tell him was what lies posterior to the stomach and that I could have done." As a result, the professor was going to make her repeat the anatomy course. Pointing out that she would have to spend the whole summer in school just to repeat one course, Ruth talked him into giving her a "D." Ruth claimed this incident relegated her to sixteenth position in her class but this close brush with failure may have been the reason for her avid interest in anatomy for the rest of her medical career. She was always ready to assist medical students such as members of the Alpha Epsilon Iota medical sorority with their anatomy studies. Later she helped her partner Peg Watkins and another doctor, Rex Howard, pass their boards by taking them at least once or twice a week to the anatomy lab to dissect specimens and share her vast knowledge of the subject.

The results showed in the surgery she performed during her practice. Each surgery, no matter how many times she had performed the operation, was performed after a careful review of the anatomy and a prayer to God to give her the strength and knowledge to do the most for the most people who need her help.

One of her patients, whose mother was associated with Greenhill School in Dallas, first saw Ruth when she was four and fell and broke her ankle. Ruth performed the surgery to restore her ankle. Years later her family took her to Mayo Clinic where after many examinations and tests by several doctors the diagnosis was mutual. None could believe that she walked without a limp after the debilitating break she had. They asked her why she didn't limp. Her answer was "Why should I?" Their next question was who did her surgery because they had never seen such a beautiful job of putting an ankle back together.

"It's because she knew her anatomy," she recalled during an office visit for one of her own children many years later, "She knew just what went where!" She was just one of many patients who were grateful that Ruth persevered during those early medical school years to earn her medical degree.[x1] Her male pre-med peers were not as hard on the four lone females, limiting their harassment to the telling of off-color stories in the presence of the ladies.

"Most of the dirty jokes I know today came from them," Ruth admits. "Even so, some of the men were helpful and some weren't. The professors gave us the most trouble." Sarcasm seemed to be the tool used most by the professors. Ruth felt the brunt of this technique used by her professor of obstetrics, Dr. C.R. Hannah. One term she returned from Christmas vacation with a gastro-intestinal problem that necessitated x-rays. She arrived late for class as a result of being in the clinic; she clambered through a myriad of male arms and legs to reach her specified seat. Just as she sat down, her mind on her recent ordeal, she heard the professor call her name. Pausing dramatically, Dr. Hannah asked

Ruth a pointed question concerning the portion of the lecture she obviously had missed. When she admitted she didn't know the answer, he raised his eyes to the ceiling in anguish. While dramatically pointing toward his head he commented: "See! See! Nothing there, absolutely nothing there!"

    Ruby Daniel and Ruth had renewed their friendship during Ruth's sophomore year at medical school. One day as Ruth was going down the stairs of the building where she shared an apartment with Kathryn Buckner, she met Ruby on the stairway. Delighted to see her friend again, the first question Ruth asked was why Ruby had dropped out of medical school. Two years ahead of Ruth in medical school, Ruby had changed her major to anesthesiology. Ruth immediately asked her where she had been and why she had not finished medical school. She told Ruth that she had spent the past two years traveling in Europe after her first two years of studying anesthesiology. At that time if a student stayed out of medical school for two years, they had to start medical school over again.

    Acting on Ruth's encouragement to

enroll, Ruby registered that fall for her junior year of medical school, much to Ruth's delight. Ruby finished with Ruth in 1928. In spite of being a diabetic and terribly obese, she did her graduate work at Lane-Stanford hospital in San Francisco, and was associated with the University of Chicago Clinic in the eye division before going to Rochester, Minnesota as a fellow in ophthalmology. She took a leave of absence to travel to China where she was connected with the Rockefeller Medical College in Peking, for two years. She eventually moved back to Dallas where she practiced medicine until her death.[xli] Ruth, Kathryn and Ruth Cudmore, one of the four female med students shared a variety of apartments during medical school. The trio lived for a while with Roberta Stovall and her husband. Roberta had been Ruth's high school teacher in McAllen. Their evening entertainment was often provided by Kathryn who had a beautiful voice. She sang at Ruth's sister, Edythe's wedding to Harold Brehm in McAllen, May 22, 1927.

During their junior year, the four

women decided to make an application for a chapter in the National Fraternal organization for women medical students, Alpha Epsilon Iota. AEI was founded as a national social fraternity for women medical students in 1890 to fill the void in the life of the student.[xlii] They received their charter and the Upsilon chapter became an active chapter of the national organization. Ruth served as treasurer and president of the Upsilon chapter, later serving as its national president in 1956.[xliii]

Ruby Daniel's father was a respected ear-nose and throat specialist in Dallas. The Daniel family lived on Swiss Avenue, the setting for some of the most lavish mansions in Dallas during the 1920s. East Dallas had such a colony of European immigrants during the late 1800s that Swiss Avenue was named in their honor. Close to Baylor Medical Center, the Daniel's home provided a meeting place for the medical students to pursue their studies. Strong coffee kept the late night study sessions going for everyone except Ruth. She had learned at the University of Texas during the

Epworth League's sunrise breakfasts out by the river to avoid the tantalizing taste of the fresh brewed coffee which accompanied the eggs and bacon cooked over an open fire. Caffeine sent Ruth into shaking spasms.

She loved the aroma of the coffee and the taste, but it didn't like her. She learned to organize her notes, go through them carefully, take leave of her all night coffee drinking zealous friends by 11:00 p.m., go home and retire for the night. The next morning she would take her exam without any qualms because she had a good night's rest.

Ruth studied hard and played hard during her senior year in medical school. Prohibition didn't stop the medical students from indulging at their parties. At one fraternity party Ruth had a date with a fellow student who sat behind her in class since their last names started with a "J." Ruth had a car, a spiffy black Model T, so she picked him up. Women's liberation had not been clearly defined as such, but Ruth always was ahead of her time. The party was in full swing and her date, a Phi Chi and a devout Baptist, guzzled thirstily from the never ending supply of punch being poured into the large crystal bowl.

What Ruth knew and he didn't was that the punch was being liberally laced with pure ethyl alcohol thoughtfully provided from the laboratory by one of the medical students. On the way back to his fraternity house, he demanded that Ruth stop the car. Thinking he was going to be sick she complied immediately. He turned to her and blearily stated his intentions: "My brothers have always told me not to have anything to do with women until I marry, but I would like to 'pet a little.'" Ruth saved his reputation by patting him on the arm and telling him she believed she'd just save herself and take him home.

The medical students were perhaps more fortunate than most of the population during Prohibition. They weren't forced to resort to purchasing the bathtub concoctions called "Panther Whiskey," or "Yack Yack bourbon" for ten times the price paid before prohibition; most of which were flavored with such lethal ingredients as fuel oil or iodine to name a few.[xliv]

Ruth's $290 Model-T took her everywhere. There was no left hand door on the Model-Ts, but there was not much danger of falling out since the top speed for the 20 horsepower engine was only 45 miles an hour. The car was a luxury item for a medical student in the 1920s, but Ruth's parents were always generous. One picture taken of Ruth in 1926 shows her dressed in a full length fur coat and stylish cloche hat, picking lemons from her mother's famous lemon tree while a palm tree can be seen in the background. She didn't need a fur coat that winter vacation in the Rio Grande Valley. If she had stayed at school for Christmas her fur would have been a welcome addition since Dallas residents reveled in a white Christmas. It would be 1975 before Dallas would, again, be covered in snow on Christmas day.

There were two Ruths in the class of 1927. Ruth Cudmore, a New York native, had failed her sophomore year in medical school, but repeated the courses and graduated a year later. The two Ruths chose surgery. Both started in general surgery while Ruth Jackson would later decide on orthopaedics.

Ruth Jackson, M.D.: A Life on the Leading Edge

Ruth had observed many interesting orthopaedic cases during her senior year at the Crippled Children's Hospital. In January 1922, ground was broken by the Texas Scottish Rite Masonic Order, which owned and controlled the Crippled Children's Hospital. The doors opened on the sixty bed hospital located on Oak Lawn Avenue south of Parkland Hospital on November 15, 1923.[xlv] With graduation planned for May 28, 1928, the women had to begin to consider the next hurdle to their medical careers: where to intern. There were no openings for women interns in surgery in most places in 1928. One of Ruth's friends was accepted as an intern in surgery until it was discovered that Occo Goodwin was fashionably gowned instead of properly suited as they had assumed by her given name that she was a male. Miss Goodwin fought a valiant fight to be accepted as a surgical intern. She won, eventually practicing in California.

Although women could not get internships in Dallas in those days, Kathryn Buckner, through the influence of her father's Methodist connections, managed to be accepted at the Methodist

Hospital in Dallas. After practicing for a while on Oak Lawn Street, she later specialized in psychiatry and moved to the East where she spent her remaining days.

One of the few women professors at Baylor University College of Medicine in Dallas between 1903 and 1943, Minnie Lee Maffett, M.D., at that time an assistant professor of gynecology, was a big influence in Ruth's medical career. Not only had she been Ruth's teacher, she was her gynecologist and good friend. It was Dr. Maffic who suggested to Ruth that she apply for an internship at Memorial Hospital in Worcester, Massachusetts. where they only accepted women interns. Until the end of World War II internships for women in hospitals were difficult to obtain, in many cases simply because sufficient facilities had not been provided. Geared toward men only, the hospitals were not equipped to provide housing for women physicians.[xlvi] Whether this was a convenient excuse is a question that can only be answered by the facts gathered by Bertha Van Hoosen who headed the American Medical Women's Association committee on Medical

Ruth Jackson, M.D.: A Life on the Leading Edge

Opportunities for Women throughout the 1920s. She paints the picture in published reports concerning the status of women in medical schools of women denied internships and residencies due to the refusal of many American Medical Association approved hospitals to open up these positions to women. Through their surgical tracking systems reports it was evident that the AMA insured that the majority of women surgeons be those trained at a woman's school.[xlvii]

When her parents arrived in Dallas to attend her graduation ceremony, they had a surprise for her. They brought her nephew, Darrell to attend the graduation ceremony with them. By the time they arrived Darrell was running a temperature. When the doctor called to examine him determined that he had pneumonia, Ruth took part in the examination. "I remember that by listening to Darrell's lungs when he had pneumonia, I was able to successfully diagnose my first case of pneumonia as an intern," she said.

With graduation and her State Board examinations behind her, Ruth left Dallas for Worcester, Massachusetts where she had been accepted as a rotating intern at Memorial Hospital. The next three years were the only time that Ruth's roots were not firmly established in her adopted home, Dallas and Baylor University Medical Center. She prepared for the next stage in the an exciting journey through her life.

"He who does not advance, falls back, He who ceases to grow greater becomes smaller."

CHAPTER VII

Ruth, probably urged by her parents, elected to make the 1700 mile trip to Massachusetts by train since she was traveling alone. She doesn't remember what happened to her trusted "Tin Lizzie" but recalls that her first year in Worcester was the only time she was without her own means of transportation. When she arrived in Worcester and was ushered into the old rambling two story home where the interns lived, she almost turned around to go home. "If I hadn't known that I was to be on general surgery, which I had set my goals toward, I think I would have walked home," she remembers, "I had a cot in the attic. I couldn't even raise my head without bumping it on the rafters." It was time for another 'good talk' with herself. "I said to myself, 'no, this is what you came for and you are going to stay.'" It wasn't too long before she was given a room where she could have some peace and quiet to study.

She was given many assignments by her clinicians that were not offered to the other women interns. Even though she was constantly encouraged to go into obstetrics and gynecology, or ear, nose and throat surgery, she steadfastly held to her ambition to specialize in general surgery. During her three months on minor surgical service, she was required to give anesthetics because of her excellent training at Baylor. The doctors knew because of her training that she was familiar with the use of nitrous-oxide which they were using instead of the more commonly used ether or chloroform to anesthetize patients. Once the nitrous-oxide was used, the ether could be used. Termed the most strenuous year due to the physical strain, the internship found Ruth instead, thriving on her schedule.

Carol Lopate states in her book, "If an intern intends to enter a residency in one of the more competitive specialties, such as internal medicine or surgery, an additional incentive for competing within the established system is provided and he or she may go to extreme lengths to catch the eye and approval of his or her chief of service."[xlviii]

Ruth caught the eye of one of her chiefs at Memorial Hospital, but not in the way she wanted to. Invited to his home for dinner one evening, Ruth arrived to find his wife out of town and his thoughts toward other appetites. She extricated herself from that situation somehow without endangering her status as an intern.

Her problem could have stemmed from the fact that she was always determined to look feminine while on duty and she succeeded too well. Determined not to practice medicine in pants and jackets, she had an outfit consisting of a dress featuring a high neck with a simple jacket, designed for her before she arrived in Worcester. On call every other night, she never went on the wards at night, even in an emergency, without appearing in her outfit and make-up.

"The nurses were always impressed with me because I was always properly dressed," she remembered.

Night calls led to midnight

suppers in the dining room. The other interns would talk Ruth into going into the kitchen to whip up a batch of her famous fudge. Months of midnight suppers, fudge orgies and little exercise caused Ruth to put on weight during her first year in Worcester. But her main concern during her internship in Worcester was finding a residency in general surgery.

In 1929 it was difficult for a woman to enter the field of surgery, particularly if she was interested in being adequately trained. Even though she knew someone at the Mayo's Clinic in Minnesota, she was not accepted. When she read in the American Medical Association Journal of an opening in the Department of Orthopaedic Surgery at the University Hospitals, at the University of Iowa, in Iowa City, she decided to apply. She knew that one of the greatest orthopaedic surgeons, Dr. Arthur Steindler, was associated with the University of Iowa. Her goal then was still general surgery.

As fast as the letters could go back and forth to Iowa City, Ruth had an internship in orthopaedic surgery in the orthopaedic department at Iowa

City. Iowa. Her goal then was still general surgery. "That was the days when we had lots of polio and all kinds of things" Ruth recalls, "I saw what we were doing with those crippled children; after three months I thought this is for me. I made my plans then to go back to Worcester in orthopaedics because I knew they had a good orthopaedic service, then to Scottish Rites over here (Dallas) the third year."

Fate had once again intervened in her behalf. Dr. Steindler, who had attended school in Vienna, and was graduated from the School of Medicine of the University of Vienna in 1902, had trained in Vienna hospitals under Lorenz, Friedlander and others until he moved to Chicago in 1907. He served as a professor in orthopaedic surgery at Drake University in Des Moines, Iowa until 1913 when he moved to the State University of Iowa. A linguist and musician he was dedicated to teaching. Medicine was his life. He worked on his final book, "Analysis of Pain in Orthopaedic Entities," until a few days before his death, July 21, 1959.[xlix]

He would be a lifelong example to

Ruth, who shared his love of music as well as his idea of the total patient concept in medicine. He saw Ruth as an eager medical student, never as a woman who was incapable of fulfilling the strenuous requirements of an orthopaedic surgeon. It was his encouragement that molded her decision, after only three months in Iowa to go into orthopaedics instead of general surgery. His liberal views of women as orthopods in the 1930s is in direct contrast with the negative atmosphere surrounding a young high school student who wrote to Ruth in 1969. Paula Bureau of Medford, Oregon wrote August 19, 1969 seeking Ruth's advice about becoming an orthopaedic surgeon. After extensive therapy and surgery on her knee, she had determined that she wanted to become an orthopaedic surgeon but most of the doctors she talked to tried to discourage her saying, "women aren't strong enough." Her therapist suggested that she write to Ruth concerning pursuing a career in orthopaedics. Ruth's prompt answer: "If you have a burning desire to study medicine no one can stop you.... Between now and the time that you will want to specialize in any field you may change your mind a dozen times, because there are so many specialties in which one may become interested. Orthopaedic surgery involves more skill and brains than brawn. If you are secure in your belief that you want to study medicine and then specialize in orthopaedic surgery, please do not let anyone talk you out of it. It is a most gratifying field of medicine and a most interesting one."[1]

The year she spent in Iowa City was an exciting one for Ruth both professionally and socially. Her goal was fixed on orthopaedics within the first three months. There were many polio cases at the University Hospital and she was impressed by the results achieved with the crippled children. One day toward the end of her internship, she and Dr. Steindler were walking down the hall together when Dr. Steindler stopped, turned to her and said, "Now Dr. Jackson have you decided what you want to do next year?" When she told him of her plans to return to Worcester for her residency because they had a good orthopaedic service, then go to Dallas to take her third year as a resident at Scottish Rite Hospital for Crippled Children, he told her that he would not worry about her. She asked him what he meant. His reply was, "Because you pay attention to the little things. These boys, all they want to do is operate, operate, but I don't worry about you."

Dr. Steindler's home was always open to the students. There were no lectureships or seminars such as are held at medical schools today, but whenever famous doctors visited the University, the students were invited to the Steindlers' home for discussions. These informal sessions, sometimes in the form of garden parties, usually ended on a musical note with Dr. Steindler at the piano. Many of the doctors had the students for dinner occasionally. In a notebook kept by Ruth during that year she recalls having dinner with Doctors Hargroves, Livingston, Adams and Olsen.[li]

Ruth's notebook is full of references to Don Keyes and Jacob 'Jake' Kulowski. When the "Three Musketeers" as they became known during that special year, met at the beginning of the year, there was an instant bonding. Her attraction to Don Keyes was like a thunderbolt and the feeling was returned. They shared a love of hunting, fishing, horses and most important, medicine. Ruth was living in the nurses' home. She had to walk to the main hospital to take her meals. In the winter she walked through an underground tunnel. With all the exercise she was getting, Ruth dropped from 158 pounds to a slim 135. Don and Jake had joined the Cavalry that year and had access to the horses for their friends and their dates to ride. Jake's date was Dr. Steindler's niece, whom he would marry. Ruth and Don also shared a sense of adventure which led them to try anything they dared to do. Ruth, the more practical one, confined her adventures to such activities as jumping barrels on horseback and taking to the air in a plane. Flying was a sport new on the scene.

After Ruth returned to Worcester, Don's escapades were a little more reckless causing him to be dismissed from the intern program. In his second year of training, after a little too much revelry, Don decided to swim across the Iowa River, still dressed in his Cavalry uniform. The journey was a success, but caused his downfall when the University officials became aware of his caper. Later he went to Northwestern, the University of Chicago where he and Edward Compere discovered that the nucleus pulposus acted as a hydro-dynamic ball bearing on the intervertebral disc.[lii]

"The Three Musketeers" weathered through good times and bad. Always able to find a fourth, bridge was one of their favorite games. She kept her dance program from the Aesculapian Frolic where the well chaperoned medical students danced in the Shadowland Ballroom April 4, 1930 to the music by Harold Austin and his New Yorkers.

They were also there to comfort Ruth when she was hospitalized one night with appendicitis. At midnight on Sunday, May 4, 1930, Ruth underwent surgery. Don and Jake kept her room filled with flowers. She recovered enough to attend the Steindlers Garden party May 16, and help Don with his research.[liii]

In romantic novels, at this

Ruth Jackson, M.D.: A Life on the Leading Edge

point, these two bright young interns with so much in common, Ruth the tiny five-foot two inches, with bright red hair in a chic Marcel wave, and Don, tall, mustached and debonair, would marry and live happily ever after. But this is not a romantic novel. This is about real life and to Ruth her only life then and forevermore was medicine. So determined was she to devote her life to medicine that in later years she would have radiation treatment to become sterile. Nothing was to interfere with her goals in life.

After spending her last hours with Don from two in the afternoon until midnight, on July 5, 1930, Ruth left Iowa City. In her open Oakland beige sport phaeton, which she had purchased for $200, Ruth drove the 1700 miles back to Worcester to start her year in the orthopaedic residency program at Memorial Hospital. Trusting her guardian angel, she drove alone over the paved roads which by now were lined with billboards, hot dog stands, home-styled diners and tourist cabins. Her four-day trip took her through Chicago, Niagara and Pittsburgh. She arrived in Worcester July 9th down to her last penny. Since the chief of orthopaedics, Dr. Charles Ayers and his wife had invited her to come to Quonochotaug beach in Rhode Island to spend the weekend with his family, Ruth wrote a check for $50 on her father, as she had always done. Her father had always allowed his seven children, even the married ones, to write checks on his bank account. Whether it was an oversight at the bank or the depression was catching up with her father's finances, Ruth never knew the reason but to her embarrassment, the check was returned: "Signature Unauthorized."

Ruth was to receive $50 a month plus her room, board and laundry while at Memorial Hospital. She had received her first pay check by the time the check was returned so she could make it good, but she had another talk with herself. "From now...from now on you are never going to ask your father for anything," she told herself. "I never asked my father for another penny. I would do extra work at the YWCA examining girls for $2 an hour. Sometimes, if a patient liked me they would give me $20 so I managed to get by on my stipend and any extra I earned."

The Ayers home was Ruth's haven away from home that year. One winter afternoon, she decided to try skiing on the hill behind their home. Borrowing a pair of skis, she donned some of Dr. Ayer's heavy pants and jacket, since she hadn't come prepared for outdoor sports and spent an enjoyable afternoon on the "ski slope." She also enjoyed a visit from her brother, Paul, who along with his wife, Velma and two sons, O.N., nicknamed "Tip" and Paul Jr., called "Honey" by family members were living at that time in New York City.

The year passed swiftly. She absorbed all the surgical knowledge Dr. Ayers had to offer, which was considerable. Well known for his work on the lower back, Dr. Ayers did many spinal fusions using superiosteal bone grafts from the patient's tibia. Ruth was kept busy, mostly because of the tree sitting craze that swept the nation where so many of the young people were trying to break the record for sitting in trees the longest. Most ended on the ground with broken limbs. It was Ruth's job to mend all their broken bones that year. She considered herself fortunate since it was good practice.

In July of 1931, it was time to return to Dallas to her next residency at Scottish Rites Hospital. This time she had a traveling companion for part of the trip. Evelyn Olsen, one of the interns, was from Iowa. An overnight stay in Chicago made it possible for Ruth and Don Keyes, who was at Northwestern, to meet again. An outing on Lake Michigan gave them an opportunity to rekindle their romance, even if temporarily. The next day the two girls drove to Evelyn's parents' home. Financially embarrassed, Ruth asked Evelyn's veterinarian father for a $50 loan. The next day she left for Dallas. When she stopped in Oklahoma for gas, two boys walked up to her and asked her for a ride to Dallas. At first she refused, but she succumbed to their request. They jokingly told her she could put handcuffs on them if she would just give them a ride. "I knew that they were fraternity brothers and could tell that they were nice young men," she laughingly remembers, "but I did tie their hands together." After an uneventful trip, she let them out on

Cedar Springs St. in Dallas and never saw them again. She drove to Scottish Rites Hospital, her temporary home for the next year. Her last year of training before she could achieve her ambition. She really felt at home because she was back in Dallas where her real life was about to begin.

"We must distrust our impulse of intervention, for the desire to make one's own will prevail is often disguised under the mask of solitude."

CHAPTER VIII

Even though Ruth's father did not originally give his blessing to her decision to become a doctor, an incident occurred during her last year in residency at Scottish Rites Hospital that made him grateful for her professional choice. White Wing dove season, two weekends in September, is a time in the Rio Grande Valley when the multitude descend to shoot its limit of the White Wing dove or anyone unlucky enough to be standing in the way. Ruth had been a resident at Scottish Rites Hospital for Crippled Children for about six weeks that September of 1931. Her brother, Harley was sitting in the breakfast room of his McAllen home getting ready for the day's hunt. His wife, Jane, anxiously called to him saying, "Harley, Marion has the gun." Seven year old Marion was holding a shotgun pointed at his nine year old brother Darrell, when his father told Jane the gun wasn't loaded.

"I'll shoot Darrell then," Marion said as he pulled the trigger.

The shotgun blast tore through Darrell's right shoulder. The plucky nine year old would not let anyone pick him up to carry him to the hospital. He somehow managed to walk to the car, then into the hospital on his own power. The only treatment he received from the doctors at the McAllen hospital was to have Mercurochrome poured over the gaping wound. Ruth's father had already contacted her asking her to come home on the first train out of Dallas to do what she could for Darrell.

"Since Darrell was recuperating from diphtheria, I couldn't give him an anesthetic to do a debridement. I had to cut away the loose pieces of bone since the blast had shot off muscle and shattered the bone," Ruth said.

During the surgical procedure Darrell kept shouting at her to stop, "I'll hate you forever if you don't," he cried over and over. Ruth kept working, talking to him all the while, and telling him to calm down, that she was sorry but it had to be done. Ruth talked to Darrell just as her mother had talked to her. She had taken an abduction arm splint with her when she left Dallas, since she knew she didn't want his arm stabilized in a downward position because she knew it would stay that way if she did. Before leaving she gave the doctors instructions on his care, and then she had another talk with Darrell. "I promised him that when he was twelve years old he could come to Dallas to live with me." Since he was always with her anyway, they could just make it permanent.

    A typical Texas heat wave was making life miserable for everyone when Ruth returned to Dallas. Ruth's room was provided along with her board, laundry and stipend of $100 a month, which soon dropped to $85 because of the effects of the depression. Her room, just off of the surgery in the Scottish Rites Hospital, was located where not a breath of air drifted through during the long, hot nights. To make matters worse the window was stuck so she couldn't open it completely. She often wandered into her friend, Lorraine Sanders's room where she curled up at the foot of her bed trying to cool off.

Ruth Jackson, M.D.: A Life on the Leading Edge

Although Lorraine was the dietician, she lived in the area reserved for the nurses. It was an innocent habit which would cause her to be labeled as a lesbian. It resulted in her losing a promised position with the Carrell-Driver-Girard Clinic where she had been working afternoons taking histories and examining patients. Dr. Carrell had been responsible for approving her residency at Scottish Rites Hospital after he made a trip to Iowa City.

"Dr. William Beall Carrell and I had an agreement that as soon as I finished my residency, I would be taken on as an assistant in his clinic on Maple," she said. "One day, Dr. Carrell asked me if I was going to open my own office when I finished my year."

She was bewildered when he added that he thought they would "work her out" of the clinic. It was a terrible blow, not only because she didn't have the financing to open her own office, but also because she felt that her work had been acceptable. Although she never doubted her capability to make it on her own, she did wonder why Dr. Carrell had reneged on his promise. One day on a routine visit to her gynecologist and friend Dr. Minnie Maffett, the puzzle was solved. Ruth told Dr. Maffett about Dr. Carrell working her out of their program. "Well, I'll tell you why," Dr. Maffett said, "The superintendent of the hospital didn't like you at all. She told Dr. Carrell that you were a lesbian, just because you slept at the foot of the dietician's bed occasionally."

Ruth was devastated by this news. It was not only men, but many women during the early 20th century also held the prevalent idea that it was "unnatural for a woman to be a doctor, ill-fitting her delicate state."[liv] Perhaps this precipitated jealousy which led to malicious gossip. It was only natural that the women physicians would seek companionship with their female peer group. As extroverted as Ruth was, there were times when the male contingent excluded her from their activities.

Later, as her friends were married, being single would find her "odd man out" on many occasions. Even at the time of this false accusation, Ruth was dating Fred Mote and several other young men. Ironically enough, Lorraine Sanders was a constant companion of Hugh McClung, who would later become Ruth's brother-in-law. As Barbara Branden said, in her book *The Passion of Ayn Rand*, "When one looks at history's great achievers one so often encounters the desperate loneliness and alienation which perhaps the emotional price paid by men and women who see farther than their brothers.... And one must wonder if they are not precisely the qualities that make possible the courage and uncompromising dedication of those who forge new paths through the unknown, enduring and persevering, shouting defiance at the enormity of the opposition which follows them at every stop of their lonely journey, and adding new glories to our world...."[lv]

Maybe it was fate's way of steering her into her own private practice. Maybe her guardian angel had an off day. Whatever! The fact that she established her orthopaedic career independently of others proved her skill even more than if she had been connected with such a prominent partnership as the Carrell-Girard-Driver Clinic.

Her first problem was money. She had vowed never to ask her father for money after her experience in Worcester. Even though she had double dated with the president of the Republic National Bank she could not ask for a loan because at that time a woman could not borrow money without a man's signature. After much deliberation she consulted with Dr. Sim Driver. She had always been treated with great respect by Dr. Driver and Dr. Percy Girard. Dr. Driver offered to co-sign her note for $400 so that she could establish her own practice.

She opened her first office, August 1, 1932 on the 18th floor of the nineteen story Medical Arts Building on Pacific Avenue in downtown Dallas. The 19th floor was a hospital. Built in 1923 by Dr. Edward H. Cary, the building had received national publicity as a medical showcase. Dr. Cary was the driving force in the Baylor College of Medicine, having served without pay as dean of the medical school from 1902 until 1920. In addition to serving as president of the Texas Medical Association, the Dallas County Medical Society and the Southern

Ruth Jackson, M.D.: A Life on the Leading Edge

Medical Association and by the time Ruth moved into the prestigious medical building, he had just completed a stint as the first Texan ever to be elected president of the American Medical Association.[lvi]

Ruth paid $35 a month for her office, sharing a common reception room with four other doctors. Ruth did have her own telephone. One secretary, Noreen Nicholas, served as receptionist for the five doctors. Noreen's pay for keeping track of records, phone calls and the many chores she was called upon to perform for five physicians was $75 per month. In 1986 after seeing Ruth's picture and an article in the Dallas Morning News about Baylor University Medical Center honoring her, Ms. Nicholas called Ruth to reminisce about those working conditions 54 years ago. She told Ruth that when she asked for a raise she was refused.

With a loan to repay, Ruth could not sit behind a closed door waiting for patients to discover her. In order to perform the extensive reconstructive surgery gratis, she gave physical examinations for $3 an hour under President Franklin D. Roosevelt's Works

Progress Administration (WPA) program. The reconstructive surgery was gratifying work as well and gave her a chance to learn new techniques. With the $2,100 she earned through the WPA program, she finished her first year in practice debt free.

    Although it was not unusual for some of her former classmates to tell her that their referral patients were refusing to go to a woman, it didn't take long for the patients to come to Ruth. It also didn't take long for the other physicians to become jealous. Edythe, Ruth's younger sister, had sent one of the poems she had written about Ruth entitled "Modern Miracle" to Don McNeil's "The Breakfast Club Program" at a radio station in Chicago. This program, heard by thousands of people was also heard by some of the Dallas doctors and their families. Ruth did not know that this poem, praising her, had been read over the national network until one of the doctors in the office building accosted her in the elevator with the sarcastic question, "How much did it cost you to get that poem read over the Chicago station?" She had to call Edythe in McAllen to get information about the incident. Edythe confirmed it by reciting the following lines from her poem *Modern Miracle*:

> You walked with certain step into the room where gleaming knives were waiting surgeon-skill and figures,
> Starched and white, began to loom about a sleeping form, well drugged to kill the coming pain.
> A silence grew, like stone, as you, with hands so trained, they felt their way, incised the tender flesh to mend a bone and plant a tendon where no tendon lay.
> You'd vision in your mind a little boy standing upon a pair of matching feet, and so with means and strength at your employ, you worked to make the withered one complete.
> You stepped aside, they wheeled the cart away, "Do wonders ever cease" you heard them say." [lvii]

She concluded their conversation by informing Ruth she told the radio station that the poem was written and dedicated to her sister, Ruth Jackson,

M.D. of Dallas, Texas.

Ruth's pride in her sister was mixed with chagrin at the adverse effect it caused. Ruth was needled in more subtle ways. She had to schedule her surgery patients either extremely early in the morning or very late, since the men always had the choice time slots for surgery. Often Dr. Driver would invite Ruth to operate with him. One morning Dr. Driver had a patient scheduled early at St. Paul's Hospital but he was running late. Since Ruth was on time she got to do the surgery. Being ahead of time for surgery was one of her strong points. "When I had surgery I was there at least 30 minutes before the surgery was scheduled. I wanted to be sure that everything was correct and that the patient was properly brought to the operating room, "I always liked to speak to the patient when they went into the operating room." she said. "I never felt stressed. I knew I had deadlines to meet. I just planned ahead and did it."

Necessity is the mother of invention. Ruth needed expensive surgical instruments which she couldn't afford in the early days of her career. Always innovative, Ruth improvised. She went to a hardware store and bought an upholstery needle. She utilized this humble tool in the Joplin operation. Her friend, Phillip Lewin, M.D. had written the book, *The Foot and Ankle* and illustrated Joplin's operation. He had designed a special operation of Hallux Valgus known to laymen as bunions. Ruth used the upholstery needle through the heel. She could then attach wires or ropes to the needle and put on the traction. She later demonstrated this procedure with a foot exhibit at the American Academy of Orthopaedic Surgeons Meeting at the Palmer House in Chicago. As an illustration, she used an upholstery needle for transplanting the long tendon of the little toe under the metatarsals and through a hole in the first metatarsal neck to act as a sling to prevent spreading of the metatarsal on weight bearing. She kept that foot on her office desk wherever she was located.

    She used a hammer to chip up bones; bought a regular chisel and had it coated with chrome and attached doorknobs to the crank and the end of a carpenter's drill. She became so attached to these items that she used them long after she could afford the expensive surgical instruments. Frugality may have been the reason for some of her homemade surgical instruments, but in one case availability was the driving force behind her inspirational choice for a surgical instrument. Ice tongs. She had been invited to go quail hunting in West Texas by a doctor whose wife had worked for Ruth at one time. The hunting season was cut short when one of the doctor's patients broke his neck. With no facilities for skull traction in the small town hospital, Ruth simply drove to the local hardware store and purchased a 25 pound set of ice tongs. After having the tongs sterilized, she injected some local anaesthetic on each side of the patient's skull. She then drilled tiny holes into his skull, "being sure," she always pointed out when telling this story that she didn't drill into his brain. Clamping the ice tongs in the tiny holes, she tied the tongs together. The rope came next, strung through a pulley over the end of the bed where the weights hung. Then it was back to the quail hunt. "That was a long time ago before the days of the halo vests which enable the patient to get up and move around," she stated.

With a growing practice, Ruth was often called by former classmates for orthopaedic consultations and to perform surgery in various parts of the state. Treating fractured hips with her method of internal fixation, the use of four special screws was in demand by many of her colleagues. She was also often asked to apply skull traction for fractures of the neck.

In Dallas, she did most of her surgery at Baylor even though she was also a member of the staff at Parkland and Methodist hospitals. She operated at St. Paul Hospital. She joined the Dallas County Medical Society and started work on her first paper, *"Painful Feet"* which was published in the *Physiotherapy Review* in 1933.

She had followed Dr. Carrell's advice to specialize in treating the foot. "When your feet hurt, you hurt all over," she said, "so I had more patients than if I had chosen another field." Even though she would become internationally known for her work with the cervical spine, she always was interested in the foot.

As busy as she was in 1934, she had not forgotten her promise made two years earlier to her nephew Darrell when he suffered the gunshot wound. She felt it was time to bring him to Dallas to live with her. He would be the first of a continuing stream of relatives and friends Ruth kept by her side. Through the years, she took in her nephew, Barney Jackson, when he worked for Braniff Airlines. Another nephew, Kieth Jackson, was her next houseguest.

O.N. "Tip" Jackson recalls that during his brief stay with his Aunt Ruth, while he attended Southern Methodist University, he had to escort her to all her social functions. He moved to the fraternity house after annoying Ruth's business manager, Marion Bouvé, who lived on the second floor of the three story house, when he got home late one night and dropped one shoe on the floor of his third floor room. Marion complained that she stayed up all night waiting for the other shoe to drop.

Ruth Jackson, M.D.: A Life on the Leading Edge

When Darrell moved in with Ruth she was living in an apartment in Judge Dick Dixon's big home at 3525 University Blvd. Centered on Southern Methodist University which officially opened in 1915, University Park adjoins Highland Park. These two autonomous municipalities were where the socially and economically elite lived. Preston Hollow completed the trio of prestigious areas. The winding roads with private lakes and beautifully landscaped homes formed country estates and summer homes for wealthy Dallasites. During the early 1930s the University Park area catered to the academic, therefore the homes could be less grand without losing prestige. Judge Dixon had divided the upstairs of his home into two large apartments. At one time Ruth's neighbor across the hall was an attorney who worked at University Park City Hall with the unlikely name of Melody Tune. Darrell distinctly remembers a young daughter whose name he swears was Tiny Tune.

Ruth, always eager to get back to the land, arranged for the two of them to go horse back riding at White Rock Park in nearby East Dallas. The trails led around picturesque White Rock Lake, at one time the city's water supply reservoir. Dallas was in for a long drought since the rains usually expected in the summer and fall had failed to materialize. Swimming at the University Park pool was a welcome diversion for the twelve year old Darrell. Believing every boy should have a dog; Ruth bought Darrell an inquisitive German Shepherd puppy named Smokey. While her home life took on a settled routine for the next few years, there was an aspect of her professional life that left her very unsettled.

"All Great people became great because they developed that facility of creative imagination! An image of what they want to be! Think big, be big! Think great, be great! Think tall of stature and be tall."

CHAPTER IX

Ruth was the only one of the "Three Musketeers", to be excluded in 1933 when an organization of orthopaedic surgeons was formed grandfathering in all orthopaedic surgeons. Ruth had the required training, limited her practice to orthopaedic surgery and had been Chief of Orthopaedic Service at Parkland Hospital for a year at that time, but none of this mattered. Although the newly formed American Academy of Orthopaedic Surgeons admitted surgeons who were not specialized in orthopaedics, the women were not included. Don Keyes and Jake Kulowski were taken in automatically, but Ruth had to wait four years until she was admitted after being made to take the boards in Cleveland, Ohio in 1937.

After taking the exams, a group of very nervous candidates was having milkshakes at a drug store when Dr. Phillip Lewin, of Chicago, an AAOS board member, walked past, winked at her and whispered in her ear "You passed."

As retiring secretary of AAOS, Dr. Lewin wrote to Ruth informing her of her membership, adding a postscript that she was the first woman elected to membership.[lviii] With this news, Ruth officially became the first woman orthopaedic surgeon to be board certified and a member of the AAOS. It would be six years before another woman, Dr. Penelope Sherwood was admitted. And another four before Ruth's partner, Dr. Margaret Watkins joined the elite organization in 1947.[lix]

The forties and fifties were called the "Great Withdrawal"[lx] The percentage of women Ph.D.s dropped drastically. It became fashionable to marry young and have large families. Many women's magazines stressed the importance of being a good mother. One by one, other women began to take the exams. Sixteen years later in 1958, Dr. Jacquelin Perry and Dr. Myra A. Peters became the ninth and tenth female orthopaedists to be board certified. Two by two the number of women orthopods admitted increased until 27 years later, in 1964, there were three admitted. The three who passed the exams were: Dr. Liebe S. Diamond, Dr. Jeane Michels and Dr. Alvina O. Sabanas. Although women were gaining ground in the 1960's; the American Stock Exchange had admitted its first female members; the Arizona Supreme Court had its first woman chief justice and Patricia Harris became the first black woman to be an American ambassador, the number of female orthopaedists was not fast forwarding; especially in view of the rise of the new Women's Liberation movement.[lxi]

The 1970s started out with three doctors, Dr. Virginia M. Badger, Dr. Maureen K. Molloy and Dr. Alice M. Murname becoming board certified. From 1971 to 1980 only eight women were admitted: Dr. Rosamond Kane, 1971; Dr. Sandra J. Thomson, 1972; Dr. Maria T. Godesky 1975; Dr. Mary Williams Clark, 1976; Dr. Mary R. McVay and Dr. Elena R. Martinez, 1978; and in 1979, Dr, Alice Martinson and Dr. Lorraine Day.

The barrier was broken in 1982

when five women: Dr. Dorothy A. Balthazar, Dr. Diane English, Dr. Helen Horstmann, Dr. Letha Hunter-Griffin and Dr. Geraldine Richter became AAOS members. Ruth lived to see the largest group of women orthopaedists, thirty-two in 1994, admitted to the American Academy of Orthopaedic Surgeons.

Even without a membership in AAOS her practice had flourished. By 1936 she felt financially capable of buying her own home. The new house on Fondren Drive, originally named Myra Jean, was located near Southern Methodist University. Taking her father's advice, she purchased the vacant lot next door to the house, both for the grand total of $5,500.

Her home was small, but perfect for entertaining Ruth's large circle of friends, including Dr. Ruby Daniel, Dr. Elsie Westley, Drs. Nina Fay and Tom Calhoun, Dr. Minnie Maffett, Drs. Magda and David Myers, Dr. Frank Brown and Kate Shodding; and many of her friends from Zonta Club. It was at a dinner party at Kate's house in April, 1938 that Ruth's date, Bill Curtis, a law student at SMU, introduced her to her future husband, Dan McClung. She had been dating Bill, who lived on a trust fund, and was always available for a good bridge game. That night Danny told Ruth that a psychic "Madame R," said, "I should marry you." Then he asked if she thought they could be happy together. Even though she thought he was too young for her, she agreed to try it.

He began the courtship by wooing her with love letters:

"My darling, may God keep me worthy of you. Always do I want to come to you clean and honorable, with nothing to conceal, with no curtains drawn across even one small part of my heart because you know I want you to be, not just my wife, but my comrade, my friend, my confidant and confessor. I can stand against the world with you by my side. I love you darling. I love you deeply and passionately and my love fills all my heart and soul so there is no room for any other emotion." He called her his "little Minx" and sometimes referred to her as Scarlet.[lxii]

The marriage, which took place July 1, 1939 in her Fondren home, was doomed from the start. For fun loving, easy going, Danny McClung it was love at first sight and until "death do us part." He adored Ruth, leaving her love notes on her dresser; waking her with songs on his banjo, writing poetry about her, and doing his very best to please his new wife.

Ruth was attracted to Danny's dark good looks, his pliability, and his *joie de vivre*. Tall with dark wavy hair, the wedding photo shows a happy, clean shaven bridegroom. Then the *"I Love You, You're Perfect, Now Change"* syndrome kicked in.

She immediately demanded that he grow a mustache. Her first effort in Danny's transformation into her former love, Don Keyes. She showered him with gifts. Gifts that pleased her, not him. Clothes like Don Keyes had worn; aftershave and cologne that Don had used. Was he in denial or did he really believe what he wrote when he refers to these gifts in a note written August 6, 1940, as knowing "how well these clothes, ties and shirts you give me express not only your love but also noble desire to keep my morale high." lxiii

There were many explanations for the marriage. One could have been that

Ruth needed a presentable escort; another that his adoration fed her ego. Women didn't attend social events at the Idlewild Club, the Calyx Club, the Dallas Country Club or the Dallas Slipper Club unless they were accompanied by a male escort. These clubs were just a few that were listed in 1938 in the *Fourteenth Annual Dallas Blue Book and Social Record* for the city of Dallas.

Dr. Ruth Jackson was listed in the prestigious Blue Book that year as being a member of the Texas State Medical Association, Texas Orthopaedic Assoc., Dallas County Medical Society, Fellow of the American Academy of Orthopaedic Surgery (only woman Fellow), A.E.I National Fraternity of Medical Women, Surgeon for Texas Society for Crippled Children, Chief of Orthopaedic Service, Parkland Hospital Ward and member of Zonta Club of Dallas. Shades of Mrs. Vanderbilt!

Whatever her reasons, after vowing never to marry or have children, the wedding was solemnized by Judge Dick Dixon, Judge of the 95th District Court in Dallas. Dr. Elsie Westley of San Antonio, was the bride's only attendant and the best man was Danny's brother, H. C. McClung. After a reception attended by family including Ruth's parents, W.R. and Belle, and friends of the bridal couple, they left for a honeymoon in Hot Springs, Arkansas.

The fact that Danny, who had attended SMU and was a member of the Phi Kappa Alpha fraternity, had no money, and even lost his job when the Home Owner's Loan Corp. folded due to the depression, didn't bother Ruth. She was capable of earning a living for the two of them. There were other strains on the marriage. She had married him for "better or for worse", but not his mother. Danny had been supporting his widowed mother even before the wedding. When a fire destroyed his mother's home, she moved in with the newlyweds.

The deterioration of the marriage can be traced through the many love letters and notes Danny left in conspicuous places throughout the house. In a letter written a month after their marriage he tells her:

"Darling I love you and all emotional upsets on the part of either of us are to be expected and forgotten. Nothing can really spoil our love." [lxiv]

Ruth Jackson, M.D.: A Life on the Leading Edge

Just a few months after their marriage, Danny began to feel the stress of trying to please Ruth.

He writes the following in a letter to her October 10, 1939:

"Everything is for you. Even the matter of a haircut that doesn't please you disturbs me so much because it makes you unhappy and I do not want to make you unhappy in any way. Sometimes I think that even now, I am not quite sure just what will please you and what will make you unhappy. Some things are not important to me but are of great importance to you. See dearest we have grown to maturity apart. I will try very hard to adjust my ways to yours as much as possible but please be patient. The long years you spent under the disciplinary demands of the medical profession are completely alien to me. It is because that profession is your life that I will attempt to conform to your manner and mode of thinking as much as possible. Since your happiness means everything to me, you would not be happy if I insisted you conform to my ways, that is continue my former way of living, my former friends, my former way of dressing, wearing my hair. You have changed many of your habits to conform to mine also, but I don't want you to change so that you would be different, because I thought you perfect when I knew you and I haven't changed my opinion. Just want you to know that I am fully aware of your deep and precious love."[lxv]

When Ruth went to a meeting in Boston, she didn't take Danny with her, traveling on to New York to see Dr. Margaret Watkins. He wrote to her every day telling her how much he missed her. "The ink is a trifle red. I loved your telegram darling, but who are the other signatures? Nice folks I hope, I am sure of course. What a lonely sort of Sunday. Our first apart. All morning I paced the house unable to read even "Orphan Annie." Do have a wonderful trip, dear, it means so much to you, these meetings. You will get much, much good out of it and I want you to extract the last ounce of that good. Don't think that you have to curtail one hour to come to me. I miss you and want you, but also know that your patients will profit from your trip and it is for them and your desire to be tops that you are there. See Peg in New

York if you want even though it means an extra day, for the little house and I will be waiting for you."

He encouraged her to live her life as she pleased, which she did anyway. He thought their problems were caused by his not being able to provide her with the beautiful clothes, furs and jewels, which he promised to buy her someday. He told her that someday she would be "so proud of me because I'll be so rich."[lxvi] Ruth already had the clothes, furs and jewels. She had bought them herself.

As Chief of the Orthopaedic Surgery Department at Parkland Hospital from 1936 to 1941, Ruth was working very hard at the hospital and at her office. She spent a great deal of time in conferences and keeping active with the resident training program she had started. She was spending a lot of time training one particular resident, Dr. Peg Watkins, who would later become her partner.

With no job, and time on his hands Danny began to brood. One evening when Ruth came home from the office to change and attend another evening conference, Danny's car was in the driveway. "I asked him if he was going out that night. His reply was, 'I do not know, that depends on you.', Ruth recalled pensively. "When I asked him why, he said 'you will have to stop seeing Dr. Watkins or I am walking out.'"

In a rush, her retort was "Oh Danny, you don't mean that," then she went into the house, dismissing his intentions. When she returned to the living room, he was gone. Ruth didn't play poker, but she called his bluff that night. She filed for divorce the next day. It was granted by the same judge who had married them. Judge Dixon left the bench telling her "If you had asked me what I thought when I married you and Dan, I would have told you that it would never work. But you didn't ask me."

It was such a friendly divorce that Ruth and Danny celebrated by going out that night to the Adolphus Hotel for dinner and dancing. Their favorite orchestra performed, whose leader and some members of the band had played at Ruth's home for a special occasion. They remained lifelong friends. Danny joined the Navy and eventually married a widow with a grown daughter.

Her view of her marriage could be summed up with a note she wrote on the envelope of a letter she received from Danny, who was repaying a loan. "I'm well convinced," she wrote, "that broken hearts, unlike most anatomical parts can be reassembled as good as new after the lapse of a day or two."

Even without a husband, Ruth managed to have a good time. Her brother-in-law, Harold Brehm recounts the story of Ruth going to an illegal gambling establishment in Dallas. Unfortunately it was raided while she was there. The account in the Dallas paper mentioned a "prominent woman" being booked in the raid, but according to a gleeful Ruth, everyone thought it was her friend, Judge Sarah Huges. (Judge Hughes would become famous for swearing in Lyndon Johnson as President of the United States after that fatal day in 1963.)

Unencumbered, Ruth immersed herself in her one true love: medicine. It had always been and would always be the main focus of her life. The early 1940s found her with more responsibilities. In May of 1940, Ruth was appointed by the Secretary of Labor, Frances Perkins, to a three year term as a member of the advisory committee on services for Crippled Children. The committee was set up to advise the U.S. Children's Bureau in the development of sound relations between the federal government and the States in extension and improvement in the health, and welfare of crippled children. Ruth had been active in the Texas Crippled Children's Society since 1933.[lxvii]

In 1941 she attended the National Meeting in Washington where she was a guest at a White House event presided over by Mrs. Eleanor Roosevelt. Ruth visited all the civilian defense offices in Washington during her stay; she taught advanced First Aid classes and many Air-Raid Warden classes to prepare Dallasites in case of air raids. She set up many simulated air raids in the training process of her classes.

In the midst of these community activities she even found time for inventions. Always a problem solver, Ruth had become upset one night when she had trouble finding a patient's house due to bad lighting in the area. She promptly decided that everyone should have luminous street signs which could be seen in the dark. She received a patent October 20, 1941 for luminous signs called "Reflecto." She formed a company called Reflecto Sign Co in January of 1940 with R.O. Walton as manager. In October 1941 he started his own company and sold her signs for which she received a thirty-five cent royalty on each sign.[lxviii]

Another idea for an invention was spawned by a couple arguing violently while driving. Ruth watched in horror as they pummeled each other in the car in front of her. After witnessing their resulting three car accident, she decided to design a headrest neck supporter for a car. She envisioned a car which would separate the two front seat passengers by enclosing them with Martian like bubble tops on the sleek, low-slung chassis. She designed it with separate compartments so they couldn't "make love or war" while driving. It was equipped with intercoms so they could communicate, but never touch. The pointed front was designed to cut down the wind factor to save gasoline. The bubble type tops were heat and cold resistant and non-breakable.

In 1966, new government regulations promulgated by the United States Government required a head rest to be provided on the back of the front seats of automobiles. Her attorney, Howard E. Moore, urged her to file for a patent as soon as possible, since there were a lot of inventors working in this field. That year she wrote a letter to Price Neeley Medical Plastics Corp., Gatesville, Texas inquiring about the feasibility of plastic models. She wanted them flexible to show resulting injuries in order to test her invention.[lxix] Ruth had been invited by the Vice-President in charge of styling & design of General Motors to come to Detroit to speak to the stylists, designers and engineers about neck injuries and confer with them about safety measures.[lxx]

Because of this connection she thought General Motors would be a good place to pitch her newly patented design. On April 16, 1968 she wrote the following to Peter Kyropoulos, technical director, General Motors Technical Center, Warren, Michigan:

Ruth Jackson, M.D.: A Life on the Leading Edge

"When I visited with you I thought you said you might be interested in the halo type head and neck safety device to be used in automobiles indicated when a patent was issued on this device you might be interested in doing the prototype there at GM. The patent has been issued, if you are still interested I would appreciate hearing from you."[lxxi]

She already had communication from two companies who she claimed were interested in promoting patents. She thought that GM's interest in the field of safety would provoke their interest in promoting patents and she wanted their reaction concerning her patent. Her design never got off the ground. In a letter written May 27, 1968 from John A. Dobb, Director of New Devices Section, GM Engineering Staff, Ruth learned that her patent #3,376,064 wouldn't fly, let alone drive. He told her that the engineering staff was working on various types of restraints and didn't feel that Ruth's would fit their present program.[lxxii]

Her busy schedule didn't keep her from taking an active part in community and social projects. A member of the

Dallas Zonta Club since 1937, she served as president twice, 1943 and 1945; was chairman of District X twice and from 1946 to 1948 was District Governor of District X.

During her first presidency, the Office of Defense requested that everyone refrain from travel because of the war so she was unable to attend the national meeting in New York. During her tenure she helped set up a War Service Committee to conduct patriotic projects such as paper collections, rummage sales and raising Victory B funds. Individual Zontians worked with the Red Cross providing food and comfort for the military personnel.

Although Ruth was never an outspoken women's liberation advocate, she worked in more subtle ways. As a Zontian officer she met with the other service clubs to arrange a survey for headquarters for Women in Service. The Status on Women Committee checked on discrimination against women in the war effort and married women teachers. In the Dallas newspaper in 1938, an article appeared asking Zonta members to attend a trial in a suit filed in the 68th District Court by Miss Stella

Gloves to establish women's right to sit on a jury.[lxxiii] Under her leadership the Zontians devoted over 3,028 hours to the war effort, including the Red Cross, war bond drives, USO, Girl Scouts, Child Welfare and Victory Gardens as well as assistance to servicemen and their wives.[lxxiv]

Being surrounded by a loyal staff in her office and home, enabled Ruth to keep her busy schedule in her medical career and her social life. Lela Mae Owens, her first housekeeper, worked for Ruth for ten years until Ruth moved to the house on Turtle Creek. Mattie Williams was her housekeeper from 1938 to March 18, 1942. In a letter of resignation dated 3-18-42, Dallas, Texas, she wrote: "Dear Dr. Jackson: It have been (sic) a pleasure and privilege to work for you the past four years. During this I have never found a person to be more kind and considerate, pleasant or cooperative than you. It is amazing to find a person as devoted as you to your life work and to know that any time day or night you are never to tired to go or to busy to go to the hospitals take emergency case, which in some cases the best had been rendered useful. They say if you give your best will come back to you. You are truly a living example. May God bless you always. Yours very truly, Mattie Williams."

Mattie's replacement was Gilbert, a gourmet cook, who also did her laundry and sewed buttons on her clothes. He was famous for his hors d'oeuvres served at Ruth's parties in her home on Turtle Creek. These behind the scenes employees kept the home fires burning. Pat Marshall, Jan Story, Lois Noll, Norma Lenk, and Helen Hopper, were just a few who kept her office running in the early years. Jan Story was with her for two years, Lois Noll, eleven years and Rita Bean in later years. Sheri Larzalere was her business manager and companion for the last years in her life.

The most dedicated of all her office staff was Tommie Lee Fields, her physical therapist and good friend, who went to work for her July 2, 1956. She was by Ruth's side until Ruth retired in 1989 then exchanged nightly phone calls until Ruth's death in 1994. Tommie Lee had worked at Methodist

Hospital but didn't like working on Sundays. All she requested when interviewed by Marion Ross Bouvé, Ruth's business manager, was that she would not have to work on Sundays. That is the only thing she didn't have to do. She helped Ruth make the first Cervipillos, accompanied her on many trips, and even fixed her lunch everyday at the office. When Tommie Lee and her husband decided to adopt her nephew, their attorney found out she worked for Dr. Ruth Jackson. Reaching into his desk drawer he pulled out Ruth's book *The Cervical Syndrome*. He explained that he had a terrible back problem, but couldn't go to Ruth for a consultation because he was an attorney with a firm who represented clients Ruth testified against in court. "I could get fired if I went to her so I bought her book *The Cervical Syndrome* trying to find out what is wrong with me," he explained. "I admire her work tremendously and would like to get you to arrange a meeting with her for me." The adoption went through, but the meeting didn't take place.

Ruth sought perfection, not only in her life, but of those around her. A hard taskmaster, she was sometimes penurious; then, paradoxically, extremely generous. Her tendency to mix friendship and business was one of Ruth's few mistakes. Marion Ross Bouvé, her business manager for 26 years, from 1943 to 1969, also lived in Ruth's house and managed her household affairs. Marion and her husband had owned and operated the Texas Country Day School in Dallas. After their divorce Marion went to work for Ruth as business manager, receptionist and according to Ruth "what not."

As long as Ruth's life ran smoothly, enabling her to devote her time to her practice, Ruth didn't question Marion's increasing control over her personal life. Friends' and relatives' calls and requests were screened by Marion without Ruth's knowledge, often denying access to Ruth. Ruth even received a letter from a patient complaining that Marion's rudeness and demeaning attitude had caused her almost to have a nervous breakdown.[lxxv]

Having a well run office, then coming home to a lovely home, decorated with many of Marion's personal antiques, suited her just fine. That is until Marion made two mistakes. In 1969 after Ruth returned from a Western Orthopaedics Society meeting in Colorado Springs, where Ruth had learned of Don Keyes' death, Marion had scheduled a non-emergency patient, this after Ruth had told her to keep her schedule free so she could get caught up with mail. Ruth informed Marion that she was terminated as of the first of the year. Marion told her, "As of now, I am through," and she walked out of the office. She remained in her suite of rooms in Ruth's house until she made her second mistake.

Returning home from an evening out, Marion walked into the library to find Ruth's friend and interior decorator, Jeani Hill, spending the night in the guest room. Flipping on the light, Marion ordered Ruth's friend out of "her house." Texas has an anti-litter slogan, "Don't Mess with Texas," and nobody messed with Ruth. Ruth informed her friend of many years that it was not "her house" and she would be expected to leave the next day. For good!

As sudden as the break was, the

problem had been simmering for some time. Although it was never mentioned at the time, Ruth's diary containing a note from Marion begging forgiveness reveals that she had been using Ruth's prescription pad to get drugs.[lxxvi] The insignificant incident concerning the house provided a good excuse for Ruth to sever the relationship without revealing the true reason.

After Marion's departure, Ruth had Jeani Hill redecorate her Turtle Creek home. The house was redone in Ruth's favorite color: red. The new red carpets, offset by white walls and draperies, delighted Ruth. "I love it" she remarked. "When I walk in I can sit down and relax." [lxxvii] In an interview with Jeani Hill, she recounts how they became friends when she redecorated her Turtle Creek home. "I began visiting her at her home. Ruth always enjoyed the organ, piano and the music. She is such a clown and we had great fun." Jeani, her husband, Tom Hill along with Marion Bouvé, would accompany Ruth to Mexico City for frequent stays at the jointly owned apartment on the Paseo de la Reforma. Jeani could play the organ and piano as well as the accordion that was in the apartment. "Of course, I enjoyed Ruth so much,"

Jeani spoke after Ruth's death. "It is nice to talk to intelligent people. There aren't that many around. We discussed literature, foreign language, art. She was very interested in Diego Rivera. She seemed to be such a giving person. I'll never forget when we were all at the apartment in Mexico City, on the Paseo de la Reforma, we were sitting out on the balcony and I said, 'Ruthie, I'm going to do your nails'. I went in and got my manicure set and I came out and worked on her nails for a while. She said, 'You know no one has ever done that for me.' We had so much fun...she is such a fun loving person."

"She was always giving and doing for every one else," Jeani continued, "and nobody does for her. She has always been so good and kind to me and my family and my friends. She has had some dreadful experiences during the years but I don't have very much input about it, because it seems that during those chaotic things that happened to her, for one reason or another, I would be out of the picture. Ruthie is so busy with her profession that she doesn't have time for that many people. I love her so dearly that I have always felt that if there was a person she was spending what ever free time she might have doing things that were important to her then I was comfortable. It is the in between times, on a few occasions when things have come up, I have tried to get on the scene, fill in the gap. Being talented, being intelligent: she is extremely high strung." [lxxviii]

    The Hills lived near Ruth on Turtle Creek near Fairmount Street at the Turtle Creek Gardens. Once again, friendship and business were intertwined. Ruth invested, with Jeani and Tom in an interior decorating company named The Triple C, which stood for Custom, Contract, and Commercial. They immediately bought a Volkswagen van and an airplane.

    In 1966 they flew to Eagle Pass, Texas to pick up Ruth's 13-year-old grandniece, Kathryn Ruth Jackson, daughter of "Tip" and Frances Jackson. Ruth had made arrangements for Kathy, an accomplished dancer, to audition for the State Fair Musicals in Dallas. Due to Kathy's skills, the 14 year age limit was lifted, but she decided she didn't want to live in Dallas.

Tom Hill, an extremely charismatic entrepreneur, earned his first pilot's license at 13. His many business ventures during the 1960s included Trojan Oil Company, which folded, as did his Hill's General Mining Corp. According to an unsigned affidavit, May 18, 1967, Tom stated that on April 27, 1965, when he was President of General Mining Corporation, he sold a four percent net working interest in and to the "Queen of Sheba Mine," located out of Shosone, California, 84 miles west of Las Vegas. for $25,000 to Dr. Ruth Jackson of Dallas, Texas.[lxxix] The affidavit goes on to state that although Ruth did not request a promissory note, Tom voluntarily delivered the note to her in order to show his good faith in the transaction because of their long time friendship.

The investment proved to be worthless, but Tom states that it was his personal thought that this purchase on behalf of Ruth represented a profitable investment from her standpoint. The affidavit ends with the following sentence: "When I delivered the note to Dr. Ruth Jackson, she asked me what it was and I told her it was just something to put with the Assignment and the other papers in the deal."

The friendship was so strong in 1965, that Ruth went through a confirmation ceremony performed by Dr. Dorsey Kelley at the Methodist Church on Pennsylvania Ave, in Oklahoma City Jeani's home church to make Ruth Jeani's Godmother. Attending, in addition to her husband, Tom were Jeani's parents, Mr. and Mrs. R.E. Malloy. Jeani said there was a special service in the church that morning due to Ruth's presence. After Tom was killed in a motorcycle accident, March 15, 1981 (RJ diary) Jeani discussed with Ruth being alone, since she was widowed. "Ruthie, I want to tell you something that I have heard you say over the years and I thought I understood, but until you have experienced it you can't really understand it. She (Ruth) had always said, 'Just because you're alone doesn't mean you're lonely.' I understand exactly what she's saying and she's right."

In October of 1985 Ruth, in a codicil to her will added Jeani Hill. Because of the dedication and devotion of those who saw to her needs, Ruth was to begin a new phase in her life.

"Let us be true: the highest maxim of art and life the secret of eloquence and virtues. To do easily what is difficult for others is the mark of talent. To do what is impossible for talent is the mark of genius."

CHAPTER X

With her practice growing and her skill in treating the cervical spine becoming recognized in the medical circles, Ruth was about to launch a new project.

Pain and determination were the key factors in the invention of the Jackson Cervipillo. A neck injury Ruth incurred in 1947 while playing with Butch, the three year old foster son of her business partner, Peg Watkins' parents, caused her to search for enough drug free relief to enable her to continue her practice the next day.[lxxx] Ruth was visiting at the home of Judge and Mrs. Royal Watkins on Bordeaux in Dallas one evening. Everyone was sitting around the fireplace talking when Butch clamored to climb on Ruth's shoulders.

"I had hold of his hands when suddenly his right foot slipped off my shoulder and all 35 pounds of his weight went on my head and neck...down and toward to the left," she recalls, "I never had such pain in all my life. I couldn't even go home."

Ruth spent the night with the Watkins, using Butch's baby pillow to cradle her painful neck. She took the pillow home with her. Each night after a long day at the clinic, she would put herself in traction with the pillow. When she began to feel better she would want to turn on her side that caused her head to fall over, then it was back to the back! The pillow cradling her neck relieved the pain. It was then she conceived the design of a pillow to make the center concave so the neck rests on the proper amount of support for comfort, leaving a bulge on either side which prevented rotation and lateral bending. The bulge at either end gave adequate support to assure comfort and to keep the neck straight. This relieved the pain by keeping the neck supported in proper alignment.

She began making the pillows for her patients in her office with the help of her therapist, Tommie Lee Fields. The pillows produced such gratifying results among her patients that Ruth and her therapist were working overtime to keep up. It was time consuming work to make the first pillows. Made of ticking stuffed with 75% feathers and 25% goose down, there were many times they would instruct the patients how to make their own pillows. One such patient was from North Little Rock, Arkansas, who first saw Ruth in 1945. Because of the war, she couldn't find the ticking, when she found it and the down, she followed the instructions from Ruth to make not only her Cervipillo, but also a neck collar designed by Ruth. On a plane trip to South Dakota, she sat next to an orthopaedic surgeon who kept looking at her collar. He not only asked her about it, but tried it on and liked it.

Ruth used her as a demonstration patient at a forum. When the doctors said she was a highly self motivated patient she wanted to tell them that Dr. Jackson motivated her. "When she tells you to do something you do it," she recalled. She also spoke of the dentist from Germany who was at the Baylor Dental College who told her that "Dr. Jackson is the one doctor who people listen to in Europe."

When the business picked up in later years, one of Ruth's patients in the upholstery business brought her some Dacron to try. After experimenting spreading the fiber with her fingers, rolling it, and then placing it in the ticking, she decided the Dacron worked better.

In 1947 Ruth described her pillow in a paper at the AAOS meeting in Chicago. She had an article, "The Cervical Syndrome as a Cause of Headache" that appeared in the *Journal of the American Medical Women's Association*. Requests for pillows began to arrive from all over the country from doctors who wanted to try them. A librarian from the Honolulu County Medical Center library wrote asking that a pillow be sent to her. When Ruth asked for comments on the pillow even the chiropractors liked them as one from New York attested.

Without a patented name, the requests were varied. One patient asking for the small "Dutch Widow" neck, another, the "contour," "the hour glass" and others referred to it as the "cervical contour pillow," the term used by Ruth at the time. She hired a woman to hand make the pillows for her and sold them for $6 plus postage. She established a company, The Cervical Contour Company. In July of 1948 she was referring her orders to the Wren Brace Shop on Maple Ave, the street behind her clinic on Fairmont. Each order was made to specifications. Height, weight and length of neck from the base to the skull were the measurements used. Some women even sent their dress size.

The pillow was gaining a reputation. Dr. Glen I. Allen of Peoria, Illinois wrote to her in 1950 saying "It has certainly been a revelation to me in the past two years after using the contour pillow and the traction, how much good we can do for these patients." In this case he was referring to patients with arthritis of the cervical spine. By 1951 inflation had set in and the pillows were selling for $7 plus shipping.

Ruth exhibited her pillow at the AAOS meeting in Chicago in 1951. The wide exposure of this exhibit boosted the mail orders. Unsolicited professional testimonials were being received. Dr. Wallace Duncan of

Cleveland, Ohio wrote to her saying that he had been very impressed by the fact that in his modifying the position of the head, in his experience using the pillow on patients who had degenerative processes in the cervical spine and nerve root compression materially influence the amount of pain that they had in their arms.

It was becoming more difficult to fill the handmade orders with the word of mouth publicity she had received. In early 1952 she sent two pillows to Louis Yellin in Philadelphia, President of Louis Yellin, Inc. He headed a family company that made and fitted surgical and orthopaedic appliances. He promised to investigate the cost of manufacturing the pillows. In May Mr. Yellin came to Dallas. By June of that year, Ruth had a contract with him to make her pillows and was referring her mail orders to his company.

The rapid increase in the use of Ruth's pillow could be linked to the fact that cervical nerve root irritation had become more frequent and increasingly trying as traffic congestion led to more of the so-called "whiplash" type of injury. The term "whiplash" was popularized about 1944 by the late Dr. Arthur Davis, an orthopaedic surgeon. Since the defendants' attorneys "saw red" every time they heard this expression, Ruth tried without success, to change the term to "necklash" in a paper given by Ruth in Atlanta Georgia in 1955 to Seaboard Air Line Railway Association.[lxxxi]

More patients were becoming involved in damage suits which further complicated the doctors' problems. Ruth soon realized that with the rapid growth of the contour pillow business she needed to protect her invention. She made inquiries in February 1952 on the advisability of registering the pillow as "The Cervical Contour Pillow," but was told by a Dallas attorney that this would be considered descriptive and not registrable as a trademark. She could file for an application covering only the term "Cervical." It might be possible on a special register set up under the recent amendment in the law. His research found only one pertinent registration similar, "Cerviplast," being used in the medical field at the time. On March 10, 1953 she received her trademark, "Cervipillo" register #571703 which has been in constant use.[lxxxii]

Ruth had signed an agreement with Lou Yellin, Inc., January 1, 1954 after having the Cervipillo approved by the United States Commissioner of Patents, serial #627136, for Mr. Yellin's company to manufacture and sell only at his factory. The pillows contained the improvement identified by the trademark. According to the agreement, Yellin was not to directly or indirectly manufacture or sell the Cervipillo or similar pillows under any other name. This point was to prove to be a festering sore some years later.

Yellin was to make the pillow to Ruth's specification, giving her a royalty of 75 cents per pillow, provide her with a written financial statement within thirty days after each six months period at which time the royalties were due. She had the right, at her own expense, to examine the books at least once each semi-annual period as well as to make reasonable inspections of the manufacturing operations to see that the pillow was being make to specifications. Either party could terminate the contract upon 30 days written notice by registered mail, restoring all rights to the pillow to Ruth.[lxxxiii]

Neither party would think that there might be problems. Lou Yellin and his wife, Beatrice had been good friends with Ruth. They socialized at the AAOS meetings where the Yellins displayed their medical equipment at the annual technological exhibits. Their young son, Arthur called her "Aunt Ruth," and spent the summer of 1958 with her in Dallas. He too was an outdoors man and often accompanied Ruth on her annual September White Wing dove hunts in the Lower Rio Grande Valley and fishing and duck hunting trips on the small lake at her Kaufman, Texas farm.[lxxxiv]

The seeds of discontent were sown between 1959 and 1961. Ruth's Cervipillo was her creative brainchild. She wanted the sales to be channeled in the most professional manner, but exclusively through the medical system. She was even willing to accept a lower royalty to keep it that way.[lxxxv]

In January 1961, without

consulting Ruth, an advertisement on the Cervipillo was inserted in a lay magazine. By the time the Yellins realized that Ruth didn't approve it, their attempts to have her name and the trademark removed were too late. Ruth was worried that the pillow was being advertised as a Yellin pillow. About the same time, Neiman-Marcus wanted to make the Cervipillo under its own label. She was adamant about not selling the Cervipillo advertised to the public under any consideration. Yellin claimed his medium would reach five million readers. She still felt the financial gains were not worth the price since her professional stature would inevitably suffer. If Neiman-Marcus did want to promote the Jackson Cervipillo under their own label and not as the Jackson Cervipillo, they, like every other department store would eventually get one of their manufacturers to duplicate it and Yellin would be left holding the bag, or in this case the pillow!

    Yellin told Ruth that he was very hurt because he had spent so much of his own money advertising in professional magazines, descriptive folders, artwork, etc; never mentioning to Ruth that her 75 cent premium was a burden. This, coupled with the fact that Ruth had complained about not receiving an accounting on the pillows in the latter part of 1959, caused a barrage of letters between Dallas and Philadelphia. The tone of the letters show the vital effort made on both sides to maintain their friendship in spite of the disagreement over the handling of the marketing of Ruth's pillows.[lxxxvi] In January of 1960 Yellin had explained that there were several reasons why she had not received an accounting from 1959 up to date; that he did not want to quit making the pillow and certainly he didn't want to lose her friendship.

Ruth had received a letter in the spring of 1959 from Lewis Silverstein, president of the Camden Fiber Mill, Inc. in Philadelphia, outlining plans for expanding the Cervipillo market to hospitals and surgical supply houses on a large scale. The possibility of a wider market appealed to Ruth and she referred him to Lou Yellin, but she left the door open by suggesting the two company presidents discuss the idea and let her know their conclusions.[lxxxvii]

The next year S.H. Camp and Company, who had a line of anatomical supports for orthopaedic conditions also was interested in the Cervipillo. Ruth had written to C.B. Clemons, vice president of the company in Jackson, Mississippi, wanting to know if it was possible for them to distribute the pillow. She had talked to a Mr. Yeakey concerning the Jackson pillow and had discussed the matter with Mr. Yellin while in Philadelphia. Yellin had given her the cost of making the pillow and she wanted to know if it were possible to get it made cheaper in Philadelphia, then the price would be cut a little.

In an attempt to explain her position she wrote to Beatrice telling her that money wasn't everything and friendship meant a great deal. She tried to explain that if Lou wanted to quit manufacturing and distributing the pillow it was all right with her. She could make a deal with plenty of people. These statements were tempered with anxious inquires over their son Art's recent car accident. As she was always apt to do with her young protégées, she admonished Art to avoid showy convertibles as too dangerous to drive. She complimented the Yellin Cervicollar which she had used on a patient with a severe neck injury and talked of plans to visit the Yellins if she got to New York to a medical meeting in the fall.[lxxxviii]

The business wounds will heal but scars will be left. In November of 1961, after enjoying a fishing trip at the Tanglewood Resort on Lake Texoma with Ruth and Ralph Sharp, Tru Wilhelm, president of Tru-Eze Manufacturing Co, Inc. of Burbank, California wrote to thank her. He told her that at the bottom of one of his orders from a surgical supply dealer for Tru-Eze traction machines was an order from a doctor for a Cervipillo. The surgical supply dealer couldn't find Yellin's address, so he ordered from Tru-Eze. By February of 1962, Tru-Eze was including the Jackson Cervipillo in their brochure on traction giving Yellin credit as the manufacturer. Although dealers were ordering the pillows from Tru-Eze, he was referring them in most part to Yellin. Since some of the orders Wilhelm deemed necessary to ship the pillow with the order, he suggested that Tru-Eze warehouse the pillow in the West Coast. Yellin replied that he was interested in receiving more particulars about the warehousing idea.

Ruth had tried for some time to talk Tru-Eze into taking over the pillow since she thought the Yellins were not promoting it enough. Wilhelm was enthusiastic about the Cervipillo. He personally sold four Cervipillos to Walt Disney. A working agreement was arranged and business transactions settled down for a time. Ruth wrote to Beatrice that she was planning to stop in New York at the Waldorf Astoria. This was to present a paper on "Automotive Injuries to the Neck," at the International College of Surgeons meeting in September, before she traveled on to Paris, then to Germany where she had been invited to lecture on the Cervical Spine at the German Orthopaedic Association meeting in Munich.

After giving the fate of the Cervipillo much thought, Ruth made up her mind to do what she considered best: sever business relations with the Yellins. Once again the wound began to fester. This time it would lead to amputation. Her letter explaining her decision to the Yellins stressed that business propositions and friendships should and could be separate. "Business is business and friendship is friendship," she wrote. She pointed out her principal reason for terminating their contract was that the Yellins' main business was making orthopaedic braces in one locale without the physical set up for extensive sales and promotions of the pillow. She also alluded to their ideas of what they wanted to do "have been discouraged by her 'for various reasons'." Ruth wanted her pillow produced and marketed on a big scale and felt that the Yellins weren't equipped to handle it. She then dangled a carrot in front of them after taking away the bunch. She offered a new agreement giving them the right to continue to manufacture and sell the pillow but revoking or eliminating their exclusive right to manufacture it. She hoped there would be no ill feelings about this arrangement but wanted to exercise her right to revoke the contract as of April 15, 1963.

From this point the correspondence was between Ruth's attorney and Yellin.

Ruth Jackson, M.D.: A Life on the Leading Edge

A new agreement was proposed by Ruth's attorney, outlining her wishes. Although Yellin felt that he had done a good job manufacturing and selling the pillow, pointing out that he had spent a great deal of effort, time and money on it, an agreement was not reached. His reply to the attorney stated that, "with a heavy heart as apparently there is no way we can come to terms so they would consider the contract canceled as of June 30, 1963 with an accounting to begin immediately."

Once again Neiman Marcus approached Ruth about manufacturing her pillow. In February she refused their offer, but did agree that they could purchase the Cervipillo from the manufacture if they would sell it only in their Special Bed Supply Department.

By this time Tru Wilhelm had learned of the canceled contract when he tried to order pillows from Yellin. He thought Ruth had made arrangements with S.H. Camp Co. She told him that as of August, 1963 no one was making the pillows. She wanted to talk to Tru in person because she had heard a rumor that the Yellins were manufacturing her pillow under their name.

After Tru's trip to Dallas, plans were made that by October 1963 the Tru-Eze company would have the exclusive rights to manufacture and sell the Cervipillo. Mr. Wilhelm would have the right to use the trademark as long as he was showing proper interest in it and continuing the promotion. By January 1, 1964, the Cervipillo had a new home in California.

Ruth's business relationship with Tru Wilhelm developed into a deep friendship with the entire Wilhelm family, including his wife, Enid and their sons, Brett and Brad. When she was invited as guest speaker on "Cervical Pain-Non Surgical Treatment" at the Cervical Pain Symposium in Stockholm, Sweden, January 25-28, 1971, Tru accompanied her. Although Tru flew first class, her ticket, paid for by the Werner-Gren Center International Symposium was coach. She did sneak up into the exclusive lounge for drinks with Tru on the way over. She was intrigued by the fact that the dinner menu listed "filet de veau a la Jackson" They enjoyed the festivities during their stay, attending the Royal Opera to hear Beethoven's *Fidelis*, and cocktail parties at their hotel, the Palace.

The strained relations with the elder Yellins didn't extend to their son, Art. His relationship with his "Aunt Ruth" remained intact. In 1968 he flew to the Lower Rio Grande Valley with Ruth and her business partner, Judy Sanders *(See disclaimer) for White Wing dove hunting. Hunters converged from all over the world to headquarter in McAllen and the surrounding small towns to participate in the Mardi Gras type atmosphere of the Labor Day weekend hunt. Hotel spaces were always at a premium, sometimes booked years in advance. Ruth always knew she could rely on her sister and brother-in-law, Edythe and Harold Brehm of McAllen, to provide accommodations for her and her guests. That year Ruth and Judy stayed in McAllen, while Art stayed in Edinburg with Ruth's nephew, Paul Jackson Jr. and family.

The wild party-filled weekends were fun but could be dangerous. Hunters who had no leases would simply line both sides of the highways and back roads twenty-five to thirty feet apart to shoot. One took one's life in one's hands getting out in public. For those who had leases or friends who shared their ranch land, the hunting was a bit safer. That fall, Ruth's group hunted on the Three Point Two Ranch that belonged to the Paul Jacksons' friend, Dr. H.D. Stephens. Sundown signaled for all guns to be put away. Hunters and non-hunters gathered around the Stephens' swimming pool for barbecue and to swap stories about "who stole whose bird in the field."

Another highlight of the hunting trip was traveling the ten miles to cross the Rio Grande River to go to Reynosa, Mexico for margaritas and dinner. The night life in Reynosa, great restaurants, entertainment and shopping were drawing cards for the hunters. There was only one bridge across the Rio Grande River and immigration stops on both sides caused traffic to back up on the narrow streets of Mexico. Art's first experience with the mass of humanity swarming through the Zona Rosa of Reynosa evoked the comment that "Times Square on New Year's Eve isn't this bad!"

Ruth Jackson, M.D.: A Life on the Leading Edge

Rounding out the weekend included horseback riding, not Texas style, but Tennessee style. The Tennessee Walking horses provided by Vale Mayes, father-in-law of Ruth's nephew made for an easier ride than the Texas quarter horse. This fact was appreciated by those who had spent a long evening the night before at Trevino's bar waiting for the traffic to abate before crossing the river back to the USA.

Art returned to New York, transporting a few chiggers he had picked up while hunting, to the Big City. He and Ruth kept in touch for a while. When Ruth returned from Sweden in 1971, she received a letter from Art informing her of his marriage "to a wonderful girl" and of his new company which he had set up eighteen months previously.[lxxxix]

Tru had suffered an embolism following surgery for a fracture, after he returned to California from the Sweden trip with Ruth. Always sympathetic and ready to give comfort, even if only through the mail, Ruth gave him medical advice, from exercising to suggesting that he take Vitamin E. She told him that Dr.

Ochsner of the Ochsner Clinic in New Orleans at one time recommended the giving of Vitamin E to all patients prior to and following surgery. Although they did this for many years, the absence of emodi probably was instrumental in their thinking on the matter and they did discontinue the vitamin E, according to Ruth. She pointed out to him that there is continued evidence in the literature that vitamin E does prevent coronary infarction or coronary thrombosis and she told him, "Perhaps it is a good precautionary measure."

Ruth was having problems of her own. With her business partner, Judy Sanders, in the hospital, financial problems in the joint ventures and upheavals in her clinic office staff, the latter part of 1971 was a disastrous period in Ruth's life. To agitate her further, one of her friends wrote in her Christmas card describing a pillow advertised in a gift catalog which Ruth suspected was her Cervipillo.[xc]

In 1975, the Cervipillo went international. Tru and Fred A. Lamb, vice president and general manager of

Ruth Jackson, M.D.: A Life on the Leading Edge

the Tru-Eze Manufacturing Co. Inc. had a very successful trip to Europe and the Middle East in the waning months of 1975. They were very enthusiastic about the future of the Cervipillo in Europe. Tru told Ruth that their principal in Zurich was buying the Cervipillo and covers in lots of 100 and sales were still growing. The pillow was being sold also in England, Canada and Puerto Rico. She had received inquiries from a company in Australia who was interested in the Cervipillo. She referred the company to Tru and by the time the American parties had come to terms, the Dunlopillo Pty. Ltd. of Clayton, Victoria, Australia had a change of management and a change of heart. International or not, Ruth was still fighting the home front battle with those who would try to copy her pillow. Some companies were those who had previously bought the Cervipillo from Tru-Eze.

In a letter to one such company she soundly trounces on them for their unlawful use of the name "Cervipillo" which was similar in sound to her registered trademark. This particular instance was brought to her attention by a patient who had purchased, as Ruth referred to it, "a poor replica of the Cervipillo."

By the fall of 1980, Art Yellin began tantalizing Ruth with letters mentioning a proposal for American Health's project. A tidbit to whet the appetite referred to "physicians who might be interested in joining our 'board' 'staff' or whatever name they may put to this venture," as well as possible remuneration." He told her, "They are going great guns with the pillow especially in the Orlando Market." The vague references weren't clarified in the correspondence and he made arrangements to be in Miami the weekend of December 5th when Ruth indicated she would be visiting friends in Miami Beach. The meeting never materialized.

Art and his partner had tabled the idea in 1981 of installing a medical advisory board for American Health and his next proposal to Ruth about the Cervical Contour Pillow scheme went over with a big thump. He wanted to use his personnel in the most profitable manufacturing areas. He said they enjoyed a substantial volume in pillow sales, but made more profits in other areas. He wanted to sell the right to his entire pillow business including customer lists, etc. to a qualified manufacturer and distributor....namely Tru-Eze! Then came the pitch.

In exchange for a relatively small dollar amount ($25,000) he would agree not to sell any pillow whatsoever on a wholesale basis, retaining the right to sell the Cervical Contour Pillow in the local Philadelphia area and purchasing these pillows, for retail sales only through Tru-Eze at the wholesale price. If he couldn't strike a deal with Tru-Eze he would stay in the business because he could not see turning his pillow business over to just anybody.

Art had been advertising an "Orthorest Pillow" sold direct to the consumer on television. Once again, Ruth geared up for battle to see that her Jackson Cervipillo was not copied. She pointed out to Art that only Tru-Eze had the contract to manufacture and sell the Cervipillo. Apparently several other companies had copied the pillow, of sorts, in an attempt to get in the business.

She pointedly remarked that

"Somehow none of them has admitted to the source of supply." Ruth saw no reason why Tru-Eze should buy Art's customer list. Art reiterated that he wanted only $25,000 in exchange for his agreement not to sell any pillow at all to any customers except on a walk-in prescription basis, with future wholesale orders being sent to Tru-Eze for processing and shipping. Once again Ruth suggested that he sell his pillow wholesale through Tru-Eze and they in turn would sell them to his customers in smaller lots.

In spite of the tough business talk, there remained between them the chatty exchange of hunting trips, news of Art's young son, Adam and the exchange of gifts. In 1983, Art sent Ruth information on his new business, the Medi-Scan Computer, Inc. for applied computer technology to practitioners of the medical arts. The relationship eventually died from lack of energy on both sides to keep it going.

The last change in the Cervipillo story came about when Tru Wilhelm retired in 1984. The Tru-Eze Manufacturing Co. was sold and his son,

Brett, became president of the newly formed company called Tru-Trac Therapy Products, Inc. Ruth's contract was still in effect with the new company which planned to continue as they had for the past twenty years. The new version of the Cervipillo was approved by Ruth and was called the original Jackson Cervipillo. In addition they manufacture the slightly varied design which she tested to be marketed as the Basic Jackson Cervipillo. The pillow's permanent cover was to be woven with the name Jackson Cervipillo, so that it could be distinguished from those who tried so hard over the years to copy it.

Although she became interested in disorders of the cervical spine in 1936, the shift in emphasis in her practice from the foot to the cervical spine became more evident when she experienced her own cervical pain and invented the Jackson Cervipillo. In 1953, Ruth gave a two-hour instructional course lecture on "The Cervical Syndrome" at the American Academy of Orthopaedic Surgeons Meeting that would lead her on her path to becoming the eminent expert on the cervical spine.

Paul Jackson Sr., six; Ruth Jackson; four and Edythe Jackson Brehm two.

Mary Ruth Jackson with her sister Edythe on a hammock

Ruth Jackson, M.D.: A Life on the Leading Edge

W.R.JACKSON FAMILY CHRISTMAS 1930'S

The Jackson families, Christmas Day 1929:
(l to r) Paul and Velma Jackson with
children, O.N. "Tip" and Paul, Jr.; Harold
and Edythe Jackson Brehm; Morris Jackson,
Marjorie Jackson, Ruby Jackson; Ruth's
parents, Belle and W.R. Jackson; Roy and
Winnie Jackson Bellcock; Jane and Harley
Jackson with their children Carol, Darrell,
Marion and Sharyn Jackson; Walter and Mabel
Jackson with twins, Herma and Hilma and
sons, Merle and Duane, McAllen, TX.

Darrell Jackson, Dr. Jackson's nephew accompanied her on many of her dates when she was in Medical School in the 1920s.

Ruth Jackson, M.D.: A Life on the Leading Edge

The Three Musketeers: Don Keyes, M.D., Dr. Jackson, and Jacob "Jake" Kulowski, M.D. at the University of Iowa in Iowa City, Iowa, 1929.

Dan McClung, Dr. Jackson's husband, makes music to entertain her at their home on Myrtle Jean Dr. in Dallas, in the 1930s.

Ruth Jackson, M.D.: A Life on the Leading Edge

Edythe Jackson Brehm with her sister, Mary Ruth Jackson, M.D.

Ruth Jackson, M.D. at her Clinic in Dallas, TX.

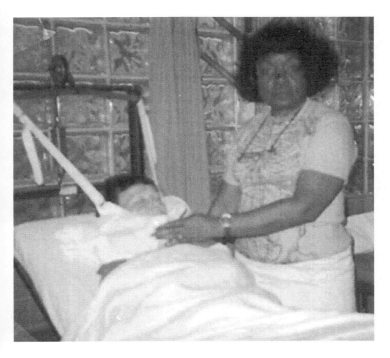

Tommie Lee Fields, physical therapist, in Dr. Jackson's clinic on Fairmont St., Dallas, TX.

Ruth and Christopher Larzalere, son of her business manager, Sheri Larzalere.

Ruth Jackson, M.D.: A Life on the Leading Edge

Ruth Jackson, M.D. with her business manager, Sheri Larzalere.

Ruth Jackson, M.D. at a Law-Science Academy meeting in Crested Butte, CO.

Dr. Jackson holds Sara Horstmann, three week old daughter of Dr. Helen Horstmann at the 1986 meeting of AAOS in New Orleans.

Exhibit of Dr. Jackson's Cervipillo by the Tru-Tract representatives at the 1986 American Academy of Orthopaedic Surgeons meeting.

Ruth Jackson, M.D.: A Life on the Leading Edge

Mary Clark Williams, M.D. , Charlottesville, VA
Liebe Sokol Diamond, M.D. Baltimore, MD, first
president of Ruth Jackson Society and Ruth
Jackson, M.D.

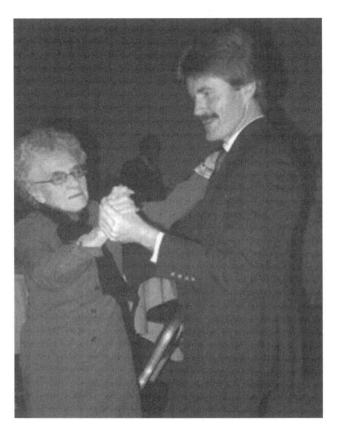

Ruth Jackson, M.D. dances with grandnephew, Donald Jackson at Kevin and Cindy Jackson Patti's wedding Sept 12, 1987.

Ruth Jackson, M.D.: A Life on the Leading Edge

Ruth vacations at South Padre Island with Sheri Larzalere, her son Christopher, her grandniece, Janis Jackson Rogers and her children, Lauren and Paul.

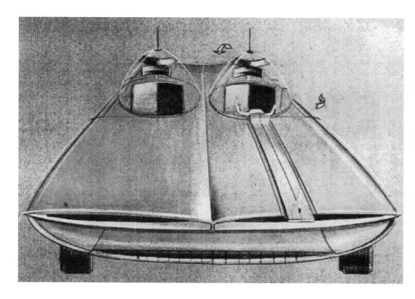

Sketch of car designed and patented by Dr. Jackson in 1966 after seeing a quarrelling couple cause a three car wreck.

Ruth Jackson, M.D.: A Life on the Leading Edge

Dr. Jackson honored with Ruth Jackson, M.D. Appreciation Day September 9, 1986 by Baylor University Medical Center. She was honored for her contributions to BUMC, especially the Ruth Jackson Orthopaedic Library and the Orthopaedic Administration Wing.

Patsy Mayes Jackson

Adrian Flatt, M.D., Chief of Orthopaedics at Baylor University Medical Center; Ruth Jackson, M.D.; Boone Powell Jr., administrator of BUMC; Lois Shelben, director of Nursing, Truett Hospital; Linda Donahue, executive assistant to the Chief of Orthopaedics at BUMC and Boone Powell, Sr. former President and administrator of BUMC at opening of the Ruth Jackson Administrative Wing at Truett Hospital

Ruth Jackson, M.D.: A Life on the Leading Edge

Dr. Jackson with her colleagues at the Werner Gren Center International Symposium on Cervical Pain in Stockholm, Sweden, January 26-28, 1971

Jacquelin Perry, M.D., Bellflower, CA with Ruth Jackson, M.D. at the RJOS exhibit in Washington, D.C.

Inauguration of the Dr. Ruth Jackson Seminar in Orthopaedic Surgery, Oct. 26, 1976 with visiting professor, David G. Murray, M.D., Chairman, Dept. of Orthopaedic Surgery, Upstate Medical Center, Syracuse, New York. Presented by The Ruth Jackson Research Foundation Fund for the Department of Orthopaedic Surgery of Baylor University Medical Center and A. Webb Roberts Center for Continuing Education.

The past presidents of the Texas Orthopaedic Association in Houston, Texas 1987 (top row: l. to r.) Albert A. Tisdale, M.D., Spencer A. Rowland, M.D., Jerry D. Julian, M.D., John A. Murray, M.D. and Lamar P. Collie, M.D. (Front row: l to r.) Ed Amith, M.D., Ruth Jackson, M.D., Hanes Brindley, M.D. and John Hinchey, M.D.

Ruth Jackson Orthopaedic Society Members attending the RJOS first seminar in Chicago, IL Nov. 2-4, 1990

First edition copy of Dr. Jackson's book *Cervical Syndrome* is signed for Judith J. Levine, M.D, which her father had among his books.

Living History taping summer of 1992, Rosemarie Morwessel, M.D.; Ruth Jackson M.D. and Mary Lloyd Ireland, M.D., Lexington, KY, co-chairmen of the project.

Dr. Jackson with some of her homemade surgical instruments she used in her early years.

At age 90, Dr. Jackson still rode her paint horse, Star Elena Blue Eyes.

Pictures from the files of Ruth Jackson MD and Patsy Mayes Jackson

"Creative Faculties become important through use-just as a muscle becomes strong if properly exercised-Exercise your imagination."

CHAPTER XI

It was these lectures on the cervical syndrome, repeated in 1954, 1955 and 1960, that prompted Dr. Robert J. Joplin to recommend to Charles C. Thomas, publisher of the American Lecture Series, that he request her monograph for publication. On February 10th, 1954, Ruth signed an agreement with Bannerstone House to publish a monograph with the tentative title *Treatment of the Cervical Spine, Shoulder, Arm Syndrome* with Dr. Joplin as editor.

Although it was a popular course, it was discontinued in 1956. After speaking to Hugh Smith, M.D. at the Campbell Clinic in Tennessee about helping her to get on the program again, he was instrumental in seeing that she returned to the lecture series. At the end of the third lecture, her old friend Phillip Lewin, M.D. once again publicly supported her.

Standing, he announced to the group attending the lecture that "this is one of the best instructional courses I have ever attended."

Ruth used the term "cervical syndrome" to signify a group of symptoms and clinical findings which occur as a result of irritation or compression of the cervical nerve roots in or about the intervertebral foramina before they divide into anterior and posterior primary rami. The other structures within the intervertebral foramina may be involved also. These include the recurrent spinal meningeal nerves, the spinal branches of the vertebral arteries and their accompanying veins, and the nearby vertebral arteries themselves.

According to Ruth in her monograph, the term "syndrome" has been used frequently with other descriptive words to indicate special conditions at specific locations when in reality the true pathology involves the nerve roots and their adjacent structures. An understanding of the anatomy of the cervical spine and of the mechanism involved in cervical nerve root irritation will assure treatment directed toward the true causative factors. Since pain is the symptom which most frequently brings the patient to the doctor and an analysis and interpretation of pain is often neglected or ignored completely it is an area to be explored.[xci]

An analysis of more than twelve thousand patients seen by Ruth who had symptoms referable to the cervical spine revealed that more than 95% had one or more injuries of the cervical spine, either recent or remote. The remaining small percentage of patients had non-traumatic disorders, metastatic lesions, spinal cord tumors or primary osseous lesions.

Encouraged and inspired to continue work in this field by Drs. Charles N. Pease, Thomas Beath, Robert Joplin, Charles W. Goff and Arthur Steindler, Ruth took to the project like a duck takes to water. The first edition of *The Cervical Syndrome* was published and distributed worldwide in 1956 by Charles C. Thomas, publisher, Bannerstone House of 301-327 East Lawrence Avenue of Springfield, Illinois. The second edition was printed in 1958 with two printings following in 1963 and 1965. The third edition was released in 1966 with a revised second printing in 1971 and 1976. The fourth and last edition was released in 1977 also in Japanese.

Arthur Steindler, M.D., internationally known orthopaedic surgeon and teacher as well as Ruth's mentor and friend wrote the foreword. He points out the great complexity of what Dr. Jackson calls the cervical syndrome. "In her quest to give the mass of symptoms which meet the eye interpretative meaning, she not only draws heavily upon information furnished by the basic sciences, but the whole structure of the work is built upon basic and recognized factors in the field of anatomy and kinetics. In her attempt to establish the causal connections between basic facts and clinical manifestations, she succeeds uncommonly well," he states in the foreword.[xcii]

Dr. Steindler had known Ruth since she was an intern in the Department of Orthopaedic Surgery, at the University Hospitals, University of Iowa, Iowa City, Iowa in 1929-30. He followed the interest she had taken in this subject and the earnest and intensive studies she had devoted to it According to Dr. Steindler, this interest and dedication made her one of the foremost authorities in this specific field.

She saw her first patient with a neck injury, the result of a sudden acceleration in a rear end collision, in 1937. Her interest grew as the number of patients with neck problems increased. She was able to follow this patient through subsequent neck injuries and to observe the progressive changes that occurred in her cervical spine. Numerous other patients, followed clinically for many years, also contributed greatly toward making the studies of the cervical spine of significant importance.

A stimulating factor in the attempt to understand the symptoms and clinical findings which the neck patients presented was a dearth of medical information in 1936 concerning the cervical spine. Since there were no immediate answers available, there were many unnecessary radiographs of the thoracic spine made in an effort to find some pathology which might explain the cause of interscapular pain and muscle spasm. Even psychiatric consultations were requested when the origin of the pain could not be established, only to find that the symptoms were not of psychoneurotic origin. With continued research and study of the anatomy of the very complex cervical spine, progress was made toward the clarification of some of the diagnostic problems. Many of the answers were found in what might be called antiquated writings.

Ruth always stressed, "Anatomy, anatomy, anatomy," to her students and interns. It is no surprise that in her book she stressed the basics: fundamental anatomy, a careful patient history, meticulous examination, and adequate radiography. In her third edition, the chapter on treatment was redone.

In a book review for the *Lawyers' Medical Journal* Charles W. Goff, M.D., professor Emeritus of Orthopaedic Surgery at Yale University, School of Medicine wrote: "Not only is Ruth Jackson direct and stimulating as a person, but her book fits her personality, which comes through to the reader. I hope the editors will not give her book to neurosurgeons to review. Such surgeons usually have one string to their violin and that is a 'cutting' string. A monograph such as this one, with few pages devoted to surgical treatment, will not appeal to them. Dr. Jackson quotes Steindler: "there are those who wish to go non-stop, and in their haste pass by the stations of indications and diagnosis, to arrive at specific operative techniques'. These surgeons will be disappointed. Physicians and orthopaedists, on the other hand will relish her work."[xciii]

After lecturing on the conservative management of neck injuries, in Las Vegas she was informed that one orthopaedic surgeon had said, "If that Goddamn Ruth Jackson would stop talking about conservative management of neck disorder I'd have a lot more surgery to do in the United States than I have."[xciv]

Ruth did as much of her surgery under local anesthetics as possible. In the early days Baylor University Medical Center had no recovery room. Patients had to take all the recovery equipment attached to them to their rooms. She liked the fact that she could, under light sedation, talk to the patients and receive their reactions.

She recalled one patient who had all the symptoms of sciatic irritation. "You could press on the ligmentem flavum, which is between the laminae of the vertebrae and if there is an extruded disc and you pressed there while they were under local, they would tell you if it sent a pain down their leg." she explained. "This young man, when she touched the synovial covering of the lumbrosacal joint, yelled 'that was the pain'. I removed the capsule and put in a Knowles support. He could get up and walk." As a result of using local anaesthetic, she almost never had infections or postoperative bleeding. Patients flocked to Ruth because she took an interest in them as a whole. One of Ruth's patients had been to many doctors who were baffled by her occasional symptoms of a sagging right eyelid, limp facial muscles and jaw misalignment which caused a pull to the right. The only diagnosis she hadn't heard was that she had an ingrown toenail.

She had a spasm one day when she was close to Ruth's clinic and decided to drop in and let Dr. Jackson take a look. She described the event in a letter to the author in 1987 as follows: "When I walked in she was strolling down the hall. She turned around, pursed her lips and that left eyebrow went up. Immediately she invited me into her office and started asking questions. The questioning went on for about five minutes, after which she sat back in her chair, absorbed in her own thoughts. It was like watching a computer go, although there was no output. Then, a light went on. She got up and poked and prodded a few minutes. She zeroed in to an area and proclaimed, There, Then, 'Let's inject it!' Okay. When she injects she looks like a mad scientist coming at you with that wicked needle. There's a standard speech. 'A little prick, then tell me where it hurts. There?

There?.. What direction? Let's try there. I want to get it all. Tommie, go get the bag.' Now I think we have it all. Let's see, look at me.'

I've never seen her so excited. 'Look at that!' Her eye works. 'Tommie

Ruth Jackson, M.D.: A Life on the Leading Edge

Lee, Look! Smile, raise your eyebrows. Amazing.'

One of the facts of injection is diathermy. You sit there with the area injected, strapped to a machine which gives off heat. During the period of time I was hooked up, the good doctor darted in and out, almost to make sure she hadn't imagined things. She was like a kid under the Christmas tree. We reconvened our visit in her office over the bowl of neck bones someone had given her. She began sputtering 'A sharp knife, that's all it would take, a sharp knife. I've seen this once before and I went in with a 'sharp knife'." She was a new person. 'Let's think about it."

I asked her to write down what she had done. She had injected 10 cc of Carbocaine into muscles attached to mastoid process and into a joint between skull and first cervical vertebra. At the next visit she put me back into my neck brace....We went to the "foot" room and she cut out a new one for me, right on the spot. I had kept records of what had happened to me after the injection essentially, the benefits wore off as the Carbocaine did. She again brought up her 'sharp knife'. There were of course, no guarantees.

After considering the proposal, the patient was forced to think through and accept responsibility for her decision. "Although Ruth cared deeply what happened, she was not dealing in Thou Shalts," she wrote. Her letter continues: "I am still transfixed by her style. It was pure art. She injected the area she intended to work on, this time with Marcaine. I lost my battle to not take her 'little pill'. She's not joking when she says it will sedate you. During her injection she fished around, intent on finding that radiated pain in the right directions, when she found it, there was a crackling noise. ....She left the needle in then got a sharp knife. Once she was at the location she began. A transformation happened, the knife became her eyes and I was sure that she could 'see' the whole area. It reminds me of the film *Fantastic Voyage* in which scientists are shrunk to microscopic size and voyage through someone's body in an attempt to repair something that is out of whack. That knife was her vessel. She found her spot and had Tommie remove the needle. Then slowly but systematically she cut the fibers, sort of like cutting the individual bands of strapping tape.

She would have me move my shoulder and arm every once in a while. ....Once she completed that task, she carefully smoothed the bone underneath the fibers she had cut. It was like a sculptor carefully chiseling a feature until it was just so. While she was doing this she was in her own world at the tip of her knife."

The patient went on to write that Ruth's explanation of the procedure, cutting the posterior belly of the diagnostric fossa of the internal mandible muscle, was relayed to her physician father, who couldn't picture how Ruth managed to get to it.

Ruth's clinic was her real home and her patients her real family. The clinic had a view of Fairmont St. It was filled with gifts from patients such as a pen and ink drawing by Jean Ferguson and a picture signed by Boone Powell, Executive Director of Baylor University Medical Center. Plaques stating her positions including one as

President in the Texas Orthopaedic Society, lined the walls. One of great amusement in the clinic was a certificate of appreciation signed in 1980 by Dr. Michael E. DeBakey president, from the American Society of Contemporary Medicine that read "In appreciation for his valuable services as a distinguished member of the faculty."

There was memorabilia as morbid as bones dissected by Ruth, filling bowls near her desk. Early in her practice the porter at Parkland Hospital would bring Ruth necks and back bones in five gallon crock jars of formaldehyde. She would x-ray and dissect them very carefully in order to correlate her findings. One patient went to her lawyer and had a will drawn leaving her neck to Ruth.

In the years prior to her retirement in 1989, Ruth's routine was sacrosanct. She arose at 6:00 a.m., drank an Instant Breakfast and was usually the first to arrive at the clinic about eight. Going through her papers she was ready to see her first patient at 9:00 a.m. An aloe vera laced glass of juice was her morning break, then at noon Tommie Lee fixed her cottage cheese, crackers, fruit and maybe some lunch meat. She reviewed her cases, dictated morning medical findings, another aloe vera gel break and out by five p.m. Tuesdays were set aside for depositions and her beauty shop appointment at 5:00 p.m. Her beautician, Oakie Rogers came to the office where Ruth had a shampoo bowl and dryer set up. Nothing interfered with her hair appointment as three lawyers and a court reporter from St. Louis, Missouri were to discover.

"A Man understands only what is akin to something existing already in himself."

CHAPTER XII

In November, 1985 three lawyers and a court reporter from St. Louis, Missouri came to Dallas to take a deposition from Ruth. The lawyer for the plaintiff, from Clayton, Missouri was a suave, dignified, courtly man in his fifties.
 The St. Louis lawyer for De Pau Hospital was a young, handsome man with a confident air. Representing the doctor was an intelligent, quietly capable young woman, a lawyer from St. Louis, Missouri. The court reporter, who had accompanied the plaintiff's lawyer on a deposition with Ruth three years earlier, was a delightful young woman. They had flown to Dallas from Missouri that morning planning to fly home after five p.m. The deposition started at 2:00 p.m. The case involved a young man who had been injured in a motorcycle accident. His claim was that he had not had proper treatment by the doctor at the De Pau Hospital which resulted in his having to have more

surgery.

It was obvious when the young lawyer began his questioning that he thought that Ruth, due to her age and delicate appearance would be easy to confuse under questioning. Little did he know he had a tiger by the tail. Of course Ruth baited him like the great fisher woman she was. She answered his long drawn out questions with a question. She made him look up her qualifications in the curriculum vitae which he had had for sometime. The plaintiff's lawyer realizing how much time the young man was taking with his questions diplomatically pointed out that he would be covering the same material and in the interest of time could they proceed to the next lawyer. The organized plaintiff lawyer was trying to keep things on track. The self-assured young man refused. During the questioning, as he slouched in his chair, he kept running his hands through his uncombed hair, scratching his chest around his loosened tie and yawning indiscriminately, Ruth finally looked at him and said, "Am I keeping you up or would you be up anyway?"

With this he sat up a little

straighter, and then proceeded to ask her pertinent questions concerning the x-rays. Ruth spun around in her chair to the x-ray screen and began to tell him in detailed medical terms why, in her expert opinion the plaintiff had a case.

The young man jumped to his feet saying "Irregardless of this..." He never finished the sentence. Ruth admonished him sternly, saying, "Young man! There is no such word as irregardless!"

With a startled look he lamely finished his questioning turning over the floor to the doctor's lawyer.

It didn't take a mind reader to see that she had benefited from his experience. Her questioning was couched in respectful terms, direct and to the point. She was helpful about clarifying files. When the plaintiff's lawyer began to speak darkness had settled in the room due to the lateness of the hour as well as the November stormy day. Suddenly Ruth stood up behind her desk, announced that it was five o'clock, she was tired and it was time for her hair appointment. They could come back tomorrow to finish.

Ruth Jackson, M.D.: A Life on the Leading Edge

If one look of consternation could hit four faces at once it happened then. They had plane reservations back to Missouri that night, no hotel reservations, no transportation and no luck in changing her mind. There was a flurry of telephone calls for hotel rooms and taxis while the women wondered what they would do with no make-up and no change of clothes.

Arrangements were made for them to return the next afternoon to finish the deposition. The next day when they returned, the young man's hair was combed, his tie fashionably knotted and his manner subdued but amiable. His comment before he entered Ruth's office was that he had thought Ruth reminded him of his grandmother, but he underestimated her: she wasn't.

"She chewed me up and spit me out!" he said ruefully.

"When the plaintiff's lawyer pointed out that he tried to avoid the situation, the hospital's lawyer replied that he guessed he had to chalk that one up to experience. The court reporter smiled and said that if he thought Ruth was tough now, he should have been there three years ago. "She has mellowed since then," she added.

Defense lawyers and insurance companies held no love for Ruth when she appeared in the courtroom for the plaintiffs. She remembers many times during depositions, the defending attorneys would always say, "Well you are a plaintiff's doctor." Her reply would always be the same: "Yes, the plaintiff is (a) patient and that is the only person I see. I do not treat the insurance company."

Her expertise in the courtroom was due, in part, to her affiliation with the Law Science Academy. The Law Science Academy was formed in 1954 as a non-profit educational corporation by Hubert Winston Smith, M.D., LL.B. In addition to his medical and law degrees from Harvard, Dr. Smith held an A.B. in economics and M.B.A. in accounting from the University of Texas at Austin. In 1954, he was a professor of Law and Legal Medicine and Director of the Law-Science Institute, Schools of Law and Medicine. The Law Science Academy was dedicated, according to his paper on "Expanding Horizons of The Law Science Movement", to integration of Law with the Physical, Medical, Psychological,

Social and Spiritual Sciences, and stimulation of the creative and performing arts and Humanities.[xcv]

In a 1956 letter to Ruth he recruits her "to participate in one of its educational programs, at the undergraduate and post graduate level, directed to developing knowledge of scientific medicine in relationship to personal injury problems."

He explained that, implementing many lecturers from various fields, the plan was to use the devise of trial sequences, using a defense counsel and plaintiffs counsel and a judge with the purpose to develop the pros and cons from the standpoint of plaintiff and defendant through direct cross examination.[xcvi]

Ruth was eager to be part of Dr. Smith's vision. Not only would it be an intellectual challenge, but the Academy's beautiful setting in Crested Butte, Colorado at the Smiths' ranch, located at the base of the Whetstone Mountain, would be the perfect spot for the only type of vacation Ruth knew how to take: a working vacation. Ruth was one of the first members to help launch the summer teaching center at the

Academy in Crested Butte in the summer of 1959.[xcvii]

In July, 1963, Ruth invited her sister, Edythe and brother-in-law, Harold Brehm to accompany her to the quaint old mining town of Crested Butte. The town had not yet been discovered by the mass of skiers who would begin infiltrating the laid back little village in the 1980s.

Ruth's mornings were spent lecturing on "Medicolegal Aspects of Injuries of Upper Extremity and of Neck", then the afternoons were free to fraternize with the lecturers, students and families gathered in Crested Butte. She also lectured at three evening sessions.

According to the brochure, these lectures covered nine areas of the bodies' organ system, considering the structure and function of each cell, its role in the bodily economy; effects of disease, toxins and trauma upon cells, tissues, organs, organ systems and the total personality. Also studied were psychiatry and psychology as pertained to the Medicolega Trial Technique. The brochure points out that the scientific lecturers were by national authorities interested in bringing trustworthy scientific information into more effective use in trial of cases civil and criminal.[xcviii]

Ruth enjoyed the company of Dr. Smith's family, his wife, Catherine and their sons, Stephen, Alan, Charles and James. An accomplished artist, Catherine's painting of Crested Butte, with a tiny figure of Ruth featured, hung in Ruth's living room at Turtle Creek in Dallas. Alan, following in his mother's footsteps, taught classes in jewelry at the Norman Art Museum in Norman, Oklahoma. Dr. Smith's Law Science Academy experiment was a giant leap into the future at a time when C.P. Snow, the British scientist-author deplored the growing gap between the humanistic-artistic culture
and the scientific-technological world in his Rede Lecture on "The Two Cultures."[xcix]

It was at this period of her life that The Ruth Jackson Research Foundation was established, the result of generous acts by two women physicians.

It all began in 1960 when a woman patient from Chicago was referred to

Ruth by a colleague, Dr. Walter Blount, of Milwaukee, Wisconsin. The patient, Dr. Eleanor Leslie was a pediatrician but had not practiced since World War I.

The Leslie family founded and owned the Signoid Steel Strapping Corporation. In gratitude for relieving her suffering from a neck problem Dr. Eleanor Leslie gave Ruth a thousand dollars in payment. Ruth did not want to accept payment from another doctor, so her attorney, John Harrison, suggested that she set up a tax free research foundation.

Ruth said, "Since I didn't want to do anything with it except research, I agreed."

From these funds and further gifts of money and stock from the Signoid Steel Strapping Corp., Ruth set up the tax free Ruth Jackson Research Foundation under charter #181810-1 on March 6, 1962. [c]

The trustees, composed of Ruth, chairman; her attorney, John Harrison, secretary-treasurer and five members appointed for a term of two or three years, met twice a year. Appointees were often Ruth's friends in the first years. Harrison, Marion Bouvé and Dr. Marianna Hood were three of the first trustees.

Every time Ruth went to Chicago to a medical meeting she and Dr. Leslie would renew their friendship. Dr. Leslie died in 1973 at which time she left additional gifts for Ruth, who commented, "She was a very generous and kind person. She was a great philanthropist, giving large sums of money to medical schools and research. The infinitesimal portion of her estate she left to me amounted to $264,000."

The Ruth Jackson Research Fund began working at the University of Texas Medical School in Dallas in 1961. Through this funding, research on growing tissue cells, then subjecting them to extracts of certain plants such as aloe vera with known anticarcinogenic properties was made possible.

In May of 1962, Ruth, accompanied by friends, Lawrence K. Handley and Ralph E. Sharpe, attended the Seventh National Congress of Orthopaedic and Traumatology meeting in Puebla, Mexico where she lectured on Villonodular synovitis of the hip. Staying at the

Hotel Maria Isabel, the trio enjoyed the festivities surrounding the historical centennial celebration.[ci]

Ruth, with her friend Dr. Marianna Hood, an ob-gyn specialist and Marion Bouvé, her business manager, had an apartment on the Paseo de la Reforma, where they spent many vacations. On one of her many trips to Mexico, Ruth had met a chemist, Hernandez Villagrán who had seen someone cure a cancer of the uterus by applying the juice of a certain cactus plant. Alfonso Hernandez Villagrán, Sr., was originally from Spain. The prospect of investigating this theory intrigued Ruth.

Mr. Villagrán, Juan Belenguer and Dr. Francisco Lozano had started this research in 1931, in Mexico. At the time Villagrán was owner and manager of Folder S.A., a 35 man factory in Mexico City. He took charge of the expenses, which were not huge because their methods were simple. During World War II, Villagrán was in the reserves of the Mexican Army thus forgoing the research.
With Ruth's interest, the project got underway again.[cii]

Among the many papers that Ruth

donated to the Archives and Special Collections on Women in Medicine at the Drexel University College of Medicine was the agreement between the Ruth Jackson Foundation Cancer Research Grant and Villagrán; reports and letters between the participants about the project.

The agreement read as follows: 11-9-65: Ruth Jackson Foundation Cancer Research Grant agreement between Ruth Jackson Foundation, Inc. as donor and Sr. Alfonso Hernandez Villagrán, Sr.; Constantino de Llano, Mexico City; and Dr. Benjamin Fleitman, Mexico City, donees. Certain funds provided to assist donees in engaging in research relative to studies concerning cancer and possible causes, treatment and cures thereof in all its forms. Sr. de Llano-pharmaceutical and industrial chemist: analyses material furnished by Villa-Gran. He will process and supply pharmaceutical alkaloids, extracts or substance to Dr. Fleitman, a homeopathic physician, surgeon and obstetrician; who will conduct chemical experiments, perform research, attempting to isolate or discover causes of-determine the effectiveness of product in cure and treatment of cancer, to keep written records, diary and logs of experiments.[ciii]

Constantino de Llano, whose nickname was "Kiki", was Villagrán's younger sister's son. A chemical engineer, on the faculty at the Centro Universitario Mexicano, professor at the Anglo-French College and head chemist at a paper factory, he was heir to a large fortune in Mexico and Spain. He had his own private industrial lab for analytical purpose according to a letter written May 20, 1964.

According to the papers in the archives, Villagrán had information that led him to believe that the pachycereus species was close to the one he was investigating (letter 5/29/1964). In another letter written May 24, 1965 he reported that the vulgar name "organo macho" was a form of torch cactus which in 1930 was identified in the Botanical garden of Mexico City as Myrtillocactus Schenkii Purpus (author's note: also known as cereus schenkii).[civ]

He began his research gathering material concerning flora in the mountain region of Mexico on the

Atlantic side, from the library at Southern Methodist University in Dallas. His research concerned a sub-region of the tropical region 150 to 1000 meters above sea level characterized by its flora.[cv] He then traveled to Xalapa, Mexico to talk to two botanists to get advice about the plants.[cvi] Then to Vera Cruz, Mexico where he went to 25 sites in an area along the Gulf coast and interior, in search of the cactus plant used in the alleged cancer cure. In a letter written August 14, 1964, from Xalapa, he stated that he had searched for the "Organo macho" plant, a name applied to more than one plant, in a chauffeured truck, but a lack of roads in the jungle area made the task difficult. He wrote that he had found a few plants, not many, in an area where it had been plentiful, but now was heavily populated and the plant had been obliterated. In his letter on August 20, 1964, he wrote that what the natives call "Organo macho" in one region is different in another.[cvii] When Ruth found that the cactus involved was unavailable she decided to concentrate on aloe vera instead. In the early

1960s, a dentist, Dr. Ellis G. Bovik from Weslaco, Texas had offered to contribute to the research of aloe vera. Ruth had turned him down. He later became instrumental in getting the aloe vera leaves sent from Mexico by "Kiki" for Villagrán's research through custom. Weslaco is only a few miles from the Mexican border. He also was helping them isolate some of the characteristics of aloe vera. Eventually Dr. Bovik had his own aloe vera fields and laboratory where the organically grown, certified pure strain Aloe Vera leaves were harvested, then processed into a gel.[cviii]

Mr. Hernandez-Villagrán set up a laboratory at the Southwestern Medical School Department of Cell biology with the original grant of $5000; monies from Ruth's foundation. His efforts, as outlined in his paper "The Sensible Approach," were "directed to find a chemical that will spur the automatic healing mechanism in the malignant cell."[cix] His ideas were a precursor to the holistic health movement which would become more widespread during the next two decades.

In his paper entitled "The

Sensible Approach" Mr. Hernandez-Villagrán states that "in consequence the sensible approach is not to try to kill the malignant cells but to try to regenerate them to normal cells. That is the approach that we follow."

He explored the theory of self-healing powers being attributed to a chemical trigger as well as what effect the emotional state of the patient had on his acquiring or overcoming cancer. He would get frozen cancer cells, some from a very famous movie star, and put the aloe vera in different strengths on the cancer cells. Cancer cells are cells that have gone wild. The nucleus breaks up and divides and wherever it goes it reproduces and becomes cancer. He had photographic equipment which he used to look at the cells under high powered microscopes. "I have seen some of those photographs where putting the aloe vera on the cancer cells, the nucleus would come right back in the center of the cell and the cytoplasm would reform and look like a normal cell." Ruth recalled.

The research premise was sound, but the mechanics of carrying it out ran into all kinds of problems: from his being moved from one lab to another, to working with various doctors and assistants. When one of the doctors said that Mr. Hernandez-Villagrán was "spinning his wheels" with his research, he was requested, once more, to move his equipment and discontinue his work at Southwestern Medical School.

In an effort to continue the connection with the school Ruth wrote a memorandum dated December 17, 1971, to Dr. Charles C. Sprague, Dean of the University of Texas Southwestern Medical School explaining in detail the purposes and work of the foundation. She stated the aim of the foundation is the study of the possible action of chemical compounds found in plants in the treatment of cancer.

She added, "The phenomenon of metastasis was what made us think that if there is any hope of total cure the approach has to be different than to try to destroy the malignant cell and we figured an <u>audacious</u> approach: to revert the malignant cell to normal."

Although not the first to look into the plant kingdom, she went on, "our originality consisted in looking into the desert plants instead of the customary way which has been the plants of the rain forests." They chose the genus aloe plant because importation of plants from Mexico presented special problems, while the genus Aloe is exploited commercially in Texas and available at any time.

She explains, "They consider that a failure until this moment, in a field in which so many failures are daily recorded this is not a disaster and we have all the reasons in the world to keep experimenting with this particular plant, and the study of others which will follow the present one." She concludes her plea by assuring him that the plan was sound, our premises are sound and scientific, our work is conducted with zeal and honesty, and our aim is both daring and original." [cx] Her plea was turned down and new arrangements had to be made.

At this time the foundation rented an apartment in the Oak Lawn area where Mr. Hernandez-Villagrán could do his work unmolested. Another researcher conferred with him in his research project.

Through all his problems, Villagrán kept on with his research, even refusing to take a raise. In a letter written January 5, 1969, he wrote "In order to increase my fee you will take money from your charities and put in the research foundation. Well I cannot be happy getting money that is intended to be for people who undoubtedly need it much more than I do. So please forget the whole thing. I shall keep working for the same money."

When Villagrán and his co-worker decided they needed animals to work with, Ruth and the trustees of the Foundation chose to phase out the research, giving all of the equipment to Baylor University Medical Center.[cxi]

Although Villagrán declined to be interviewed for the biography, in a letter he had written to Ruth January 9, 1982, he spoke of his admiration for her.

"...I have always admired you as a person and as a scientist. Very specifically I admire your outspokenness, your daring and your indefatigable love for your work."[cxii]

Meantime, Ruth learned of the need for an electronic microscope at the

University of Texas Medical School. The cost was $10,500. She wrote to Dr. Leslie and told her about the need for the microscope and Dr. Leslie sent the money. The microscope was donated to the Southwestern Medical School in the names of Dr. Leslie and the Ruth Jackson Foundation for Hernandez-Villagrán to use. Another doctor at Southwestern Medical School assisted him in its use while he worked on the project at the school. Because Baylor University Medical Center placed a high priority upon its operation of an educational facility for those practicing medicine and related sciences, they needed to be able to receive instruction in their respective fields. An excellent physical facility for the purpose of conducting programs in continuing education in the health sciences was completed in January 1973. The A. Webb Roberts Center for Continuing Education consisted of a 400 capacity auditorium, four adjoining seminar rooms, all near the existing library which houses 20,000 volumes and 700 monthly scientific journals. The auditorium and seminar rooms are to this day well equipped with projection facilities and other teaching aids. Office facilities provided a full-time Dean of Continuing Education and related personnel. Southwestern Medical School also participates in the program and shares a portion of the cost of the personnel required for its operation.

Ruth, always interested in contributing to the development of her chosen specialty, wanted to become involved in establishing programs to further her interest in educational opportunities for physicians in the Southwest. A distinguished lecturer and teacher, she supported the residency program, guiding many young doctors in Orthopaedic surgery.

In 1936, as Chief of Orthopaedic Service at Parkland Hospital in Dallas, Ruth received a letter from Dr. Leo Mayer, whom she had met when she was with Dr. Steindler in Iowa City. He asked if she could find a residency in Orthopaedic Surgery for Dr. Wilhelm Zuelzer, a German trained orthopaedic surgeon who was doing some post-graduate work with him at the Hospital for Joint Disease. She wrote in the 1975 Historical Background of the Orthopaedic Residency Program in

Dallas, which Parkland needed to set up a residency program but there were no funds appropriated. Dr. Zuelzer needed a salary. After discussing this with the Medical Board at Parkland it was decided that inasmuch as funds had been provided in the budget for a Physical Therapist at a salary of $75 per month, and inasmuch as there was no Physical Therapy Department, the salary could be diverted to Dr. Zuelzer, as long as he supervised some physical therapy. He agreed and became the first resident in Orthopaedic Surgery at Parkland in 1936, thanks to Ruth's efforts. [cxiii]

With this goal in mind Ruth and the directors of the foundation established the Ruth Jackson, M.D. Education and Research Fund in connection with Baylor University Medical Center in July of 1975. [cxiv] Through the fund, Baylor received $3,500 a year for the purpose of providing expenses and an honorarium for lectureships at Baylor University Medical Center and at Scottish Rite Hospital, as well as the University of Texas Southwestern Medical School in Dallas. The ten-year donation to Baylor Medical College provided seminars in orthopaedic surgery for students and professionals to encourage the residents to work in research. A committee was formed to function under the general direction of the Chief of Orthopaedics at Baylor and the Dean of Continuing Education for the responsibility of administering this endeavor.

The agreement drawn with Baylor University Medical Center by Ruth and the Foundation stated that within ten years, or upon the death of Dr. Jackson, all the monies accrued by the Foundation would be turned over to Baylor Medical University Center. The inaugural seminar was presented October 20-21, 1976 with David G. Murray, M.D. as guest lecturer. Dr. Murray of Syracuse, New York is noted for his contributions to the design and implantation of knee prostheses. A second seminar was held in December, 1976 with Charles A. Rockwood, M.D. speaking on the "Treatment of Shoulder Problems."

The subject for the third seminar held December 7-8, 1977 presented the status of oncology related to orthopaedic surgery. Guests lecturers included John A. Murray, M.D.,, Houston, Texas.; Melvin Tefft, M.D., Hugh G. Watts,M.D., Philadelphia, Pennsylvania.; and Marvin Stone, M.D.

In 1978 at the October 11-12th seminar, James H. Dobyns, M.D., Rochester, Minnesota and George Omer, M.D., Albuquerque, New Mexico spoke on "Problems of the Elbow, Wrist, and Hand." The fifth seminar was held October 24-25, 1979 with Charles Neer, M.D., New York and Hugh Tullos, M.D., Houston, Texas presenting "All Aspects of the Shoulder."

"Surgery of the Knee" was the topic for the sixth seminar held October 29-30, 1980 by David MacIntosh, M.D. and Peter Fower, M.D. London, Ont. Canada. E. Shannon Stauffer, M.D., Springfield, Illinois and Douglas W. Jackson, M.D., Long Beach, California lectured at the seventh seminar, October 14-15, 1981.

Dr. James Funk Jr., associate of the Peachtree Orthopaedic Clinic of Emory University School of Medicine in Atlanta, Georgia and team physician for the Atlanta Falcon Football Club was the guest speaker in 1982. One of his topics was "Football Injuries of the

Cervical Spine." This, the eleventh seminar, focused on the lower limb and the cervical spine, areas of special interest to Ruth.

In 1983, Dr. David G. Murray, Chairman of the Dept. of the Upstate Medical Center, Syracuse, New York spoke at the seminar that centered on reconstructive procedures for the knee. His research interests covered a wide field including experimentally induced arthritis, cellular dedifferentiation by very small electrical currents, fate of liquid silicone in the rabbit knee joint, hemodynamics of fat embolism and the surface interaction between hydrophilic gels and articular cartilage. His contributions to the design and implantation of knee prostheses have become internationally known. His topic was "Surgery for the Arthritic Knee: Pitfalls and Pratfalls."

The Chief of Foot Surgery at the Children's Hospital and Samuel Merritt Hospital in Headland, California, Dr. Roger A. Mann, presented the program on "Gait and the Foot" at the September seminar in 1984. His program centered on the reconstructive procedures for the foot and the biomechanics of human gait and of running.

"The Surgical Rehabilitation of the hip and knee" was the topic presented by Dr. David Hungerford at the eleventh seminar presented by the Ruth Jackson Research Foundation in 1985. An associate professor of orthopaedic surgery at the Johns Hopkins University and Chief of the Division of Arthritis Surgery at the Good Samaritan Hospital in Baltimore, Maryland, Dr. Hungerford has published numerous books, papers and abstracts relating to the musculoskeletal system with particular emphasis on arthroplasty procedures in the lower limbs.
Many orthopaedic surgeons and others have attended these informative and educational seminars, held while Ruth was still involved in the Foundation.

Other objectives of the Fund's money included acquiring and maintaining texts, reference books, visual aids and other educational materials for the use of physicians, nurses and related personnel in the field of Orthopaedic Surgery. This was intended to conduct research activities as projects were approved by the Medical Center's Research Committee and the Advisory committee of the Department of Orthopaedic Surgery. In addition, there was an effort to conduct such other educational activities approved by the Committee.

A committee was composed of the Chief of the Medical Center's Department of Orthopaedic Surgery as chairperson; two orthopaedic surgeons appointed by the Chief of the Orthopaedic Surgery; the Chief of the Medical Center's Department of Internal Medicine. These included Mr. Boone Powell during his lifetime, and thereafter the Director of the Medical Center or his representative; the Dean of the Center for Continuing Education or his representative; and Dr. Ruth Jackson during her lifetime or her designate and thereafter the Vice Chief of the Department of Orthopaedics of The Medical Center would be responsible for directing the use of the funds, to be invested. Ruth had a great input about where the money would go.

A new hospital, the Kaufman Community Hospital, a "satellite hospital" of the Presbyterian Hospital

Ruth Jackson, M.D.: A Life on the Leading Edge

in Dallas, was built in Kaufman where Ruth had her farm. For over 30 years she had spent one day a week doing orthopaedic surgery with Dr. Ed Hall of Kaufman and other doctors in the area. From the time she first "nailed a hip" behind Scott's Drug Store in Kaufman, to using the modern facilities, she was faithful to the people in the area.

In an interview with Dr. Ed Hall he tells how he and Ruth crossed paths when he was discharged from the Navy. "I got off down here in the country with the only medical facility within 12 miles one way and 40 the other. She came down with Peg Watkins.... From then on she came down by herself and did my orthopaedics including nailing hips, open reductions, closed reductions and what have you in a 25' by 40' room. We knew about sterility but there wasn't any there. It's amazing how well those people got along. It was in the old drugstore, and then we moved to the old bank building," he continued.

Ruth took up the tale, "They had a surgery behind Scott's Pharmacy. The first hip I nailed down here for you was in that operating room behind

Scott's Pharmacy. About 1943 or 44."

"From then on she took pity on me and came down whenever I got in trouble." Hall said, "She came down pretty regularly because we had a lot of trauma. People had just found out that bottled and bond whiskey was better than white lighting. It kept up an awful active night."

"Ruth taught me all, or what little orthopaedics I know." He continued, "I know enough to most times to call her."

An intern when Ruth was at Baylor, Ed talked about how special she was to the interns. "We weren't afraid of her but we weren't looking for her animosity," he recalled. Interns ask a lot of questions and Ruth would always help them. She taught them anatomy while training them at the same time. She never went into an operation, no matter how many times she had done the surgery without reviewing the anatomy.

The conversation evolved into a comparison of practicing medicine prior to the 1960s and after. Ed and Ruth agreed that there are things that couldn't be done then that, due to all the technology can be done now.

Ruth Jackson, M.D.: A Life on the Leading Edge

"It was a lot more fun practicing medicine then." Ed stated, "When you spend your nights without sleep because you're afraid some idiots going to sue you for everything you've got... Back then you took care of people, you knew they weren't going to pay you anyway...especially down here. These people, if they needed taken care of about all it took was my time. Sometimes we even took care of their hospital bills. When Bill and I sold that hospital we wrote off $670,000 worth of bad debts...and that was at $10 a day and $25.00 for the operating room. Nobody griped about it. If they needed taken care of they got taken care of."

Ruth called Ed one day in 1948 and told him to "buy me a farm." About two weeks later he found her 225 acres. He called her and after confirming the price, she agreed to go look at it. After she bought it, borrowing the money from her father, Ed's brother came from Tennessee to begin working on it in January 1950.

With the farm house livable, Ruth spent many weekends in Kaufman and was always available to help Ed and his office partner William Dlaning, M.D. Ed and Dr. Bill had built a 16 bed cottage type hospital that opened in 1948. Ruth remembered the call for help with a 220 pound patient with a dislocated hip.

"I said, 'Don't move him, leave him on the x-ray table, I'll be there.' When I got there they hadn't moved him. Of course the x-ray table was high. They knew I couldn't stand on a stool and work, so I said move him very carefully onto the floor so I didn't have to stand on a stool. I just very carefully got a hold of his leg and pulled it back in place," she recalled. Hall interjected, "He wasn't fat; all muscle. A little bitty girl like her did a pretty good job on him."

During their reminiscing about a malpractice suit brought against one of the doctors, it was noted that Ruth had practiced for 55 years and had never been sued for malpractice.

"Ed, you know very well that I never put my hands in the wounds" Ruth said, "I used the instruments because there was too much danger of tearing the gloves. We never had any infections..... In this day and age, Ed, with all the high technology going on today I am glad I don't do any surgery anymore.... I do a lot of second opinions. Should this be done. I sure am careful about it. I want a good examination. I want to see if what this doctor has recommended needs to be done."

In December of 1978 the Foundation donated $10,000 for equipment for the orthopaedic equipment room to the new Presbyterian Hospital of Kaufman. The hospital board had a plaque placed on the door designating that the equipment was donated by Ruth.

Another project, "The Cervical Spine Stability Study," an investigation carried out jointly by the University of Texas Southwestern Medical School and Yale University School of Medicine received $6,000 for the two year study. It was for the harvesting, storage and transport of the specimens as well as for the interpretation of results and publication of data. Begun in 1979 by Dr. Robert W. Bucholz, assistant professor, division of orthopaedic surgery at the University of Texas Health Science Center at Dallas and Corry Payne III, resident at the time, the paper, presented in 1981, was well received.

The Foundation also funded, in part, the presentation of the paper at the September 1984 Conference on Engineering and Medicine Biology in Los Angeles by Mark Strauss, engineering student, UTA.

The Baylor Dental School, connected with Baylor University Medical Center, received a donation of $5,000 in 1984 to the TMJ Dysfunction Research for research in temporal mandibular joint, as related to neck injuries and neck disorders. An award was given to the resident who presented the best paper at the North Texas Chapter of the Western Orthopaedic Association. The trustees decided to continue this project because it perpetuated an area of interest to Ruth and inspired residents to further their research. Five thousand dollars was given to the North Texas Chapter of the Western Orthopaedic Association to be used in the future for this purpose.

On December 10, 1985, three days before Ruth's eighty-third birthday, the board of Trustees, Dr. M. Paul Goodfried, Dr. Robert Bucholz, Dr.

Adrian Flatt and Dave F. Hunt, attorney, met at Dr. Jackson's home for the last meeting. Their purpose was to determine the status of each of the Foundation's ongoing projects and to make the final arrangements for turning over the money to Baylor University Medical Center on the thirty-first of December.

Dr. Flatt presented a proposal to donate $55,000 to improve and upgrade the quality of the new conference center authorized by Baylor University Medical Center. The Conference Center and the library were to be named the "Ruth Jackson Orthopaedic Education Center."

In addition to the $5,000 grant given to the Baylor Nurses' Library fund, the trustees voted to grant the Ruth Jackson Library's Fund of Baylor University Medical Center $15,000 for use of purchasing books, supplements and other literature for the Ruth Jackson Nurses' Library and the Ruth Jackson Orthopaedic Library.

The North Texas Chapter-Western Orthopaedics Association received $5,000 for use during the years 1985-86. The last $13,000 of the original

$19,679.56 grant was sent to the Baylor Orthopaedic IBM computer program. An additional $2500 was granted to the Baylor Orthopaedic Department for replacing equipment, bringing the total to $8,000. The Foundation's new projects were in the form of an $8000 grant to the Audiovisual Orthopaedic fund for slides to be prepared and the overall need for audio-visual props, as well as a grant of $7000 to Dr. Dan Loyd's project bringing the total to $17,195.57.

In 1981 or 1982, under a merger plan, the Signoid Steel Strapping Corp. stock was called, and the Foundation received $53 per share for its holding. This was placed in certificates of deposit at the BancTexas of Kaufman. When Boone Powell, Executive Director of Baylor University Medical Center, received the cashier's check endorsed to Baylor Medical Research Foundation it was for $287,213.10. Over $100,000 had been donated to Baylor University Medical Center Foundation in the past year. Effective December 31, 1985 these funds established the Ruth Jackson Research Foundation Fund at Baylor University Medical Center.

When asked why she chose Baylor to receive her gift, Ruth quickly replied, "Baylor Hospital is my interest. I am interested in Baylor and also in research. Everyone in Baylor has been good to me and my loyalty is to Baylor." Ruth's generosity could also cause her problems. She had a tendency too often to mix business with friendship.

"The Soul moralizes the past in order not to be demoralized by it."

CHAPTER XIII

For all the business deals that turned out well, there were a few which caused Ruth great pain and great financial problems. Like the proverbial "girl with the curl in her hair. When she was good in choosing her business dealings she was very, very good and when she was bad at it, she was horrid." Such was her partnership with her good friend, Judy Sanders*. Ruth met Judy Sanders when she came to Ruth as a patient in 1965 for back problems. At the time Judy was in charge of training the stewardesses for Braniff Airlines in Dallas. Judy called Ruth "Lightning." They soon became great friends, sharing many interests such as hunting and fishing. Once when they went deer hunting on a ranch in Menard Judy shot two deer in one day. They took the deer to Judy's hometown in Northwest Texas to be processed and the hides to a taxidermist.[cxv]

Judy had back surgery at Baylor University Medical Center in February

1966. She then went to Europe, in the fall of 1966, with her parents. Soon after, Judy lived with Ruth at various times. It was then that they decided to go into business together. Ruth agreed to become her partner in the Sandruth Company.

A partnership agreement was drawn March 1, 1967 and signed March 13, 1967 between Ruth Jackson and Judy Sanders. It was called the Sandruth Company, a partnership to buy, own, lease, rent or sell real and personal properties to establish a mobile home park or parks or any other business mutually agreeable. The principal place of business was 4001 Turtle Creek Blvd., Ruth's home. They each put in $1,500.00 at the First National Bank in Mineral Wells.

All net earnings and/or losses of Sandruth were to be shared equally. Article 8 said that neither of the partners shall attempt nor purport to cause the partnership to become security, endorser or guarantor, nor shall either partner lend, spend or give away any part of the partnership property. And no assignment, mortgage or pledge of the firm property shall be made without the consent in writing of both partners and such consent shall be evidenced by the signature of each partner to any such proposed assignment, mortgage or pledge. Article 9 stated all matter of policy shall be decided by mutual discussion and agreement. The Sandruth Company was located at 400 Stemmons Tower South, Dallas, Texas. 75207.

Somehow things didn't work out that way. By July 3, 1967 Sandruth Company owed Ruth $21,920.60. Listed as part of the Sandruth equipment was a T-Bird and Volvo automobile.

Pecan Lake Mobile Village was in Kleberg, Texas located on Belt Line Road 1.3 miles west of Hwy 175. On October 1, 1967 Ruth's net worth was $669,725.00. This included a 295 acre Kaufman farm with four houses, barns, tractors truck, machinery and livestock; one-half interest in Park Central Duplex, Vandalia property, Winona Gardens property, Fondren property, ten acres in Hidalgo County, as well as stocks, bonds, personal property; royalties from inventions, books, etc. $14,000.00; oil and gas royalties, and annuities. The Sandruth partnership listed Ruth's investment as $51,847.00.

On Ruth's birthday, December 13, 1967, Judy was in an automobile accident: the first disaster to occur. On October 11, 1968 Ruth and Judy were advised by the Dallas Bank & Trust Co. that their loan for $205,000.00 at 8 1/2% had been approved with security, the 102 acres on Pipeline Road and 7 acres, Town and Country Mobile Home Court at Mineral Wells subject to appraisal of collateral.

In February 1970 Judy was trying to get FHA financing on the Kleberg mobile home project. She was trying to buy approximately 70 acres which would require a sewer life station and approximately 1,000 feet of deep lines after the topography had been changed. She was trying to get Mrs. Dorothy Bush of Dorothy Bush Property in as a partner in a joint venture agreement with the understanding that Judy Sanders would be named co-broker in the land transaction. The Sandruth Company or her personal corporation would be named as general contractors in the development of the property in order to control sub-contract fees; and that the

Sandruth Co. or her personal corporation would be in charge of management, receiving a management fee deducted from the 25-30% operating fee.

Judy owned Sanders* Construction Co. which was named general contractor for the park development and Judy Sanders* Investment Corp. which provided the management contract for the park operations.

Since Ruth had been listed, in addition to Judge Sarah Huges, in the first edition of Who's Who in 1959, she felt Judy should have that honor.[cxvi]

She nominated Judy for Who's Who in American Women in February of 1970. She listed her as Partner of Sandruth Co., President of Sanders Construction Co., Inc.; President, Sanders Investment Corp., Director M.R. Properties, Inc.; ASE Dermetetics Clinic Inc., managing agent, Excalibur Venture, a group of real estate investors; and trustee of Ruth Jackson Foundation.[cxvii]

On February 17, 1970 Ruth wrote to Judy sending her a financial statement in order for her to go on Judy's bond as a general contractor or principal owner of a contracting corporation which is in the formative stage. In April Ruth wrote to Judy saying that the amount of money owed Ruth by the Sandruth Company was in error by $70.38, because it did not figure the cost of the Volvo correctly. This payment was to discharge all financial indebtedness to Ruth by the Sandruth Co.

A contract between Lone Star Gas Co. and Raintree Construction Co. was signed to furnish all labor and equipment to install 356 services in the Pecan Lake Mobile Village in Kleberg.[cxviii] In September 1971, Kaufman Co. Tax Assessor-Collector, Mrs. Doris Dunn, was dunning the Sandruth Co. for delinquent taxes, which was taken care of eventually.

Other problems surfaced when it was found that some of the lines installed to the Lone Star Gas Co. had been put in improperly. Walter Charette, office manager, and Ruth had to make a special trip to Mesquite to get approval of 1/2 inch pipe from the meter to the mobile home connection. If the mobile home was moved the 1/2 inch pipe was to stay in the ground and the gas to be cut off at the riser. An agreement proposal was presented November 26, 1971. Notes taken by office personnel point out problems in Denton, Copperas Cove, Crowley, Garland and Kleberg projects with cave ins, cut TV cable lines, water cut off because proper tests weren't made and digging the main too long before they put the line in. The main problem was, while putting in the sewer line, a large hole was covered stopping up the sewer lines.

Judy had been ill for some time, due in part to her automobile accident and had not been taking care of the business. In the first few months of 1971 she had been having trouble with a kidney stone which could not be removed. This had kept her incapacitated to the point that she could not take care of her many responsibilities. She had just completed a mobile home park in Roanoke, west of Dallas. She was a general contractor on an FHA project for a couple of developers as well as starting to develop Sandruth's property on Belt Line Road at Kleberg. The weather was not co-operating with spring rains stopping construction work. In July Ruth took Judy to Hot Springs, Ark. for a vacation to get away from the stress of her businesses.[cxix]

Ruth was concerned about the amount of drugs that Judy was taking to relieve the terrible pain of her kidney condition. The first part of August Ruth wrote to the head of the Narcotic Treatment Administration in Washington, D.C. to inquire about the effectiveness of Methadone treatment against withdrawal symptoms of all drugs of opium derivation including the synthetic ones. [cxx]

By the end of the month Judy was feeling well enough to return to work daily. She had promised to go to the hospital if she was not better, but Ruth thought that she felt threatened by the idea of being hospitalized. Her doctors were trying to prevent surgery until the stone was placed where it could be removed without harming the kidney. The situation was status quo until Judy had to be hospitalized for three weeks in November.[cxxi]

She tried to resume her business activities. In order to meet her obligations of the Sanders Construction

Corp. in which Ruth had no interest, Judy was mortgaging everything.[cxxii]

 Walter J. Charette was managing the Sandruth Co. during Judy's absences, taking care of things in Mineral Wells and Cleburne. As of October 20, 1971 the projected accounts payable for Judy's companies through November 26 would be $232,137.45 with an existing bank loan of $100,000.00 due, while the accounts receivable were only $167,174.97 leaving a deficit of $164,962.48. The bank loans Judy had made to the Dallas B&T and Kaufman Banks; M.R. Properties, the Ruth Jackson Research Foundation and Ruth personally in the amount of $39,339.02 were all due before the end of 1971. On November 8, 1971 the bank balances were Dallas B&T. $65.00; Seagoville, $150.00; T&C at Mineral Wells, $500.00. Walter Charette wanted to know how to pay a bank note due for $18,500 plus $401.87 interest.

 November 23, 1971, Ruth renewed a $33,434.44 note from Dallas Bank & Trust for Sandruth Co. By then it was too late. Judy took her own life November 30, 1971.[cxxiii]

 Ruth gave the following written

account of the events leading up to the day that Judy committed suicide in Ruth's bedroom on Turtle Creek.[cxxiv] "On Friday, October 22, 1971 Judy called me on the car telephone saying she would be home in five minutes. I had everything ready in my car to go to her parents' home. When Judy arrived home she slumped over the steering wheel of her car-crying of pain in her right kidney area. I had to help her from the car and into my car. (I had to go to Wichita Falls the next day to give a deposition in re: "Excalibur Ventures.") She was in such pain that she begged for some Demerol for relief. This was obtained at Skillern's Pharmacy and she took 2 cc by hypo. Before we got to Grapevine she was begging for more because of such severe pain. Another 1 cc was given and we made it to her parents' home. Her mother gave her or she took more during the night. I left early Saturday a.m. for Wichita Falls and returned about 3 or 4 p.m. Judy needed more pain medication and her mother and I went to the pharmacy for it...and again on Sunday before we returned to Dallas. Monday and Tuesday she stayed in bed and her niece came and sat with her on Tuesday and Wednesday. I called her mother and asked her to come. She did and took Judy back home to the hospital on Wednesday, the 27th. She remained there until the 18th of November-taking Methodone as directed by her doctor there. On the 5th of November she called a friend from Houston who had moved to Austin and had called Judy two or three times here at Turtle Creek, wanting Judy to spend a weekend with her, which Judy did not do. She spoke of another friend and Judy told her, "I never want to see her. She has almost ruined my life." Yet Judy talked to her on November 5 for some time- $7 worth. While she was in BP Hospital. I saw her on one occasion only-for a few minutes- the doctors there sent her to a psychiatrist in Ft. Worth.

On November 18 about 1 p.m. Judy called on the car phone saying she was on her way home and we would have dinner together. She was taking Methodone as recommended by the psychiatrist and continued to do so until November 30. On November 29th she was very upset with James Martinson and Jim Watson and the pressures created in

Sanders Construction Co. She asked many questions about how people committed suicide-and later that night said, "I will never commit suicide. It was the next morning, November 30, 1971 sometime between 9 a.m. when I left and noon when Gilbert found her bleeding in bed.[cxxv]

She had shot herself with Ruth's gun which Ruth kept in her room.[cxxvi] The bullet hit the clock by the side of the bed. It remained there, cracked and stopped at 11:30 a.m.

Judy had just had her 32nd birthday. From then on Ruth's affairs were in disarray. As a guarantor on Judy's performance bond for Sanders Construction Co., Ruth was liable for all the debts of Judy's companies. The bonding company would have to complete the unfinished construction work contracted at the time of Judy's suicide.[cxxvii] It would take more than two years, with Ruth losing part of her Kaufman Farm, and entering a marriage contract to save her Turtle Creek home, before she had her affairs untangled.

One such suit concerning an agreement made in August 1970 between the Pecan Lake Mobile Home Park and the

Texas Power and Light Company wasn't settled until June of 1973. In August 1974 she was trying to sell the Town and Country Mobile Home Park in Mineral Wells. At one time the eight remaining mobile homes had been clear of indebtedness, but now were mortgaged along with the park itself. She was making monthly payments on the note against the Mobile Home Park and interest only on the note against the park and these were becoming burdensome.[cxxviii]

Ruth confirmed her oral authorization to the bank to pay the draft in the amount of $18,640.44 against her note of $33,434.44 dated March 1972 but in May 1972 she turned over the seven acres of land in Palo Pinto County. Although Ruth fought the insurance companies, she had to pay on the bond issue. In order to meet these obligations she had to sell her farm at Kaufman. D. Priest bought all but 67 acres. Ed Nash, Ruth's banker at Kaufman took care of the sale arranging for D. Priest to give Ruth a life estate in the lake house. The insurance company got $260,000.00. After her finances were in better shape, she bought back the two and one-half acres where the lake house and one farm house are for $6,000.00. A patient of Ruth's from Miami, Florida, became Ruth's partner when Ruth bought another 57 acres and 73 acres. Ruth eventually bought her one-half of the 73 acres where the main house and the lake house area. The insurance company got the Pecan Lake Mobile Home Park at Cleburne.

Judy's absences from the business because of her illness, which Ruth thought chaotic at the time, were a blessing in disguise. Her absences paved the way for Walter Charette, an astute businessman who insisted on keeping impeccable records, to oversee the business during those last downhill months. Without his documentation, Ruth could have been liable for possibly as much as 30 million dollars instead of the half million it finally cost her.[cxxix] According to a letter from David Ford Hunt, April 9, 1974, M.R. Properties, Inc.'s ownership of the valid shares of stock issued in the corporation were as follows: 1,380 shares-Ruth Jackson; 100 shares, Marion Bouvé; 5 shares, Marianna Hood, M.D.;

and 10 shares, John F. Harrison. The total number of shares came to 1,495 out of a possible 1,500 authorized.[cxxx] There had been no stockholders' meeting since August 1972. He wanted the date that the loan from M.R. Properties, Inc., to the Sandruth Company had been paid.[cxxxi]

According to Dave Hunt, there were no meetings between 1972 and 1974. Later, when Ruth decided to use Henry Klepak as her lawyer, after Dave Hunt refused to return her calls, she tried to have the legal papers, including the minutes of the Research and M.R. Properties meetings returned to her. When Mr. Klepak sent a courier over to Hunt's office with a letter requesting the return of the M.R. Properties, Inc. books, Dave complied. Upon examining the books, Ruth discovered many pages were missing. Walter Charette said in an interview, that it was one reason why he resigned from the board. The board of directors, or trustees, the terms were used intermittently, was always intermingled between the Research Foundation and M.R. Properties, Inc. Most of the board members, who served from 1976 through

1985, were Ruth's friends in the medical field. Serving on the board at various times were: Drs. Leon Ware; Paul Goodfried, Robert Bucholz, and Adrian Flatt.[cxxxii] In order to solve some of her financial problems, she inadvertently created another. She married Raleigh Regley Mayfield to keep from losing her Turtle Creek home to the bond company.

"Do not stop, do not hesitate-push forward with belief and aplomb to reach your goal. Do not stop for triviality-look forward, not backward, look upward not downward- always forward"

CHAPTER XIV

The wedding took place during White Wing dove season in Edinburg, Texas, August 31, 1972. The reception: a bridge game with her sister and brother-in-law, Edythe and Harold Brehm in their McAllen home. Bridge and the courts of law were what brought the unlikely couple together. Ruth met Raleigh, a court reporter, while testifying in many court cases. Both avid bridge players, they soon sought each other out when a fourth was needed for bridge. So, when she looked around for a male to marry, there was Raleigh right across the table from her, with a three no-trump bid in his hand. She explained to him that she needed a temporary husband, due to a vague Texas law that allowed only male homestead owners to keep their homes when threatened with a lien. The marriage would be dissolved as soon as her financial problems were resolved.

She assumed he thought that her assets had been seized, so she didn't bother to tell him that most of her assets had been transferred to her sister, Edythe. The platonic relationship went well for a while. He moved into her Turtle Creek home; went quietly about his business, and was always available for bridge. Other than a 1972 New Year's Eve visit from Edythe and Harold, Ruth's social life was affected by her financial problems.

According to Ruth's 1973 journal, usually filled with dinner engagements with friends and notes about who called or whom she called, the pages are blank for months. Her only recorded social event in February 1973 was an unusual one for Ruth. She attended the American Academy of Orthopaedic Surgeons Meeting in Las Vegas from January 31 to February 5. One entry for the evening of February 4th simply says: "To see Elvis." She met Dr. Theda Dowell, an orthopaedic surgeon who also was an engineer, at the AAOS meeting.

By April, a steady diet of married life began to grate on Ruth's nerves. A comment recorded in her journal states "Bridge E. Clammons, R. showed his colors at the bridge table." The entry for the next day, Aril 7, 1973 states: "Today R wants to move out-wants a place of his own. But will stay until my problems are settled-he says-we shall see-."

No more entries until October 1973 when she made a trip to Los Angeles. Her friends, Tru and Enid Wilhelm took her to their La Quinta home where they coddled Ruth with lakeside lunches, shopping trips and much needed down time. She met Dr. Theda Dowell who extended the kindness with dinner at the Fireside Inn after a tour of her new office. She spent the night with Theda and husband, Mike Glenden, M.D. in their Culver City home. The next day Ruth and Theda drove to San Diego to the Western Orthopaedic Association meeting. Ruth returned home October 24 and settled into her routine: seeing patients and studying at home. She never went to bed without several medical journals or her writing material splayed around her on her bed.

By Christmas Eve Raleigh was still living in Ruth's house despite his desire to leave. They attend Christmas Eve dinner at a friend's house, but

Ruth wanted to leave at 10:30 citing a "terrible pain in her left shoulder." She notes in her journal that R.K. went on to a man friend's house. Edythe and Harold arrive for the New Year holiday. Ruth wrote in her journal that "R.K. did not show & had never returned except to get his things in early January."

Raleigh must have known that Ruth was close to the end of her financial difficulties. While at the American Academy of Orthopaedic Surgeons meeting in January 1974, Ruth received word that her Kaufman farm was sold and the Bond Company got $101,000.00 from the proceeds. Her brother-in-law, Harold Brehm, claimed Ruth had to give Raleigh between $5,000 and $10,000 to "get rid of him." At 72 years old, Ruth was still working hard. She wanted all her Kaufman farm back and she needed to recoup her losses. She was busy, not only with her medical practice, but with dispensing the infusion of funds from Dr. Leslie's bequest to her. The Research Foundation enlarged its focus on many new projects. Long days at the clinic with patients, then night meetings in her home with the board of directors kept her at a pace even a young person would shudder to take on.

Ruth was always interested in helping the young medical residents. She spoke to the residents at Columbia University in September of 1962 when she stopped in New York City to present a paper to the International College of Surgeons meeting on her way to Germany to present a paper to the German Orthopaedic Society.

Through the efforts of her friend, Dr. Mary Sherman, Director of the bone pathology laboratory at Oschner foundation Hospital in New Orleans Ruth gave a speech to the residents in New Orleans during a 1950s AAOS meeting. In Dallas, she took many of them under her wing, counseling them, teaching them, taking them on weekends to her house on the remaining acres she retained in the Kaufman farm. They went fishing and shot ducks, doves and rabbits, all of which Ruth then cleaned. Ruth took the students' problems to heart, loaned them money and ran interference when they had problems with school, parents and chiefs of staff.

Carole Gordon, M.D. of Waco, Texas

was one such medical student. Inspired to become a physician by her father, a surgeon practicing in Waco, Carole arrived, full of anticipation, in Dallas in 1982 to attend medical school. "During the first week of our school, the Dallas County Medical Society threw a medical dinner, an annual event, whereby fresh new medical students are introduced to a member of the private medical community in Dallas." Carole recalled, "This practicing physician would be a sponsor; a mentor; a friend; someone to call for moral support or for contacts within the community. I arrived that evening to be given a name of a woman orthopaedic surgeon, Dr. Ruth Jackson. I was immediately surprised, I had never known a female surgeon, much less a female specialist in orthopaedics!"

She continued, "Today there are not many women orthopaedic surgeons. Of course we all made generalizations of what specialty doctors are. An internist uses his brain; a surgeon uses his hands, an orthopaedic surgeon uses brute strength to manipulate joints and bones. Most of the orthopaedic surgeons I have known were over 6 foot, ex-football players. My first thought was that this is bound to be a tall woman. Over 200 doctors gathered in the lobby. I searched for a woman who would stand out, perhaps be Amazon in appearance. My surprise was great when a five foot one inch, frail looking 74 year old woman approached and stuck out her hand. 'I'm Ruth Jackson,' she said, 'so Carole you want to be a surgeon.' Looking her eye to eye I responded, 'Yes, But Dr. Jackson, they tell me I'll have to stand on a stool to reach the table. Do you do that?' 'Hell no, I just tell them to lower the table.'"

Carole remembered an invitation Ruth extended for her to visit the clinic. She entered and saw Ruth; gray hair properly pinned up, wearing a white jacket. "Whew," Ruth sighed as she sat, "Everyday I see patients with such problems. I hope that I help them."

"They come to me every day, referred or by request to give a second opinion of their problems. I don't know what other doctors do, but some of these patients have never been examined. Pay attention to the little things, be thorough and you will do well.

I said, "Everyday I hear,' But doctor, I have never been examined like this before." Ruth peered at her over her glasses and said to Carole, "Medicine has changed a lot. High technology and more tests than you can imagine. What happened to touching the patient and examining them for the diagnosis? Listen, you must remember this: listen, look and touch. These things you must remember and above all you must care. Too many doctors don't care these days."

The caring staff at the clinic impressed Carole. She wondered whether the physical or spiritual therapy helped them more. As Carole observed, Ruth examined her patients, she was impressed with how Ruth methodically and completely she obtained their history; manipulated and examined their particular ailment. "Her understanding of human anatomy was masterful as well as the quickness of her mind." Carole said.

At least once a month for the three years that Carole was in Dallas she and Ruth drove to the farm in her

1978 gold Thunderbird. Sometimes twelve year old Sandy Curtis, the son of Ruth's current office manager accompanied them. Ruth taught Carole and Sandy how to use a knife to whittle, use a 16 gauge shotgun for hunting and how to skin a rabbit. Carole remembered what a great respite it was to go to the farm after the strenuous week of studies. The fishing tank, large enough for a trip around in a rowboat was stocked with catfish; the old green lake house nestled among the trees was waiting for them to come in for resting and great conversations. Their time was spent in quiet meditation, talking of the past and the making of a doctor.

In looking back at the three years of mentoring by Ruth, Carole summed up her feelings in a 1987 interview. "She, who is well into her senior years as a physician, and I, a neophyte in the medical profession found a common bond in our unique position. She, who had come long before, was one of the few. She fought, not only family and friends, well meaning but horrified that she was not a normal woman, but also academia and society who thought a woman's place was in the home. She did not speak bitterly or with resentment, but fondly of her medical training days. I knew that she had fought many battles and had won, this small dynamic woman sitting with a fishing pole bedside me. Times have changed; however I still feel the frustration, the social pressures of being a perfect spouse, mother and professional. I anger at the professors who have looked at females as second class citizens and at society in general who feel that a "small girl" is not big enough to be a doctor much less a surgeon. It is difficult now, but what she endured I cannot even imagine.

This one whose love of medicine she married, no ambition of family ever swayed her from medicine and never wanting nor needing a life. She paved the way for the new generation of female physicians who now can "have it all." Dr. J. was one of the rare ones. Throughout the years she has reached back helping many; given of herself, her money and her heart, medicine or non medicine to better themselves. And I am one of those."

Ruth's largess is legendary. Dr.

Theda Dowell relates the time she went to Dallas to a 1974 Western Orthopaedic Society meeting and Ruth handed Theda the keys to her 1971 Thunderbird. When Theda protested that she couldn't afford it, Ruth told her to take it; she wouldn't drive it anymore. She had an accident in the car after dreaming that she had been killed in it. She refused to drive it, buying herself a new '74 Thunderbird.[cxxxiii] She gave, not only a car away at the WOA meeting, but ten gallon cowboy hats, to those who attended her cocktail party at her Turtle Creek home. The big Texas welcome was not so welcome the next morning as Tru remembered it. He had to help Ruth pour several people, still wearing their hats, onto the plane.

It was during the party that a conversation between Ruth and Theda helped Ruth make the decision to stop performing surgery. Ruth didn't perform surgery unless there were specific indications and she was certain that there was a surgical necessity.

"I might have one patient in Baylor Hospital and would have to make rounds once or twice a day and walk and walk, then go to my office," She recalled, "That was too much so I decided I would not do surgery anymore." It was Theda's question, "Why do you go on doing surgery when you don't do it much anymore?" that put the seed in her mind.

With more free time and the loss of her houseman, Gilbert, Ruth spent more and more time alone. Although she professed not to regret having radiation on her ovaries when she was young so she wouldn't have children, the house was empty and work took up less of her time. She generously had taken many of her young relatives into her home, but the price they paid was having Ruth take control of their lives. None stayed for very long. Marion Bouvé had fostered the idea that Ruth's relatives weren't welcome so many had quit trying to contact her.

Ruth soon found, not one, but two women to mentor and nurture. Two, who would be there to take care of her in various capacities until her death in 1994.

"Absolute independence is a poor chimera, a stoic who withdraws into the fortress of his will and closes the gate."

CHAPTER XV

Lucy Bentley* drew Ruth's name out of a hat. She didn't realize then that her lucky draw would change her life.

In 1981, Ruth called a security company to have someone come to her office to talk about installing security alarms in her home and office.
"There were three other sales representatives there that day and we all had call-in leads." Lucy recalled, "The leads were always put into a hat for the sales reps to draw. I drew Dr. Jackson's name. I had never heard of her and didn't know what to expect."

She didn't expect a little old lady After Lucy gave her an estimate for the clinic, Ruth asked her to go to the house to continue to demonstrate her product, a process that usually took an hour. Seven hours later, the two had become friends, delving into subjects from reincarnation to drug and alcohol abuse. They exchanged life stories, Ruth's about her medical career and Lucy's about her problems with manic depression. They discovered they both had an interest in the outdoors and horses. "I felt a lot of warmth and compassion for her (Ruth), for what she had done and what she had been through. I admired her and I knew I would definitely see her again." Lucy said. "It was like two old friends had come together who hadn't seen each other in a long time. *De ja` vu* or whatever."

Lucy lived alone in an apartment. Ruth was alone in her ten room house. After six or eight months; months spent driving Ruth to the Kaufman farm every weekend, Lucy moved into Ruth's home. Once again Ruth had someone to teach to hunt, fish and clean rabbits. She supported Lucy through difficult times. Lucy admitted to being "spiritually, emotionally and physically in real bad shape" when she met Ruth. Consumed by alcohol and drugs, she didn't know any other way of life, didn't even realize it was a problem. Ruth tried to help her by paying her bills. Ruth showered Lucy with gifts and Lucy showered Ruth with her time. After a year, Lucy's feeling of obligation and her restlessness kicked in. She was wrestling with her conscience. A friend wanted her to move to Florida with her and Lucy wanted to go. She was looking for something different in her life. What, she didn't know.

When she decided to go, she felt as if she was abandoning Ruth, and this was difficult for Lucy. Before Lucy left in 1983, she introduced her to Sheri Larzalere. Ruth was about to inherit an instant family.

Lucy took Ruth to Sheri's home in Canton, Texas where she was living with her daughter, Kim and son, Christopher. Sheri had a secretarial job in Dallas and was trying to find a house in Dallas to be closer to her work. Lucy told Sheri she wanted to introduce her to Ruth because she wanted Sheri to check on Ruth after she left. Lucy's move to Florida left Ruth alone, once again.

During Ruth's and Sheri's twice a week phone calls, Sheri mentioned she was going to move to a house being renovated in Kaufman by Ruth's banker, Ed Nash, because Kaufman was 30 miles closer to Dallas. Two weeks after Lucy left, Ruth told Sheri to meet her at the Kaufman farm and they would look at the rent house. Ruth took one look at the house, disapproved and suggested that Sheri and five year old Christopher move in with her so Sheri would be even closer to her work. Sheri's teen age daughter, Kim had gone to live with her father, Rick.

Ruth's new family moved in with her on a Saturday, September 17, 1983 in what Sheri believed would be a temporary arrangement. The company Sheri worked for was in financial trouble and Sheri was looking for a job with a law firm to make more money, be closer to downtown and afford her own apartment. Ruth came home from the clinic everyday to find Sheri reading the want ads and calling to inquire about jobs. Ruth didn't like what she heard. She was lonely. The house, which had been in benign neglect for the past few years, was shaping up under Sheri's organized care.

"She didn't want me to move," Sheri said, "I wanted to move. I could see the writing on the wall and I didn't want to stay."

After Sheri and Christopher had

been there two months, Ruth came home devastated. Lois Knowles, who had been her office manager for 12 years had quit after an altercation with another employee. Ruth pleaded with Sheri to take the job. She needed her: at work as well as at home. Sheri resisted for three days, then since Ruth had been so kind to her, agreed to take the job until Ruth found someone else. Sheri gave two weeks notice at her job, and then went to work for Ruth the last week of October 1983.

"I look back and think it was meant to be," Sheri said. "Ruth was very busy when that happened. I kept the books and ran the office for her."

What started as a business proposition, a partnership, a business obligation, became a friendship, then deepened into a loving family relationship.

"I lost my grandmother about a year after I moved into the house with Ruth. No one will ever take the place of my grandmother, but it seemed to fill a void there." Sheri said.

As Christopher and Sheri settled in, Ruth's lifestyle changed subtlety. Her "Ba Humbug" attitude about

Christmas was unacceptable to Sheri. Christopher was little and Santa Claus had to come. Sheri recalled it was like "pulling teeth" to get her to let her put up a tree. Ruth just didn't want Christmas festivities. It was the closest that Sheri ever came to moving out.

Sheri held her ground and by Christmas Eve, Ruth was up in the middle of the night helping Sheri play Santa Claus. Sheri remembered Lois Knowles telling her that Ruth never wanted to let her employees take off for holidays. They agreed that Ruth hated holidays because with the clinic closed she would go home to an empty house. In the years Ruth was on the staff of the hospital she was busy during the holidays. As Sheri pointed out, "hospitals don't close on holidays."

Other lifestyle changes were made: at home and the office. The house got new paint, sterling silver was brought out and used, flowers were placed on the grand piano and a guest room was redecorated. Sheri hired a maid to live in the garage apartment. The house came to life again. Christmas had come year round at 4001 Turtle Creek Dr. The office benefited when Sheri hired more employees, which pleased everyone.

However, not everyone was pleased all of the time. Although Ruth wanted everything done for her at home and in the office, she didn't like to lose control. Sometimes in the beginning, Ruth got belligerent with Sheri, one of the first persons to be able to stand up for her own rights. One of Ruth's patients was a psychic who had told Ruth that "she will live to be 90 and then come back and I may tell you 102." psychic told Sheri, "The only reason Ruth gets belligerent is because she thinks you will leave her. That there are times she feels that you are going to take advantage of her and not be there when she needs you." [cxxxiv]

Sheri admitted that this made her understand Ruth and helped her be more patient. Christopher had become a big part of Ruth's life. She always gave Sheri advice on raising him, telling her, "Remember I raised a boy," referring to her nephew, Darrell.

If Sheri had access to Ruth's scribbled notes, she might have understood sooner. One such note,

Ruth Jackson, M.D.: A Life on the Leading Edge

written Saturday, April 5, 1986 stated: "During the past 2 1/2 hours I have been sitting here at my work table listening to some of my music cassettes and, may I add, contemplating what I must do. I am alone, but with my head bowed I pray that I will be able to go on doing the most for the most people who need my services-at the moment I have no friends & no family with whom I can communicate-no one to whom I can turn for even a small bit of consolation. Why do I need any? Well, I am alone & lonely. My penchant for helping others has been responsible for my present status. But-one must not look back-only forward. 'Adelante siempre adelante.' An old Spanish saying -forward always forward- certainly I am cognizant of the fact that my material possessions are all that those around me desire-so down the drain it goes with no recourse for restitution-now. I know there must be change and with God's help the changes will occur. My destiny is not to be left alone-changes must be made. It is gratifying to know in spite of all the mistakes I have made, I have become an internationally known and respected doctor-and I plan to continue on the same trail-but some corners must be made straight to avoid collapse. I want no more stumbling blocks-although they may be necessary as a challenge to climb to ever greater heights!!"

Ruth's problems became Sheri's problems. When Ruth became ill about the time the note was written, Sheri, not knowing who to call for help, turned to Ruth's lawyer, Dave Hunt. He informed her that "he wasn't to be bothered at home." A call to Dr., Marianna Hood, Ruth's friend, elicited the response: "What's the matter is Ruth pregnant?"

A lawsuit resulting from Ruth's signing a note for two young women to go into business had drawn on for the first three years Sheri lived with Ruth. When Dave Hunt didn't return her calls concerning subpoenas, Sheri called a prominent lawyer, Henry Klepak, who would pick up the phone. He explained the situation to the judge and the problem was solved.

Concerned because of the stress it caused Ruth, Sheri convinced Ruth to hire Henry Klepak, whom Ruth had known for 20 years. He persuaded her to settle the lawsuit out of court, which was accomplished in October 1987. Klepak told Sheri he had warned his staff of twelve attorneys, ten years previously, "that if you have a case and Ruth Jackson is the doctor involved, settle out of court. Do not ever put that woman on the witness stand because she was rough and tough."

In February 1984, four months after Sheri and Christopher came to live with Ruth, Lucy returned from Florida, stopping by for a short visit before heading for Austin.

Lucy remembered she didn't want anybody to see her. She was extremely suicidal and "right at the bottom with drugs and alcohol." Four months in Austin made everything worse. One day she woke up, called, "Doctor" as she always referred to Ruth, and told her she was going through a really difficult time. Ruth assured her she was there for her, to come back to Dallas and she would do anything to help. Ruth and Sheri wanted Lucy to live with them, but Lucy wanted to be alone. Ruth sent her to the Kaufman farm hoping the rural atmosphere would help. Leaving nothing to chance, Ruth sent her a video tape on alcoholism. Finally recognizing her real need for help, Lucy decided to go to the Terrell State Hospital. Ruth had just received a newsletter from Baylor University Medical Center about a new drug-alcohol treatment center at Baylor Parkside in Argyle. Two days later, thanks to Ruth's influence, Lucy entered the center to begin treatment with Ruth's and Sheri's moral support.

While at Baylor Parkside, it was recommended that Lucy be sent to a woman's program near Colorado Springs, Colorado, a private program that cost $10,000 and lasted from three months to a year. Ruth brooked no nonsense from Lucy, telling her she was going to enter this program. Lucy had a profound experience in the Outward Bound program and felt capable of returning home after three months.

"Ruth has always propelled me to go forward. I am real grateful," Lucy said. After returning to Dallas in August 1985, Lucy moved in the garage apartment at Ruth's, got a job at the Bank of Dallas and Ruth bought her a shiny new car. Ruth supported Lucy, not only with money, but with encouragement.

"Doctor was always here and told me how proud she was and how far I had come," Lucy said. "She is probably the only one in this world who still tells me how proud she is of me and that is something I really need to hear."

After three months, Lucy felt strong enough to try living on her own. She moved to the Kaufman farm where she was surrounded by the animals she loved: Five dogs, chickens, rabbits and seven horses. Ruth had bought a champion paint horse, Star Elena Blue Eyes, for Lucy to show. With Lucy's hard work and Ruth's encouragement, they took the paint to several horse shows winning several awards. Now that Lucy had turned her life around and Sheri had Ruth's home and office running smoothly, Ruth's thoughts turned to their futures.

After being bedridden in 1986, an unusual occurrence for Ruth, she worried about being put into a nursing home. She wanted to die in her own bed. She realized that Sheri had no power to keep someone from doing just that if Ruth was incapacitated. When she recovered, she drove herself to the attorney's office, had him write a will and a living will. The will left the Turtle Creek house to Sheri and gave Lucy the right to live on the Kaufman farm until Lucy's demise, and then it would be turned over to Baylor University Medical Center. Sheri had the power of attorney for the living will.

A meeting at Ruth's home was attended by Boone Powell, Jr., Executive Director of Baylor University Medical Center and the administrator of Psychiatry, with whom Lucy had been working. Sheri and Lucy attended and they discussed the possibilities of using the Kaufman farm to develop some type of therapeutic environment for young people's recovery, similar to the Outward Bound program.

"Everyone was so nervous. You could feel the tension in the air. Maybe it was my own," Lucy recalled, "Then Dr. Jackson started dancing. I thought 'Oh my God!' but it was so great. Just what was needed because it broke the ice and everyone started laughing."

Ruth felt at ease. She had taken care of the futures of her live-in family and the love of her life Baylor University Medical Center. She also had a new interest in life. One that had her name on it. In 1983, The Ruth Jackson Orthopaedic Society was conceived, labored, was born and continued to grow.

"What you are is what you believe you are, a failure? A success!"

CHAPTER XVI

The concept for the women's orthopaedic organization was conceived on December 21, 1982 when Mary Louise Morden, M.D., assistant professor of pediatric orthopaedics at Johns Hopkins University, the Johns Hopkins Hospital, Baltimore, Maryland, wrote a letter to her American Academy of Orthopaedic Surgeons female colleagues, stating that she would be establishing a female orthopaedists organization that would meet at the Academy's 1983 annual meeting in Anaheim, California in March at its 50th anniversary celebration. The basis for the meeting was to organize a national women's information network.

The idea evolved when Dr. Morden met two other female orthopaedists at a board review meeting in 1981. Dorothy Balthazar, M.D., assistant professor of orthopaedic surgery at the University of Massachusetts in Worcester, and Catherine Hawthorne, M.D., who practiced in Gallup, New Mexico, found that they had many similar experiences in going through their residencies, even though they had very different backgrounds, practices, clinical experiences and types of training programs. "It was fun to find somebody to sit and talk with for the first time," Dr. Morden exclaimed.

Their next step was to go through the American Academy of Orthopaedic Surgeons roster for female members. This task proved to be formidable since the women weren't listed separately. It became a challenge to decide if the Leslies, Dales, Marions, or Ashleys were female or male. They settled on twenty-two of the more obvious female sounding names and sent out the first letter. A notice was placed in the AAOS bulletin and the word was out.

The formal society for women orthopaedic surgeons was organized at the California meeting and was named The Ruth Jackson Society, changed in 1990 to the Ruth Jackson Orthopaedic Society. The name was chosen to honor Ruth's efforts to become the first female orthopaedic surgeon to be board certified in 1937.

Liebe Sokol Diamond, M.D. of Baltimore, Maryland was elected the first president with Mary Morden, M.D., Baltimore, Maryland, treasurer and Sandra Thomson M.D., Boston, Massachusetts, as secretary. Serving on the committee as members at large were: Ruth; Jacquelin Perry M.D. Downey, California; and Mary Ann Shannon M.D., Minneapolis, Minnesota, resident.

The labor began. By the end of 1983, the articles of incorporation of the Ruth Jackson Society, Inc., were drawn. Its stated purpose was to encourage, promote and advance the science and medical art and practice of orthopaedic surgery amongst women. Its assets were to be used exclusively to enable the corporation to perform its functions and to carry out its stated purpose. But the broader aspects of the Society were explained in the May 17, 1983, issue of *The Medical Post*. In this interview with *The Medical Post*, Dr. Morden emphasized that the original intent was for the organization to act as a support and information group and not a feminist faction. Dr. Jacquelin Perry, Downey, California, echoed the sentiments by stating in the article that one of the reasons some of the first women orthopaedists felt no need to organize was because by the time one was at the state of organization, one had already won the battle.

"With most battles won, it would be divisive to set up The Ruth Jackson Society as a political, feminist faction," she pointed out, "If I had a major axe to grind, I'd be perfectly willing to go into battle, but I don't think we have one," she concluded.

"No woman at the meeting wanted to be separate from the men in the Academy....but what they wanted to do was establish a social group to share common experiences that is really necessary and to set up an information network for women who are interested in orthopaedics or women who are in orthopaedic residencies. Because that is what has been missing for women," Dr. Morden was quoted in the article. She pointed out that there was no 'old boy' system like the men has and it is a problem for all the women trying to find the kind of practice position they wanted. "These annual meetings will give the women an opportunity to compare many common problems such as the wisdom of various career moves, the effects of orthopaedic residency programs on marriages, appearance and self-image as well as practical adjustments to a male-dominated profession," she explained in the article.

The charter was drawn up by Dr. Diamond's father, a lawyer who "likes to help lady doctors," according to a letter to the members in April of 1983. The second meeting of The Ruth Jackson Society was held Saturday, February 11, 1984, in the Westover Room of the Omni International Hotel in Atlanta, Ga. At this meeting the articles of incorporation and constitution and by-laws were accepted by the membership. It was decided that an additional category for corresponding members would be added for those members from foreign countries who wished to join the Society and that there should be no membership fee for honorary members. The Society members voted to publish a quarterly newsletter, to include lists of those positions seeking women partners and other news of interest to the members.

Jacqueline Perry, M.D. of Downey,

California, was elected president with other officers: Mary Williams Clark, M.D., of Charlottesville, Virginia, vice-president; Melanie Sanders, M.D., Shreveport, Louisiana and Dorothy Balthazar, M.D., Worcester, Massachusetts as members-at-large. Dr. Thomson and Dr. Morden remained as secretary and treasurer respectively. Ruth had told the board that the Ruth Jackson Research Foundation would be donating $10,000 to the Society. Legal difficulties due to RJOS's tax status delayed the ability to accept the gift. By then Ruth had turned over the Ruth Jackson Research Foundation to BUMC in 1985. The legal problems were eventually solved and the funds were made available in 1986.

The possibility for The Ruth Jackson Society to sponsor a lectureship or an Academy paper presentation with monies to come from the Ruth Jackson Research Foundation was explored. The members decided to contact the Academy and individual resident programs to ascertain how many women were involved in residency programs across the country in order to inform the program directors of the organization's interest in new members. There were sixty-eight members at the first RJOS meeting: 35 active members, 11 associate members, 20 affiliate members; one emeritus and one medical student. Twenty-five of these were married, twenty-eight single and the marital status of the remaining fifteen was unknown. Thirty-four of the members were affiliated with institutions, eight involved in group practices, eight practiced on their own, and four were in the military. The major specialty interests of the group included pediatrics, general orthopaedics, scoliosis/backs, hands, sports, knees-arthroscopy and tumors.

Various membership categories were defined as active members, associate members, affiliate members, emeritus members and honorary members. An active member was limited to women physicians certified by the American Board of Orthopaedic Surgery and members of the American Academy of Orthopaedic Surgeons, practicing exclusively orthopaedic surgery principally in the United States of America. Women physicians not certified by the American Board of Orthopaedic Surgery or who were not yet eligible to be members of the American Academy of Orthopaedic Surgeons, but practice exclusively orthopaedic surgery in the U.S. were qualified as associate members. A woman physician engaged in residency training programs for orthopaedic surgery was qualified for an affiliate membership. Those active or associate members who had attained the age of sixty-five, were emeritus members. Upon written request to and by approval of the Board of Directors, members who had withdrawn from active practice could also become emeritus members. Honorary members were those persons, both male and female, practicing orthopaedic surgery, other branches of medicine, or in the basic sciences, making significant contributions to the orthopaedic education of women. The Ruth Jackson Orthopaedic Society was born!

Membership had grown to 100 by the next meeting in Las Vegas, Nevada, January 26, 1985. RJOS started on a positive note by deciding to honor those who had helped women orthopods reach their goals. Vernon Nickel, M.D., San Diego, California, had been elected the first honorary member, citing his commitment and training of women orthopaedists. The tradition holds and in the next ten years the following orthopaedic surgeons were elected honorary members: 1987, Augusto Sarmiento, M.D., Los Angeles;1988 Patsy Mayes Jackson and Donald Wiss, M.D., Los Angeles; 1989, Roger Mann M.D., San Leandro, California; with three honored in 1990: Michael Schafer M.D., Chicago; Edwin Guise, M.D., Los Angeles; and Dennis Coughlin M.D., Knoxville, Tennessee; 1991, McCollister Evarts M.D., Hershey, Pa.; 1992, Henry Mankin, M. D., Boston, and in 1994, Thomas J. Scully, M.D., El Paso, Texas.

The next ten years, under the leadership of the following presidents: 1984-85, Jacquelin Perry, M.D., Downey, California.; 1985-86, Mary Williams Clark, M.D., Charlottesville, South Carolina ;1986-87, Mary Morden, M.D., Baltimore, Maryland;1987-88 Dorothy Balthazar, M.D., Baltimore, Maryland.; 1988-89, Helen Horstmann, M.D., Philadelphia, Pennsylvania.; 1989-90, Diana Carr M.D., Sebring, Florida ;1990-91 Mary Ann Keenan, M.D., Philadelphia, Pennsylvania; 1991-92

Laura Tosi, M.D., Washington D.C.; 1992-93, Diane Gilles, M.D., Scottsbluff, Nebraska.; 1993-94, Janet Walker, M.D., Lexington, Kentucky.; and 1994-95, Vicki Kalen, M.D., Gainesville, Florida; RJOS matures to become an organization with a powerful voice.

A new category, "Corresponding member" was added to include women orthopaedists residing and practicing outside continental North America. This result boosted the membership from 112 RJOS members in 1986 to 507 names on the 1990 RJOS newsletter mailing list.

There were 395 female orthopaedic surgeons from the United States; 28 from Canada, and 70 corresponding members from Australia, Belgium, Brazil, England, Israel, Japan, New Zealand, Norway, Russia and South Africa.

Six international guests attended the 1990 meeting. Ulla Choler, M.D., the first woman orthopedist in Sweden was at the RJOS meeting along with Hanne Hedin, M.D. and Margaretha Rodin M.D., and Rigmor Julliasson, M.D., all of Sweden. Linda Ferris M.D. of Adelaide, Australia, the first woman to complete her orthopaedic training in Australia was there. Nanny Allington, M.D. came from Brussels, Belgium.

Ruth was presented with a cake and a standing ovation, noting her retirement from practice in 1989. As of February 1990, 170 information sheets had been returned with the following breakdown for type of practice: academic, 31; group, 32; hospital, 14; HMO, 12; military, 15; solo, 31; research, six; EMG, one. Thirty-three were on fellowships and the balance of those who supplied information was residents.

Specialty groups were broken down into the following categories: arthroscopy, 29; foot and ankle, 31; general, 30; hand, 38; hip, six; knee, 17; shoulder, 16; pediatric, 36; spine, 17; sports, 40; trauma, 27; wrist, nine; oncology, three; fracture reconstruction, one; lower extremity, one; total joint arthroplasty, one; and biomedics, one.

There were 149 board certified female orthopaedic surgeons, six of whom were deceased; and 124 who were active or had been active fellows of the American Academy of Orthopaedic Surgeons. There were 13 candidates for AAOS at this time. Eight years after the Ruth Jackson Orthopaedic Society was organized in 1983 in the Marriott Hotel in Anaheim, California by a handful of female orthopods the organization returned to Anaheim. It continued under the leadership of its president, Mary Ann Keenan, M.D., Chairman of the Orthopaedic Department of Albert Einstein Hospital in Philadelphia, as an international organization.

The first two years RJOS members spent organizing; the next two focused on getting information on women in orthopaedics and disseminating that information to the medical community.

At the 1986 meeting held in New Orleans, Helen Horstmann, M.D. reported on a paper "Women in Orthopaedics" compiled by Dr. Horstmann, Peggy Naas, M.D. and Wendy Bastings. The report was the result of a questionnaire regarding the attitude of residency programs in the viewing and the screening process for women applicants to determine opportunities that existed for women in orthopaedics and any biases toward women that still persisted.

One woman's comment, after being told that the staff's policy was to hire only one woman every two years, is "Women physicians may be a hot item, but I doubt that it is true for orthopaedics."

A precedent was established with the first AAOS exhibit, a chart listing the first fifteen women AAOS members.* The exhibit was by Peggy Naas, M.D., who presented the 1987 AAOS exhibit on "Contributions of Women to the Orthopaedic Literature." These educational projects continued each year.

Letters were sent to 240 chairmen of orthopaedic programs in the United States and Canada, requesting residents' names. A free trial membership to RJOS was offered to all the residents. Advice ranging from "Leadership Roles for Women in Orthopaedics by Jacqueline Perry, M.D. to "The Business of Orthopaedics" by Helen Horstmann, M.D., was the topic for the meetings. Contrasting practices from Lorraine Day, M.D.'s trauma practice in San Francisco; Ronnie Dowling, M.D.'s solo isolated mountain practice and Susan Swank, M.D., and Francesca Thompson, M.D. group practice and academic practice gave members an insight into various problems and benefits.

There was even proof that fathers do encourage daughters to become orthopaedic surgeons. Member, Judy Wright, M.D., brought her father, orthopaedic surgeon John Wright, to a meeting. Other father-daughter orthopaedic duos included: Bess Brackett, M.D., Oak Park, IL; Michelle James, M.D. and her father, Preston James, M.D, San Francisco; Susan Stephens, M.D.; and Elaine Barber, M.D., who was in practice with her father and uncle.

In 1988 the RJOS board authorized a newsletter. Patsy Mayes Jackson, a former Woman's Page Editor of a daily newspaper, volunteered her services to publish the newsletter to create the networking which would enable the organization to grow, and through communication provide the support system for which the organization was founded.

And grow it did. As the membership increased, so did the medical community's awareness of its female orthopaedic surgeons. In 1989, Amy Ladd, M.D., Chief resident at the

University of Rochester, Rochester, NY, was elected as a member of the AAOS membership committee. She reported that Richard Gelberman M.D., Chairman, wanted to open a forum for women in orthopaedics. Stressing that the committee was very receptive to residents and young physicians and was willing to address the needs of these individuals, Dr. Ladd requested input from the RJOS members.

The members received a report on the forum at the first RJOS retreat held in Chicago, November 2-4 1990. Rosemarie Morwessel, M.D., M.D. Charleston, S.C., who organized the retreat, cited a need for a continuing forum to address the issues which evolved from the AAOS Women's Forum. It was seeking solutions to these problems relating to residents and fellows, a lack of female orthopods in leadership roles in organizations and academics; and maternity leave.

Holly Duck, M.D. was named Fellowship Mentor Coordinator to compile information from members on fellowships for further reference. The Mentor Program got a boost when Diana Carr, M.D. had informational brochures designed and mailed to all students in the American Medical Women's association.

A standing Scientific Committee was created. Mary Lloyd Ireland, M.D. and Ro Morwessel, M.D. produced a video, *A Tribute to Dr. Ruth Jackson,* based on a 1982 interview with Ruth in Dallas. Ruth's portrait by artist, Martha Robbins of Denton, Texas, which hangs in the Baylor University Medical Center was photographically reproduced and with the proceeds from the sales of Ruth's portrait to go to create an endowment fund.

Janet Walker, M.D., received feed back from members when she was asked to testify at the hearing of the National Institute of Health on recruitment, retention, re-entry and advancement of women in biomedical careers.

The first fall retreat was such a success that it became a biennial event, with the second retreat held October 16-18, 1992 in Chicago and the third was held Oct 7-9, 1994 in Lisle, Illinois.

By 1991, RJOS was too large to be administered by volunteers. RJOS hit the big time. Under the umbrella of the AAOS, RJOS joined the other Specialty organizations. Now, with an Executive Director, Priscilla Majewski, and Sandra Brahos to oversee the administration of the organization, publishing the newsletter and directory, and establishing a website, the officers looked to the future. A long range planning session was held September 10-12, 1993 at the home of chairperson, Laura Tosi, M.D., Washington, D.C.

By 1994 RJOS was preparing for the 21st century and Ruth had seen it happen.

"Doing the most for the most people."

CHAPTER XVII

She rose to her feet, to thunderous applause, and stood, still erect at the age of 83, head cocked to one side. She looked through a blur of tears, at the group of her peers, friends and family members, who had come to honor her for her contributions to the field of orthopaedics. It was September 9, 1986 and Baylor University Medical Center had proclaimed it "Ruth Jackson Day," to dedicate the Ruth Jackson Conference Center at BUMC.

For the past fifty-four years, this diminutive woman with hands like steel, had devoted her life to her orthopaedic practice, had gained national recognition as the first female certified by the Board of Orthopaedic Surgeons and had become internationally known as a clinician, educator and researcher.

She had just seen her life flash by in pictures on the large screen behind the head table, while her friend and colleague, Dr. Leon Ware paid tribute o her accomplishments. The last picture that appeared on the screen had seemed incongruous: a picture of the Cotton Bowl, Dallas's famous football stadium, filled with people. Dr. Ware was quick to explain that these stands would not hold the unbelievable number of people to whom her two hands had ministered. Not mass production treatment, he explained since each patient had been talked to, had hands-on treatment, then talked to again. Her philosophy, "doing the most for the most people" had propelled her through life. A life she had lived to the utmost in every capacity. There were many in the audience who had been the recipients of her "doing the most;" some through her orthopaedic skills, others through her humanitarian efforts.

The head table was filled with her colleagues who had risen through the ranks along side her. Boone Powell Sr., her friend and confidant, started as the Assistant Administrator of Baylor University Medical Center in 1945 had become a Senior Consultant at BUMC. He had seen his son, Boone Powell Jr., Master of Ceremonies for Ruth Jackson Day, become president of BUMC. Dr.

Adrian Flatt, Chief of Orthopaedics, spent time with Ruth's mentor, Dr. Steindler in Iowa City before arriving in Dallas in 1982. He not only joined Ruth's research foundation, but became one of Ruth's special friends. His collection of bronze-coated casts of the hands of nationally and internationally famous persons, including U. S. presidents: Eisenhower, Truman, Johnson, Ford and Carter; Philippines' Corozon Aquino; England's royalty; as well as many persons from sports, science and art world is known internationally.

The cast Dr. Flatt sculpted of Ruth's hands had been brought from the Adrian E. Flatt Hand Collection display case #21 in the lobby of the George W. Truett Memorial Hospital to the Folsom room for the night's festivities.

Coming from the University of Arizona School of Medicine was assistant professor of surgery, Robert B. Dzioba, M.D., the 1986 speaker for the Dr. Ruth Jackson Seminar in Orthopaedic Surgery.

There also were those whose personal lives she had taken into her hands to manipulate, just as she manipulated the bones of her patients.

Her first glance stopped on Tommie Lee Fields, who, July first, had celebrated her thirtieth anniversary as a physical therapist at the Jackson Clinic, the one person who had been most constant in Ruth's life. The mutual respect they felt for each other was based on years of sharing everyday problems. As Ruth had dedicated her life to orthopaedics, Tommie Lee had, in many respects, dedicated her life to Ruth's goals too. Ruth's gaze shifted from Tommie Lee, to her nephew, Darrell Jackson, who had flown from California with his wife, Miriam, to share his special aunt's special day. She remembered the day, still a resident at Scottish Rites Crippled Children's Hospital in Dallas where she had received the call from her father to come home to McAllen to repair ten year old Darrell's shoulder, shattered by a shotgun blast. It was the first time her father admitted to being glad that she had chosen to study medicine over his objections.

Her brother-in-law, Harold Brehm, McAllen, Texas with his friend, Maria Lamantia were in the audience along with Harold's grandson, Alan Brehm

Ph.D., and his wife, Gwen of Fort Worth. Her nephew, Paul Jackson Jr. and his wife, Patsy Mayes Jackson came from Edinburg, Texas to help Ruth celebrate. Ten year old Christopher Larzalere grinned impishly at "Doctor." Impeccably groomed in suit and tie, he was Ruth's escort for the evening. The son of Ruth's business manager, Sheri Larzalere, Christopher and his mother had shared Ruth's home for the past three years, converting the ten empty rooms into a welcome teeming turbulence of family life.

Lucy Bentley, the troubled young woman who had come to Ruth's office one day to sell her a security system and had her life turned completely around by Ruth's support and guidance, was there to share Ruth's triumph. Patients had come from near and far for Ruth Jackson Day. Stuart and Edith Newman brought Ruth's favorite fruit, mangoes, with them when they flew in from Miami. Lucy Jones, spoke through teeth wired together as a result of a car accident, paid her respects, while hungrily eyeing the sumptuous dinner denied to her.

The Folsom Room was a perfect setting

for the appreciation dinner. The spectacular view from the electrically controlled windows on the seventeenth floor of the Roberts Hospital took in the Dallas skyline and overlooked the Baylor University Medical Center's complex. A skyline that Ruth grumbled about constantly since it fenced her in the sixteen block area around which her home life and work revolved. She hated the high rise buildings whose green, gold and blue walls of glass flashed kaleidoscopic lights from the sun's rays into her eyes as she drove to and from her clinic. She preferred instead the memory of the once lovely wooded area where cows had grazed on land belonging to the Catholic Diocese and the highest buildings were three story homes.

Ruth had heard Dr. Ware extol her accomplishments: Lecturer and writer, beginning in 1933 with an article published on painful feet and others including subjects on fractures, headaches, TMJ joint, neck and back problems Twenty articles in the *American Journal* as well as articles in German, Sweden and Japan were published. She had given an instructional course for the Academy and had a science lab program in the library of the AAOS. She had lectured more than 60 times, all by invitation, to such organizations as the AAOS, Southern Medical Assoc., American College of Surgeons, Oschner Clinic, International College of Surgeons, as well as medical societies all over the country.

She made three trips to lecture in Mexico, one each in Munich and Stuttgart, Germany and in Sweden. The business world, General Motors; and the government, the United States Air Force, sought her out for her lectures. Dedicated to teaching, her efforts were instrumental in setting up the residency program at Parkland where she was chief for several years. Her research foundation had not only funded research and purchased various physical needs for the orthopaedic department, but had supported the very important Ruth Jackson visiting professorship, Dr. Ware pointed out, "Through this, she has welcomed more than 18 outstanding men to this campus, the 'Who's Who of orthopaedics' and in bringing them to this campus has helped our residents, this staff and orthopaedists in the sections of this country."

Ruth established a permanent orthopaedic library at BUMC to be used by medical students and professionals. " The records show that she has ministered to between 18,000 and 20,000 necks and backs, give or take a few," he added. He ended his introduction by saying that if all her patients, who could overflow the Cotton Bowl, were here they would each one say singly or together, "Dr. Ruth, we thank you. We appreciate you and we love you." It had been just five months since Ruth scribbled the note to herself detailing her lack of friends and family. She finally accepted the fact that she was surrounded by people who cared about her. Not only her BUMC family, which included Boone Powell, Sr. and Boone Powell, Jr., administrators; Dr. Flatt, Dr. Ware, Dr. Hall and Linda Donohue, the executive assistant to the Orthopaedic Department, but, also her relatives, who she finally had allowed into her life.

The last eight years of Ruth's life were spent attending the Ruth Jackson

Orthopaedic Society meetings, whether in San Francisco or Washington D.C.; playing gin with anyone she could find who didn't mind being "skunked" every hand, and having her evening cocktail of vodka and aloe vera juice and her cigarillos. She watched Christopher grow. Spent a week at the Jacksons' beach house on South Padre Island with Sheri, Christopher, her nephew, Paul and his wife, her grandniece Janis Rogers and her husband Mike and their two children, Lauren and Paul. She fished in the bay, sat on the beach while the children played and seemed to have a good time. Sheri looked at her and said, "See Ruth, this is what retired people do. Isn't it great?" Ruth admitted only to enjoying seeing the children have fun, then added: "I'd rather be at work at the clinic!"

When she became ill in August 1994, she agreed to let Sheri take her to her second home, BUMC. It is there she spent her last days, surrounded by those who had helped her through the last years of her life: Sheri and Lucy, her grandnephew, Alan Brehm and his wife, Gwen; her nephew, Paul and his wife, Patsy; and her grandniece,

Paulanna Jackson Watson.

  The day before Ruth died, she talked Sheri and Lucy into taking her on the roof of the hospital so she could have one last cigarillo. She wouldn't inhale, she promised. In dying, just as in living, Ruth did it her way.

THE END

LIST OF BOARD CERTIFIED WOMEN ORTHOPAEDISTS IN AAOS

1937 TO 1994

1937 Ruth Jackson MD
      Dallas, TX

1943 Penelope Sherwood MD
      Newburgh, NY

1947 Margaret Watkins MD
      Dallas, TX

1949 Mary Sherman MD
      New Orleans, LA

1951 Frances Brennecke MD
      Rockville, MD

1953 Isabel Bittinger MD
      Winston-Salem, NC

1955 Ruth M. Waring MD
      Chassell, MI

1957 Doris E. Chambers MD
      Raeford, NC

1958 Myra A. Peters MD

Tulsa, OK
1958 E Jacquelin Perry MD
Downey, CA

1962 E Anna M. Brady MD
Philadelphia, PA
1962 Alice L. Garrett MD
Pasos Robles, CA

1963 Mary M. Powell MD
Villanova, PA

1964 Liebe S. Diamond MD
Baltimore, MD
1964 Jeane Michels MD
Lompac, CA
1964 E Alvina O. Sabanas MD
Sun City, AZ

1967 Roshen N. Irani MD
Philadelphia, PA

1968 1968 Mary E. Conroy MD
Grosse Point Farms, MI
1968 Kathleen M. Robinson MD
Tilton, NH

1970 Virginia M. Badger MD
Breckenridge, CO
1970 Maureen K. Molloy MD

         Shelburne, VT
1970   Alice M. Murname MD
         New York, NY

1971   Rosamond Kane MD
         New York, NY

1972   Sandra J. Thomson MD
         Boston, MA

1975   Maria T. Godesky MD
         Kingston, NY

1976   Mary Williams Clark MD
         Charlottesville, VA

1978   Mary R. McVay MD
         Portland, OR
1978   Elena R. Martinez MD
         Miami, FL

1979   Alice M. Martinson MD
         Oakland, CA
1979   Lorraine J. Day MD
         San Francisco, CA

1980   Jeanne Pamilla MD
         New York, NY

1981   Anca Popa MD

Patsy Mayes Jackson

North Bergen, NJ

1982 Dorothy A. Balthazar MD
Worcester, MA
1982 Diane M. English MD
Brighton, MA
1982 Letha Hunter-Griffin MD
Atlanta, GA
1982 Geraldine Richter MD
Manassas, AR
1982 Mary Morden MD
Baltimore, MD

1983 Catherine Hawthorne MD
Las Cruces, NM
1983 Winfried M. Berger MD
Huntingdon, PA
1983 Susan Swank MD
Downey, CA
1983 Leela Rangaswamy MD
Boston, MA
1983 Janaleigh Hoffman MD
San Diego, CA

1984 Ruth Anne O'Keefe MD
Redlands, AR
1984 Melinda M. Gardner MD
Washington, D.C
1984 Carol Claire Teitz MD
Seattle, WA

1984   Joyce E. Johansson MD
        Westmount, Que. Canada
1984   Mary Lloyd Ireland MD
        Lexington, KY
1984   Ruth Anne O'Keefe MD
        Monroeville, PA

1985   Marie Ann Czaplicki MD
        Toms River, NJ
1985   Victoria Marie Dvonch MD
        Chicago, IL
1985   Diana Lynn Kruse MD
        Prairie de Sac, WI
1985   Mary-Blair Matejczyk MD
        Cleveland, OH
1985   Elizabeth Quinlan MD
        Honolulu, HI
1985   Roberta E. Rose MD
        Warsaw, IN
1985   Claudia Thomas Carty MD
        St. Thomas, Virgin Island
1985   Jean Walsh MD
        Fresno, CA
1985   Sandra Marie Abda MD
        Monroe, NC

1986   Dorrit E. Ahbel MD
        Kent, WA

1986   Charlotte E. Alexander MD

Oakland, CA
1986 Barbara Jean Campbell MD
Somerset, PA
1986 Diana Deane Carr MD
Bartow, FL
1986 Mary Ann Keenan MD
Bellflower, CA
1986 Sandra Propst-Proctor MD
Honesdale, PA
1986 Susan Puls MD
Delray Beach, FLA
1986 Margaret Mary Rich MD
St. Louis, MO
1986 Karen Sue Seale MD
Mooresville, IN
1986 Margaret R. Albanese MD
Utica, N.Y

1987 Lorraine K. Doyle MD
Worcester, MA
1987 Marybeth Ezaki MD
Dallas, TX
1987 Maureen A. Finnegan MD
Ottawa, Ont. Canada
1987 Carol L. Hulett MD
Mount Clemens, MI
1987 Vicki Kalen MD
Gainesville, FL
1987 Lucie M. King MD
Tuscaloosa, AL

Ruth Jackson, M.D.: A Life on the Leading Edge

1987 Jan Elizabeth Leo MD
     Denver, CO
1987 Nancy R. Otto MD
     Haddonfield, NJ
1987 Suzanne Ray MD
     Fargo, ND
1987 Francesca Thompson MD
     New York, NY
1987 Kathleen Kopach MD
     Berwick, PA
1987 Evelyn Davis Witkin MD
     Southampton, PA
1987 Carol Mowery Cammy MD
     Seattle, WA
1987 Mary Lloyd Ireland MD
     Lexington, KY
1987 Denise O. Holmes MD
     Gallipolis, OH

1988 Lesley J. Anderson MD
     San Francisco, CA
1988 Tee Selmon Campion MD
     Hills AFB, UT
1988 Andrea B. Crawford MD
     Gloucester, VA
1988 Jacquelin Emmanuel MD
     Jamaica, NY
1988 Laura B. Flawn MD
     Austin, TX
1988 Michelle Foltz MD

	Butler, PA
1988	Wendy Michelle Hughes MD
	Portland, OR
1988	Julie Isaacson MD
	Newburg, OR
1988	Kathleen A. McHale MD
	Alexandria, VA
1988	Margaret Jane Ripley MD
	Jacksonville, FL
1988	Brenda L. Sanford MD
	Pontiac, MI
1988	Cynthia Ann Schneider MD
	Morehead, KY
1988	Linda F. Staiger MD
	San Francisco, CA
1988	Elizabeth Ann Szalay MD
	Beaumont, TX
1988	Linda Thompson MD
	Beaver, PA
1988	Laura Lowe Tosi MD
	Washington D.C.
1988	Christine Indech MD
	Dunwoody, CA ABOS not AAOS
1988	Lynn Froome Ferletic MD
	APO New York
1988	Margaret A. Landy MD
	Needham, MA. ABOS not AAOS
1988	Elizabeth Arendt MD
	Minneapolis, MN

1989 Margaret Elfreing MD
     Santa Maria, CA
1989 Barbara Freeman MD
     Brooklyn NY
1989 Charlotte J. Harris MD
     Maysville, KY
1989 Marcia Lynn Hixson MD
     Little Rock AR
1989 Elise Smith-Hoefer MD
     Woodland, CA
1989 Kathleen Raggio Gavin MD
     New Hyde Park, NY
1989 Nancy Cullen MD
     London, Ontario, Canada
1989 Sandra Eisele MD
     Knoxville, TN
1989 Diane E. Gilles MD
     Gallipolis, OH
1989 Barbara Grugan Frieman MD
     Philadelphia, PA
1989 Sally A. Knauer MD
     Fort Collins, CO
1989 Victoria Masear MD
     Birmingham, AL
1989 Ruth Barrington Nauts MD
     Aurora, CO
1989 Elizabeth Regan MD
     Denver, CO
1989 Sally Rudicel MD
     New Haven, CT

1989 Marie S. Olestad MD
      Minneapolis, MN

1990 Teresa V. Balcomb MD
      Albuquerque, NM
1990 Aimee V. Hachigian MD
      Great Falls, MT
1990 Ilona Ruth Hirsch MD
      Beverly Hills, CA
1990 Lynn Carole Garner MD
      New York, NY APO
1990 Kristine Kaga MD
      Franklin, NC
1990 Victoria M. Langa MD
      Oakmont, PA
1990 Judith J. Levine MD
      Elmhurst, NY
1990 Nina M. Nijus, MD
      Akron, OH
1990 Diana M. Rothman MD
      Ann Arbor, MI
1990 Angela Dorman Smith MD
      Wilmington, DE
1990 Rosemarie Morwessel MD
      Charleston SC
1990 Diane Von Stein MD
      Charleston SC
1990 Diane Von Stein MD
      Wilmington, OH
1990 Victoria Stevens MD

	Globe, AZ
1990	Dale L. Maples
	Grand Rapids, MI
1991	Charlotte B. Alexander MD
	Houston, TX
1991	Ann Babbitt MD
	Yarmouth, ME
1991	Deborah Bell MD
	Toronto, Ontario Canada
1991	Gail Chorney MD
	New York, NY
1991	Dale Dedrick MD
	Ann Arbor, MI
1991	Karen S. Duane MD
	Tampa, FL
1991	Barbara Frey MD
1991	Patricia A. Gorai MD
1991	Wanda Lee Gorsuch MD
	Great Falls, MT
1991	Shelia Love MD
	St. Petersburg, FL
1991	Sharon Menkveld MD
	Milwaukee, WI
1991	Elizabeth Meyerdierks MD
	Greensboro, NC
1991	Amarilis Durieux Millard MD
	Santurca Puerto Rico
1991	Judith R. Oppenheim MD
	Dallas, TX

1991 Elizabeth A. Ouellette MD
     Miami, FL
1991 Mary Ann Shannon, MD
     Nederland, TX
1991 Sharron Sussman MD
     San Rafael, CA
1991 Joanne R. Werntz MD
     Orlando, FL

1992 Lydia Coffman MD
     Sierra Vista, AZ
1992 Beth M. Dollinger MD
     Elmira, NY
1992 Grania Feddis MD
     Bellflower, CA
1992 Nancy D. Garber MD
     Smithfield, NC
1992 Gaia Georgopoulos MD
     Englewood, CO
1992 Charlotte Harris MD
     Maysville, KY
1992 Regina O. Hillsman MD
     Westport, CT
1992 Denise Holmes MD
     Gallipolis, OH
1992 Christine Indech MD
     Atlanta, GA
1992 Barbara A. Jackson MD
     Norton, MA
1992 Colleen A. Kennedy MD

	Springfield, VA
1992	Delores Kirkpatrick MD
	Roswell, GA
1992	Patricia A. Kolowich MD
	Detroit, MI
1992	Francisca Van Geloven Lytle MD
	Smithville, TN
1992	Ellen C. Maitin MD
	Penn Valley, PA
1992	Peggy L. Naas MD
	Minneapolis, MN
1992	Donna P. Phillips MD
	New York, NY
1992	Mary L. Scovazzo MD
	Pittsburgh, PA
1992	Elizabeth Sirna MD
	Clearwater, FL
1992	Barbara Van Winkle MD
	Houma, LA
1992	Anna Voytek MD
	Greensboro, NC
1992	Janet Walker MD
	Lexington, KY
1992	Virginia Wintersteen MD
	La Crosse, WI
1992	Michele M. Zembo MD
	New Orleans, LA
1993	M. Beth Bathgate MD
	South Pasadena, CA

1993 Roberta Brockman MD
     Settle, WA
1993 Yolanda A. Cillo MD
     Temecula, CA
1993 Frances Cuomo MD
     New York, NY
1993 Ellana D. Delgado MD
     Daly City, CA
1993 Jean M. Eelma MD
     Bloomington, IN
1993 Rosalind Epstein MD
     Albuquerque, NM
1993 Bobbi A. Farber MD
     Columbus, GA
1993 Cathleen A Godzik MD
     Los Angeles, CA
1993 Cherie A. Holmes MD
     Washington, DC
1993 Caren R, Ires MD
     Canyon Lake, CA
1993 Michelle A. James MD
     Mill Valley, CA
1993 Margaret M. Landy
     Needham, MA
1993 Anne J. Miller-Breslow MD
     Englewood, NJ
1993 Laura A. Mitchell MD
     Albuquerque, NM
1993 Patricia Morales-Wright, MD
     Elko, NV

1993	Mary Lynn Newport MD Lubbock, TX
1993	Christine S. O'Donnell MD Levittown, PA
1993	Iris E. Schlesinger MD Woodmere, NY
1993	Naomi N. Shields MD Albuquerque, NM
1993	Liz A. Z. Stark MD Arcadia, CA
1993	Ann C. Stein MD Rutland, VT
1993	Carol A. Walker MD Lawrenceville, GA
1993	J. Denise Wells MD Seattle, WA
1993	Susanne White-Spunner MD Mobile, AL
1993	Audrea H. Wynn II MD Winchester, VA
1994	Mary Johanna Albert MD Atlanta, GA
1994	Donna M. Boehme MD San Antonio, TX
1994	Mary Beth Cermak MD Erie, PA
1994	Alice R. Coyle MD Scranton, PA
1994	Jessica Cohen-Brown MD

Santa Barbara, CA
1994 Dona M. Alvarez MD
Oakland, MD
1994 Mary Lynn Brown MD
Orlando, FL
1994 Jeanne L. DelSignore MD
Rochester, NY
1994 Nancy J. Ensley MD
Farkville, MO
1994 Maylene M. Glidewell MD
Los Angeles, CA
1994 Lee D. Hieb MD
Yuma, AZ
1994 Candace Jennings MD
Boston, MA
1994 Annabella Juhasz MD
Michigan City, IN
1994 Amy L. Ladd MD
Stanford, CA
1994 Nancy A. Miller MD
Houston, TX
1994 Cheryl Rubin MD
Suffern, NY
1994 Judith W. Smith MD
Atlanta, GA
1994 Linda H. Specht MD
Vallejo, CA
1994 Ruth Lourdes Thomas MD
Little Rock, AR
1994 Colleen M. Fay MD

	North White Plains, NY
1994	Suzanne E. Hall MD Bronx, NY
1994	Serena S. Hu MD San Francisco, CA
1994	Susan L. Jolly MD Littleton, CO
1994	Linda T. Kirilenko MD Springfield, VA
1994	Berisse Lester MD Bronx, NY
1994	Carol L. Prchal MD Burlington, WI
1994	Tamara A. Scerpella MD Jamesville, NY
1994	Patricia M. Solca MD Providence, RI
1994	Joan Sullivan MD Tacoma, WA
1994	Laura J. Trombino MD Oneonta, NY
1994	Serena Young-Nguyen MD Rancho Palos Verdes, CA
1994	Debra A. Zillmer MD La Crosse, WI

The above information was compiled from Dr. Ruth Jackson's, the first board certified woman orthopaedist and the American Academy of Orthopaedic

Surgeons program and report books from 1944-45, 1946, 1947, 1948, 1950, 1951, 1952, 1953, 1973, 1986, 1987 and 1988 as well as the AAOS Directory for 1985 and 1988, plus list from AAOS 2004. Some names were acquired as a result of a query for information on women orthopaedist printed in the October 1988 issue of the AAOS Bulletin. Residences are listed at time of induction.

Only obvious female names were selected so there may be others who are not listed. I do not have access to the AAOS program books for years other than those mentioned above. I am sure there are more female orthopaedists than I have listed. .

*Isabel Bittinger was listed in the January 1946 revised edition of the 13th annual AAOS report, but was neither on the 14th annual report issued in April 1946 nor any other until the 1953 AAOS program book. Ulla M. Fortune was listed 1975, but was dropped.

BIBLIOGRAPHY

American Studies Class of McAllen High School, A Bicentennial Reflection 1974-75

Branden, Barbara. The Passion of Ayn Rand, Anchor Books, New York, 1986.

Brown, Stanford J. *Getting into Medical School*, Kaplan Paperbacks, 2001

Ernest, R. May 1998. . *War, Boom and Bust: The Life History of the United States 1917-1932*, New York, Time Inc., 1963.

Ferrell, Robert H. *The Twentieth Century: An Almanac*, World Almanac Books, New York 1985.

Fishbein, Morris. The History of the American Medical Association, 1847-1947, WB Saunders Co., Philadelphia, 1947.

Jackson, Ruth. "Treatment of Cervical Spine, Shoulder, Arm Syndrome," 1946.

Jackson, Ruth. Papers of ACC 213,

Archives and Special Collections on Women in Medicine, Drexel College of Medicine, Philadelphia, PA.

Jones, Johnny. Interview, Weslaco, TX

Henderson, Lana. Baylor University Medical Center: Yesterday, Today and Tomorrow, Waco, TX 1998

Keller, Robert B. M. D. "Orthopedist Exceeds HMO Needs," *AAOS Bulletin*, Vol. 42, January 1, 1994.

Lopate, Carol. *Women in Medicine*, Josiah Macy Jr. Foundation Series, 1968.

Lynch, Dudley. "The Saga of Tom Hill's 106 Million Debacle." *D: The Magazine of Dallas*, May 1975.,

Morantz-Sanchez, Regina Markell. *Sympathy and Science*, Oxford University Press, New York, 1985.

Morgan, Elizabeth: *The Making of a Woman Surgeon*, Berkley Publishing, 1987.

Morsund, Walter H. M.D. *History of Baylor College of Medicine: 1900-1953*, Waco, TX 1954.

Peavy, John R. *Echoes from the Rio Grande*, Brownsville, TX, Springman-King, 1963.

Robertson, Brian P. *Rio Grande Heritage: A Pictorial History*, Norfolk-Donning, 1985.

Robertson, Brian P. *Wild Horse Desert: The Heritage of South Texas*, Edinburg, Texas, Hidalgo Texas County Historical Museum, 1985.

Stillman, E. B. *Past and Present History of Greene County Iowa*, 1979.

Thomas, Charles C. *The Cervical Syndrome*, Springfield, Ill. 1956

ADDITIONAL SOURCES

"Acute & Chronic Neck Pain" American Medical Assoc. Dallas, Texas. 1976
"Arthritis of the Cervical Spine," and "Disorders of the Cervical Spine," four hour tutorial course, American Soc. of Contemporary Medicine and Surgery, Orlando, Fl. March 1981.
"Back Injuries," Courtroom Medicine, Charles C. Thomas, Springfield, Ill. 1956.
"Bracing of the Cervical Spine," American Limb Manufacturers Assoc. Dallas, Texas. 1959.
"Cervical Pain-Nonsurgical Treatment," Symposium on Cervical Pain, Stockholm, Sweden 1971.
"Cervical Spine and Arthritis Symposium, New York University, New York City 1968.
"Cervical Spine Disorders, Greater Boston Medical Soc., Boston, Ma. 1967.
"Cervical Spine Disorders-TM Joint" Tucson, Ariz. 1985 Examined patients to show connection between trauma to neck and TM Temporomandibular joint dysfunctions and orofacial pain-Orthodontists.
"Cervical Spine Injuries in Vehicular

Crash Accidents", General Motors Corp. Safety Designers and Engineers Detroit, Mich. 1966.
"Cervical Spine Injuries" Young Lawyers Assoc. of America, Acapulco, Mexico 1972.
"Cervical Spine Injuries," Ohio State Medical Soc. Columbus, Ohio, 1971.
"Cervical trauma: Not just another pain in the neck" Geriatrics, vol. 37 #4, April 1982.
"The Cervical Syndrome" Dallas Co. Medical Journal Vol. 35 1946.
"The Cervical Syndrome" Physical Medicine Staff, University of Ohio Medical School, Columbus, Ohio, 1971.
"The Cervical Syndrome," Clinical Orthopaedics, Vol. 5, 1955.
"The Cervical Syndrome," The American Academy of Orthopaedic Surgeons, Instructional Course Lectures, Vol. 12, 1953.
"Clinical Orthopaedic Society, Dallas, Texas.1936.
"Comparative Study Treatment Compound Fractures" From Journal of Southern Medical Assoc. Vol. 34 #3, 1941.
"Dallas County Medical Society, Dallas, Texas. 1933, 1935, 1946
"Dental Assoc. for Study of

Temporomandibular Joint Dysfunctions, "Dallas, Texas. 1968.
"Department of the Air Force, Lackland Air Force Base, Instructional Courses, San Antonio, Texas. 1967
"Diagnosis of Whiplash" Vol. 1 #6 Medifacts Tape-The Voice of Medicine, 1975.
"Die Konservative Behandlung bei Vertelzungen der Halswirbelsaule, Verlog, Stuttgart, Ger, 1963
"Disorders of the Cervical Spine," four hour tutorial course and "Traumatic Lesions of the Cervical Spine" American Soc. of Contemporary Medicine and Surgery, Orlando, Fl. 1980.
"Fifth Western Medical Assembly of Mexico, Guadalajara, Mexico. 1959
"Foreword: "Medical-Legal Report," by Robert M. Fox Little Brown & Co., Boston, Ma. 1969
German Orthopaedic Soc., Munich, Germany, 1962
"Guest Editor of Symposium on disorders of the Cervical Spine preface, Clinical Orthopaedics #24, 1962
"Headache Associated with Cervical Spine Disorders" Headache, January 1967.
"Injuries of the Cervical Spine,"

Trauma, Matthew Bender & Co., Inc. N.Y. City, Vol. 2, 1960.

"Injuries of the Cervical Spine-The Structural Changes," Archives of Physical Medicine and Rehabilitation, Vol. 40, September 1959.

"Injuries of the Upper Portion of the Cervical Spine," Supplement of Lawyers Medical Cyclopedia Vol. 8 1965.

"Joint Injuries and the Cervical Syndrome," Wisconsin State Medical Meeting, Milwaukee, Wis. 1967.

"The Mechanism of Cervical Nerve Root Irritations, " Dallas Medical Journal, Vol. 38, 1952.

"Painful Feet", Physiotherapy Review 1933;"Poliomyelitis, Dallas Co Medical Journal 1935.

"The Positive Findings in Alleged Neck Injuries" The American Journal of Orthopaedics Aug-Sept 1964.

"The Scope and Extent of Neck Injuries," De Paul Review, Vol. XXI, 1971.

"Special Stand for Treatment of Fracture of Clavicle" Journal of Bone & Joint Surgery 1937;

"The Syndrome of Cervical Nerve Root Compression," Arthritis, Lea and Fabiger 1960, 1966, 1972, 1977, 1984.

"Traumatic Arthritis of the Cervical Spine," American Soc. of Contemporary Medicine and Surgery, Las Vegas, Nevada March 1979.
"Traumatic Arthritis of the Cervical Spine," Comprehensive Therapy, Vol. 7 #2, February 1981.
"Updating the Neck" Trauma, June 1970.
"Whiplash Injuries of the Neck-an Editorial," Dallas Co. Medical Journal, Vol. 46, October 1960.
"Whiplash Injuries" Journal of the Western Medical Assembly of Mexico, 1960.

LECTURES

LECTURES GIVEN BY INVITATION TO FOLLOWING MEDICAL ORGANIZATIONS:

American Academy of General Practice, Oklahoma City, 1960.
American Academy of Orthopaedic Surgeons, Chicago, Il. 1949.
American Academy of Orthopaedic Surgeons, Instructional Course Lectures, 1953,1954, 1955,1960.
American Academy of Osteopathic Orthopaedists, Guest Instructor, Detroit, Mich.1965.
American Association for the Study of Headache, Chicago, Ill. 1966.
American College of Surgeons, Omaha, Neb. 1954.
American Institute of Ultrasonics, Dallas, Texas. 1963.
American Medical Assoc. Chicago, Il and San Francisco, Ca.
American Rheumatism Assoc. of Northern California, San Francisco, Ca. 1961.
American Rheumatism Assoc., New York City, 1960.
American Society of Safety Engineers,

Dallas, Texas. 1961-62.
Los Angeles Medical Soc., Los Angeles, Ca. 1958
Mississippi Orthopaedic Assoc., Biloxi. Miss. 1963
Neck Sprains" American Medical Assoc. Clinical Meeting, Las Vegas, Nev. 1966.
North Texas Orthopaedic Assoc., Ft. Worth, Texas. 1956
Orthopaedic Club of Chicago, Chicago, Ill. 1961
Orthopaedic Club of Miami, Fl. 1959
Instructional Course Lectures, Vol. 12, 1953.
"The Knowles Vertebral Support Operation for Low Back Pain" Texas Orthopaedic Assoc. 1970
"The Non-Surgical Therapeutic Aims for Treatment of Cervical Pain," Four Lectures on the Cervical Syndrome for the Sound Slide Library of the American Academy of Orthopaedic Surgeons, 1966-1969
International College of Surgeons, Chicago, Ill. 1961
International College of Surgeons, New York City, 1962
Law-Science Academy of America, Medico-Legal Lectures, Crested Butte, Co., 1959 through 1969.

Physical Medicine and Rehabilitation
Assoc., Philadelphia, Pa. 1958
Physical Medicine and Rehabilitation
Symposium, Denver, Co. 1961
Post Graduate Groups, Southwestern
Medical School, Dallas, Texas.
Proceedings of the International
Symposium, Stockholm, Sweden,
1971.
Resident Staff, Oschner Clinic, New
Orleans, La. 1959
Resident Staff, Presbyterian Medical
Center, New York City 1962
Resident Staff, University of Denver,
Denver, Co. 1961
Seaboard Airline Railroad Surgeons,
Savannah, Ga. 1954
Sixth Congress of Orthopaedics and
Traumatology, Mexico City 1960
Seventh Congress of Orthopaedics and
Traumatology, Pueblo, Mexico, 1962
Southern Medical Assoc., Dallas,
Texas.; Louisville, Kentucky and
Houston, Texas.
Southern Medical Assoc., General
Practice Section Houston, Texas. 1965
Southwestern Surgical Congress,
Houston, Texas. 1958
Symposium on Cervical Spine Trauma,
Institute for Medical Education, Los

Angeles, Ca. 1967
Texas Orthopaedic Assoc., Houston, Texas. 1956
Texas Traumatic Surgeons Assoc., San Antonio, Texas. 1954
Tri-County Medical Soc., Grand Rapids, Mich. 1955
Tri-County Medical Soc., Tuscaloosa, Ala. 1959
Tri-county Medical Society, Beaumont, Texas. 1952, 1967
University of Texas Law School-Guest Lecturer in Legal Medicine, Austin, Texas. 1960-64

ENDNOTES

[i] Keller, Robert B., M. D. "Orthopedist Exceeds HMO Needs" AAOS Bulletin, Vol. 42, January 1, 1994.

[ii] Stillman, E. B, Past and Present of History of Greene County Iowa 1907, pg. 24.

[iii] Ernest, May L. War, Boom and Bust: The Life History of the United States 1917-1932, pg.82

[iv] Robertson, Brian P. Rio Grande Heritage: A Pictorial History, pg. 186.

[v] Robertson, Brian P. Wild Horse Desert: The Heritage of South Texas, pg. 266.

[vi] Peavey, John R. Echoes from the Rio Grande: King County, pg. 83.

[vii] Story related by Johnny Jones, Weslaco banker, on local television show, Weslaco, Texas

[viii] Robertson, Brian P. Rio Grande Heritage: A Pictorial History, pg. 150.

[ix] Tuckman, Barbara. Zimmerman Telegraph, pg. 3.

[x] Perry, Daniel. McAllen: A Bicentennial Reflection, American Studies Class 1974-75, pg. 115

[xi] Robertson, Brian P. Wild Horse Desert: The Heritage of South Texas, pg. 270.
[xii] Perry, Daniel. McAllen: A Bicentennial Reflection, American Studies Class 1974-75, pg. 72.
[xiii] Papers of Ruth Jackson M.D., Acc.213, Archives and Special Collections on Women in Medicine, Drexel University College of Medicine.
[xiv] Papers of Ruth Jackson M.D., Acc.213, Archives and Special Collections on Women in Medicine, Drexel University College of Medicine.
[xv] A Bicentennial Reflection, American Studies Class 1974-75, pg. 46-47.
[xvi] Robertson, Brian P. Wild Horse Desert: The Heritage of South Texas, pg. 263.
[xvii] University of Texas Registrar's Office.
[xviii] Morris Fishbein, *The History of the American Medical Association 1847-1947*.
[xix] Lopate, Carol, *Women in Medicine*, pgs. 12-13.
[xx] Lopate, Carol, *Women in Medicine*, pg. 26.
[xxi] Lopate, Carol, *Women in Medicine*, pg. 178.

[xxii] Lopate, Carol, *Women in Medicine,* pg. 7.
[xxiii] Lopate, Carol, *Women in Medicine,* pg. 8.
[xxiv] Lopate, Carol, *Women in Medicine,* pg. 15.
[xxv] Lopate, Carol, *Women in Medicine,* pg. 14.
[xxvi] Morantz-Sanchez, Regina Markell. *Sympathy and Science,* pg. 234.
[xxvii] Lopate, Carol, *Women in Medicine,* pg. 21.
[xxviii] Lopate, Carol, *Women in Medicine,* pg. 18.
[xxix] Henderson, Laura, *Baylor University Medical Center: Yesterday, Today and Tomorrow,* pg. 94.
[xxx] Lopate, Carol, *Women in Medicine,* pp. 23.
[xxxi] Brown, Stanford, J. *Getting Into Medical School,* pgs. 7
[xxxii] Brown, Stanford, J. *Getting Into Medical School,* pgs. 7-12.
[xxxiii] Brown, Stanford, J. *Getting Into Medical School,* pgs. 240
[xxxiv] Morgan, Elizabeth, *The Making of a Woman Surgeon,* pgs. 11-12.
[xxxv] Dianne Pingree and Charmian Akins, Texas Woman Magazine, June 1978, pg, 30

[xxxvi] Henderson, Lana, *Baylor University Medical Center: Yesterday, Today and Tomorrow,* pg. 68
[xxxvii] Morsund, Walter H., M. D., L.L.D. *History of Baylor University* College of Medicine: 1900-1953, pg. 73.
[xxxviii] Morsund, Walter H., M. D., L.L.D *History of Baylor University* College of Medicine: 1900-1953, pg. 81.
[xxxix] Morsund, Walter H., M. D., L.L.D. *History of Baylor University* College of Medicine: 1900-1953, pg. 73
[xl] Patient, December 1986 interview
[xli] *Dallas Journal,"* Friday, June 7, 1940
[xlii] Papers of Ruth Jackson M.D., Acc.213, Archives and Special Collections on Women in Medicine, Drexel University College of Medicine.
[xliii] Papers of Ruth Jackson M.D., Acc.213, Archives and Special Collections on Women in Medicine, Drexel University College of Medicine.
[xliv] Ernest, May L., War, Boom and Bust: The Life History of the United States 1917-1932, pg.89
[xlv] Morsund, Walter H., M. D., L.L.D. History of Baylor University College of Medicine: 1900-1953, pg. 81.

[xlvi] Lopate, Carol, *Women in Medicine*, 21-22.
[xlvii] Morantz-Sanchez, Regina Markell. *Sympathy and Science*, pg. 317.
[xlviii] Lopate, Carol, *Women in Medicine"*, 107-08.
[xlix] AAOS *"The Bulletin,"* Vol. 7, #3 August 1959.
[l] Papers of Ruth Jackson M.D., ACC. 213, Archives and Special Collections on Women in Medicine, Drexel University College of Medicine.
[li] Papers of Ruth Jackson M.D., ACC. 213, Archives and Special Collections on Women in Medicine, Drexel University College of Medicine.
[lii] Taped interview, date: September 22, 1984 page 6 of transcript.
[liii] Papers of Ruth Jackson M.D., ACC. 213 Archives and Special Collections on Women in Medicine, Drexel University College of Medicine.
[liv] Lopate, Carol, *Women in Medicine*, pg 22.
[lv] Branden, Barbara, *The Passion of Ayn Rand*, pg. 330.
[lvi] Henderson, Lana, *Baylor University Medical Center: Yesterday, Today and Tomorrow,* pgs. 67-70.

[lvii] Brehm, Edythe, Heart Wrought Filigree, pg.28
[lviii] Papers of Ruth Jackson M.D., ACC. 213, Archives and Special Collections on Women in Medicine, Drexel University College of Medicine.
[lix] Papers of Ruth Jackson M.D., ACC. 213, Archives and Special Collections on Women in Medicine, Drexel University College of Medicine.
[lx] Bernard, Jessie, Academic Women, pg. 37.
[lxi] Ferrell, Robert H. *The Twentieth Century: An Almanac* p.352
[lxii] Papers of Ruth Jackson M.D., ACC. 213, Archives and Special Collections on Women in Medicine, Drexel University College of Medicine.
[lxiii] Papers of Ruth Jackson M.D., ACC. 213, Archives and Special Collections on Women in Medicine, Drexel University College of Medicine.
[lxiv] Papers of Ruth Jackson M.D., ACC. 213, Archives and Special Collections on Women in Medicine, Drexel University College of Medicine.
[lxv] Papers of Ruth Jackson M.D., ACC. 213, Archives and Special Collections on Women in Medicine, Drexel University

College of Medicine.
[lxvi] Papers of Ruth Jackson M.D., ACC. 213, Archives and Special Collections on Women in Medicine, Drexel University College of Medicine.
[lxvii] Papers of Ruth Jackson M.D., ACC. 213, Archives and Special Collections on Women in Medicine, Drexel University College of Medicine.
[lxviii] Papers of Ruth Jackson M.D., ACC. 213, Archives and Special Collections on Women in Medicine, Drexel University College of Medicine.
[lxix] Papers of Ruth Jackson M.D., ACC. 213, Archives and Special Collections on Women in Medicine, Drexel University College of Medicine.
[lxx] Papers of Ruth Jackson M.D., ACC. 213, Archives and Special Collections on Women in Medicine, Drexel University College of Medicine.
[lxxi] **Letter from** papers of Ruth Jackson M.D., ACC. 213, Archives and Special Collections on Women in Medicine, Drexel University College of Medicine.
[lxxii] Papers of Ruth Jackson M.D., ACC. 213, Archives and Special Collections on Women in Medicine, Drexel University College of Medicine.

[lxxiii] Papers of Ruth Jackson M.D., ACC. 213, Archives and Special Collections on Women in Medicine, Drexel University College of Medicine.
[lxxiv] Papers of Ruth Jackson M.D., ACC. 213, Archives and Special Collections on Women in Medicine, Drexel University College of Medicine.
[lxxv] Papers of Ruth Jackson M.D., ACC. 213, Archives and Special Collections on Women in Medicine, Drexel University College of Medicine.
[lxxvi] Mary Barr taped interview, Aug. 8, 1988, Dallas, TX. Copies of MB's confession, prescription and details included in file.
[lxxvii] Jeani Hill Interview, tape 15, side A, May 11, 1987
[lxxviii] Jeani Hill Interview, tape 15, side A, May 11, 1987
[lxxix] Papers of Ruth Jackson M.D., ACC. 213, Archives and Special Collections on Women in Medicine, Drexel University College of Medicine.
[lxxx] Papers of Ruth Jackson M.D., ACC. 213, Archives and Special Collections on Women in Medicine, Drexel University College of Medicine.
[lxxxi] Papers of Ruth Jackson M.D., ACC.

213, Archives and Special Collections on Women in Medicine, Drexel University College of Medicine.
[lxxxii] Papers of Ruth Jackson M.D., ACC. 213, Archives and Special Collections on Women in Medicine, Drexel University College of Medicine.
[lxxxiii] Papers of Ruth Jackson M.D., ACC. 213, Archives and Special Collections on Women in Medicine, Drexel University College of Medicine.
[lxxxiv] Papers of Ruth Jackson M.D., ACC. 213, Archives and Special Collections on Women in Medicine, Drexel University College of Medicine.
[lxxxv] Papers of Ruth Jackson M.D., ACC. 213, Archives and Special Collections on Women in Medicine, Drexel University College of Medicine.
[lxxxvi] Papers of Ruth Jackson M.D., ACC. 213, Archives and Special Collections on Women in Medicine, Drexel University College of Medicine.
[lxxxvii] Papers of Ruth Jackson M.D., ACC. 213, Archives and Special Collections on Women in Medicine, Drexel University College of Medicine.
[lxxxviii] Papers of Ruth Jackson M.D., ACC. 213, Archives and Special Collections

on Women in Medicine, Drexel University College of Medicine.

[lxxxix] Papers of Ruth Jackson M.D., ACC. 213, Archives and Special Collections on Women in Medicine, Drexel University College of Medicine.

[xc] Papers of Ruth Jackson M.D., ACC. 213, Archives and Special Collections on Women in Medicine, Drexel University College of Medicine.

[xci] Jackson, Ruth, *Treatment of the Cervical Spine, Shoulder, Arm Syndrome*, 1960.

[xcii] Jackson, Ruth, *Treatment of the Cervical Spine, Shoulder, Arm Syndrome*, 1960.

[xciii] Goff, Charles W., Lawyers Medical Journal, Vol. 4, No. 2, Aug. ,1968, pg. 193

[xciv] Taped interview with Tru Wilhelm, Date: March 2, 1987

[xcv] Taken from the Summary of the Profit and Loss Statement by Alan Winston Smith

[xcvi] Papers of Ruth Jackson M.D., ACC. 213, Archives and Special Collections on Women in Medicine, Drexel University College of Medicine.

[xcvii] Papers of Ruth Jackson M.D., ACC.

213, Archives and Special Collections on Women in Medicine, Drexel University College of Medicine.
[xcviii] Law Science Academy brochure (author's file).
[xcix] Ferrell, Robert H., *The Twentieth Century: An Almanac*, pg.
[c] Papers of Ruth Jackson M.D., ACC. 213, Archives and Special Collections on Women in Medicine, Drexel University College of Medicine.
[ci] Papers of Ruth Jackson M.D., ACC. 213, Archives and Special Collections on Women in Medicine, Drexel University College of Medicine.
[cii] Papers of Ruth Jackson M.D., ACC. 213, Archives and Special Collections on Women in Medicine, Drexel University College of Medicine.
[ciii] Papers of Ruth Jackson M.D., ACC. 213, Archives and Special Collections on Women in Medicine, Drexel University College of Medicine.
[civ] April 28, 1964 report.
[cv] Letter of June, 7, 1964.
[cvi] Letter of July, 27, 1964,
[cvii] Papers of Ruth Jackson M.D., ACC. 213, Archives and Special Collections on Women in Medicine, Drexel University

College of Medicine.
[cviii] Brochure: Cr. Bovik's (Is) "Field Fresh at Valley Aloe Vera" (author's file.)
[cix] Author's File.
[cx] Papers of Ruth Jackson M.D., ACC. 213, Archives and Special Collections on Women in Medicine, Drexel University College of Medicine.
[cxi] Papers of Ruth Jackson M.D., ACC. 213, Archives and Special Collections on Women in Medicine, Drexel University College of Medicine.
[cxii] Letter from author's file.
[cxiii] Papers of Ruth Jackson M.D., ACC. 2Notebook of Jack13, Archives and Special Collections on Women in Medicine, Drexel University College of Medicine.
[cxiv] Notebook of Jackson files.
[cxv] Papers of Ruth Jackson M.D., ACC. 213, Archives and Special Collections on Women in Medicine, Drexel University College of Medicine.
[cxvi] Papers of Ruth Jackson M.D., ACC. 213, Archives and Special Collections on Women in Medicine, Drexel University College of Medicine.
[cxvii] Papers of Ruth Jackson M.D., ACC.

213, Archives and Special Collections on Women in Medicine, Drexel University College of Medicine.
[cxviii] Contract in author's files.
[cxix] Papers of Ruth Jackson M.D., ACC. 213, Archives and Special Collections on Women in Medicine, Drexel University College of Medicine.
[cxx] Papers of Ruth Jackson M.D., ACC. 213, Archives and Special Collections on Women in Medicine, Drexel University College of Medicine.
[cxxi] Papers of Ruth Jackson M.D., ACC. 213, Archives and Special Collections on Women in Medicine, Drexel University College of Medicine.
[cxxii] Papers of Ruth Jackson M.D., ACC. 213, Archives and Special Collections on Women in Medicine, Drexel University College of Medicine.
[cxxiii] Papers of Ruth Jackson M.D., ACC. 213, Archives and Special Collections on Women in Medicine, Drexel University College of Medicine.
[cxxiv] Sandruth file and Chapter 13
[cxxv] Copy of written statement, author's file. Gilbert was cook and housekeeper_)
[cxxvi] Papers of Ruth Jackson M.D., ACC.

213, Archives and Special Collections on Women in Medicine, Drexel University College of Medicine.
[cxxvii] Papers of Ruth Jackson M.D., ACC. 213, Archives and Special Collections on Women in Medicine, Drexel University College of Medicine.
[cxxviii] Papers of Ruth Jackson M.D., ACC. 213, Archives and Special Collections on Women in Medicine, Drexel University College of Medicine.
[cxxix] Walter Charette taped interview Feb. 15, 1987.
[cxxx] Letter David F. Hunt April 9, 1971.
[cxxxi] Letter from Ruth Jackson's Research Foundation file.
[cxxxii] Papers of Ruth Jackson M.D., ACC. 213, Archives and Special Collections on Women in Medicine, Drexel University College of Medicine.
[cxxxiii] Telephone conversation with Theda Dowell April 4, 1988.
[cxxxiv] Taped interview with Ruth Jackson, M.D. on Dallas television during the mid 1980s.

INDEX

A
A. E. I. National Fraternity of Medical Women, 151

A. Webb Roberts Center for Continuing
   Education, 263
Abda, Dr. Sandra Marie, 353
Adams, Dr., 120
Adolphus Hotel, 156
Aesculapian Frolic, 122
Ahbel, Dr. Dorrit E., 353
Albanese, Dr. Margaret R., 354
Albert, Dr. Mary Johanna, 363
Albert Einstein Hospital, 33
Albuquerque, NM, 267
Alexander, Dr. Charlotte, 353, 359
Alice, TX, 41
"All Aspects of the Shoulder" (Tullos), 267
Allen, Dr. Glen I., 178
Allington, Dr. Nanny, 332
Aloe Vera, 7, 242-243, 253, 258-259, 261
Alpha Epsilon Iota medical sorority, 100, 105
Alvarez, Dr. Dona M., 364
American Academy of Orthopaedics Surgeons
   (AAOS)
  meetings of, 12-13, 57, 139, 145-146, 148, 151
  members of, 177-178, 182, 297, 299-300, 322-
     323, 328-329, 332-333, 345, 365-366
  women's forum, 336-337
American Association of Medical Colleges
   (AAMC), 92
American College of Surgeons, 95, 345
American Health project, 196
American Hospital Association, 95
American Journal, 344
American Lecture Series, 230
American Medical Association, 80-81, 111, 116,
   135

American Medical Women's Association, 86, 110-111, 337
American Red Cross, 86
American Society of Contemporary Medicine, 242
American Stock Exchange, 147
American Women's Medical Association, 65
Ames, IA, 16
Anaheim, CA, 322
Analysis of Pain in Orthopaedic Entities (Steindler), 117
Anderson, Dr. Lesley J., 355
Anesthesiology, 103
Anglo-French College, 256
Anthony, Susan B., 65
Aquino, Corozon, 341
Archives and Special Collections of Women in Medicine, 255
Arendt, Dr. Elizabeth, 356
Argyle, TX, 318
Arizona, 47
Arizona Supreme Court, 147
Arkansas, 152, 176, 287
ASE Dermetetics Clinic, Inc., 284
Atlanta, GA, 180, 267, 326
Atlanta Falcons (football team), 267
Austin, Harold, 122, 290
Austin, TX, 69, 72, 76-77
Australia, 331-332
Automobiles, 29, 37, 106, 108, 113, 123, 306
Automotive Injuries to the Neck" (Jackson), 187
Ayers, Dr. Charles, 124-125

B
Babb, Caroline Arabelle. *See* Belle Jackson
Babb, Valentine, 5

Babbitt, Dr. Ann, 359
Badger, Dr. Virginia M., 147, 350
Balcomb, Dr. Teresa V., 358
Balthazar, Dr. Dorothy A., 148, 322, 327, 330, 352
Baltimore, MD, 269, 322, 324, 330
Bannerstone House, 230, 232
Baptist General Convention of Texas, 94
Barber, Dr. Elaine, 335
Bastings, Wendy, 333
Bathgate, Dr. M Beth, 361
Baylor Board of Trustees, 94
Baylor Orthopaedic IBM computer program, 278
Baylor University Hospital, 87-88, 95
Baylor University Medical Center (BUMC)
 drug-alcohol treatment center, 318, 320
 Executive Director of, 241
 Parkside, 318
 Ruth as honoree, 73, 277, 337, 339-340, 343
 Ruth Jackson, M.D. Education and Research Fund, 265-266, 278-279
 Ruth's career at, 95, 112, 135, 269-270, 306
 Ruth's influence at, 236, 262-263, 272, 321, 327, 346
Baylor University Medical School
 admission requirements to, 91-92
 College of Dentistry, 88, 94, 176, 276
 dean of, 96, 134
 Ruth as student, 72, 90, 93, 96-100, 103-106
 School of Nursing, 94. 275
 School of Pharmacy, 94
 treatment at, 280
 women at, 1-3, 97-99
 women professors at, 110
Bean, Rita, 164

Beath, Thomas, 232
Beethoven, Ludwig von, 190
Belenguer, Juan, 254
Belgium, 331-332
Bellcock, James, 24
Bellcock, Roy, 35
Bellcock, Winnie Jackson, 9, 23-24, 35
Bell Dr. Deborah, 359
Belt Line Road, 96
Bentley, E. R., 55
Berger, Dr. Winfried M., 352
Bernard, Jess, 89
Bible study, 68
Bittinger, Isabel, 349
Blackwell, Dr. Elizabeth, 83-84
Blount, Dr. Walter, 252
Boehme, Dr. Donna M., 363
Boston, MA, 5, 82, 154, 324, 330
Boston Female Medical College, 82
Bouvé, Marion Ross, 142, 165-168, 253-254, 293, 307
Bovik, Dr. Ellis G., 258
B Brahos, Sandra, 338
Branden, Barbara, 133
Braniff Airlines, 142, 280
Brazil, 23, 331
"The Breakfast Club Pro
gram", 136
Brehm, Alan, 343, 347
Brehm, Gwen, 343
Brehm, Harold, 73, 104, 157, 191, 250, 296-297, 299, 342
Brennecke, Frances, 349
Brockman, Dr. Roberta, 362
Brothels, 76-77

Brown, Dr. Frank, 148
Brown, Dr. Mary Lynn, 364
Bryan, Williams Jennings, 69
Bucholz, Dr. Robert W., 275, 277, 295
Buckner, Kathryn, 71, 75, 96-98, 103-105, 109-110
Burbank, CA, 186
Bureau, Paula, 118
Bush, Dorothy, 283
"The Business of Orthopaedics " (Perry), 334
Brackett, Dr. Bess, 335
Brady, Dr. E. Anna, 350

C
Calhoun, Dr. Tom, 148
California, 13, 104, 109, 171, 186, 190, 193, 267-268, 298, 322-324, 326-329, 333-334, 342
Calyx Club, 151
Campbell Clinic, 230
Camden Fiber Mill, 184
Cammy, Dr. Carol Mowery, 355
Campbell, Dr. Barbara Jean, 354
Campion, Dr. Tee Selmon, 355
Canada, 24, 267, 331, 333
Cancer, 254-257, 259
Canton, TX, 310
Card playing, 39-40
Carnegie Foundation, 90
Carr, Dr. Diana, 336, 354
Carranza, Venustiano, 46
Carrell, Dr. William Beall, 131, 141
Carrell-Driver-Girard Clinic, 131, 133
Carter, Jimmy, 341
Carty, Dr. Claudia Thomas, 353
Cary, Dr. Edward H., 96, 134

Cavalry, 121-122
Central Medical College of New York at Syracuse, 83
Centro Universitario Mexicano, 256
Cermak, Dr. Mary Beth, 363
Cervical Contour Company, 178, 180
Cervical Pain Non-Surgical Treatment, 190
Cervical Pain Symposium, 190
Cervical Spine Stability Study, 275
Cervical syndrome, 231-235
The Cervical Syndrome, 165, 232-233
"The Cervical Syndrome as a Cause of Headache," (Jackson), 177
Cervipillo, 165, 174-190, 193-200
Cerviplast, 180
Chambers, Dr. Doris E., 349
Charette, Walter, 285, 288, 293-294
Chicago, IL, 28, 117, 122-123, 126, 136, 139, 146, 178, 251-253, 330, 336-337
Child Welfare, 16
Children's Hospital and Samuel Merritt Hospital, 268
China, 4, 104
Chiropractors, 177
Choler, Dr. Ulla, 331
Chorney, Dr. Gail, 359
Christmas, 102, 108, 194, *203,* 239, 298, 313
Church, 6-7
Cillo, Dr. Yolanda A., 362
Civil War, 82-83
Civilian defense offices, 158
Clark, Dr. Mary Williams, 147, 327, 351
Clayton, MO, 244
Cleburne, TX, 288, 293
Clemons, C. B., 185

Cleveland, Grover, 66
Cleveland, OH, 145, 179
Coffman, Dr. Lydia, 360
Cohen-Brown, Dr. Jessica, 363
Colorado, 167, 249
Colorado Springs, CO, 167
Columbia Theater, 61
Columbia University, 300
Compere, Edward, 122
Conroy, Dr. Mary E., 350
"Contributions of Women to the Orthopaedic Literature", 333
Copperas Cove, TX, 286
Coughlin, Dr. Dennis, 330
Coyle, Dr. Alice R., 363
Crawford, Dr. Andrea B., 355
Crested Butte, CO, 249-251
Crippled Children's Hospital, 109
Crops, 33-34, 48
Crowley, TX, 286
Cudmore, Ruth, 104, 108
Cullen, Dr. Nancy, 357
Cuomo, Dr. Frances, 362
Curtis, Bill, 148-149
Curtis, Sandy, 304
Czaplicki, Dr. Marie Ann, 353

D
Dallas, TX
  Baylor College of Medicine in, 90, 94-96, 108
  District Court, 151, 162
  family in, 58, 136, 142-144, 244, 301, 309-310
  Fairmont clinic, 28
  Greenhill School, 101
  Highland Park, 143

Judge Watkins, 174
Methodist Hospital, 109-110
Preston Hollow, 143
Presbyterian Hospital, 271
Ruby Daniel in, 104-105
Ruth's practice in, 28, 70, 112, 119, 129-130, 134-135, 141, 179, 182, 184, 190, 264-265, 300, 303
Scottish Rites Hospital, 120, 126-127, 130, 342
Social Record, 151
State Fair Musicals, 170
Stemmons Tower South, 282
Texas County Day School, 166
Turtle Creek, 1, 40, 163, 168, 170, 251, 281, 289-290, 295, 297, 306, 314
University Park, 143-144
University of Texas Medical School, 253, 275
White Rock Park, 143
Zonta Club, 148, 151, 162-163
Dallas Bank and Trust Co., 283, 288
Dallas Country Club, 151
Dallas County, TX, 96
Dallas County Medical Society, 134, 141, 151, 301
Dallas Morning News, 135
Dallas Slipper Club, 151
Dance, dancing, 25, 56-58, 74, 122, 156, 170, 320
Daniel, Ruby, 72, 103-105
Daniels Dr. Ruby, 148
Darwin's Theory of Evolution, 69
Davis, Dr. Arthur, 180
Dawson, Dr. Cleo, 48
Day, Dr. Lorraine, 147, 334, 350

Dayton, Tennessee, 69
De Pau Hospital, 244
DeBakey, Dr. Michael, 242
Dedrick, Dr. Dale, 359
Delgado, Dr. Ellana D., 362
DelSignore, Dr. Jeanne L., 364
Denton, TX, 286, 337
Des Moines, IA, 117
Detroit, MI, 160
Diamond, Dr. Liebe Sokol, 147, 324, 326, 350
District Court
  68th, 162
  95th, 151
Dixon, Judge Dick, 143, 151, 156
Dlaning, Dr. William (Bill), 273-274
Dobb, John A., 161
Dobyns, Dr. James H., 267
Doctors. *See* Physicians
Dollinger, Dr. Beth M., 360
Dowell, Dr. Theda, 297, 305-306
Dowling, Dr. Ronnie, 334
Doyle, Dr. Lorraine K., 354
Drake University, 117
Drexel University College of Medicine, 83, 254-255
Drinking, 7, 106-108
Driver, Dr. Sim, 134, 136
Duane, Dr. Karen S., 359
Duck, Dr. Holly, 336
Duncan, Dr. Wallace, 178-179
Dunn, Doris, 285
Dvonch, Dr. Marie Victoria, 353
Dzioba, Dr. Robert B., 341

E
Eagle Pass, TX, 170
Edinburg, TX, 296, 343
Eelma, Dr. Jean M., 362
Eisele, Dr. Sandra, 357
Eisenhower, Dwight, 341
El Paso, TX, 330
Elfreing, Dr. Margaret, 357
Emmanuel, Dr. Jacqueline, 355
Emory University School of Medicine, 267
England, 5, 195, 331
English, Dr. Diane, 148, 352
Ensley, Dr. Nancy J., 364
Epstein, Dr. Rosalind, 362
Epworth League, 72, 106
Europe, 46, 81, 103, 176, 195, 281
Evarts, Dr. McCollister, 330
Excalibur Ventures, 284, 289
Ezaki, Dr. Marybeth, 354

F
Faculty Club, 56
Falls Congressional Committee, 46
Fantastic Voyage, 240
Farber, Dr. Bobbi A., 362
Fay, Dr. Colleen M., 364
Fay, Dr. Nina, 148
Feddis, Dr. Grania, 360
Female Medical College of Pennsylvania, 82-84
Ferguson, Jean, 241
Ferletic, Dr. Lynn Froome, 356
Ferris, Dr. Linda, 331
Fidelis (Beethoven), 190

Fields, Tommie Lee, 164-165, 175, 238-239, 241, 243, 342
Fifty-sixth Evacuation Hospital, 87-88
Finnegan, Dr. Maureen, 354
Flatt, Dr. Adrian, 277, 295, 341, 346
Flawn, Dr. Laura B., 355
Fleitman, Dr. Benjamin, 255
Flexner, Abraham, 90-91
Flora, 254-261
Florida, 196, 293, 310, 317, 330, 331, 343
Foltz, Dr. Michelle, 355
The Foot and Ankle (Lewin), 139
Foot and Ankle Society, 57
"Football Injuries of the Cervical Spine" (Funk), 268
Ford, Gerald, 341
Forth Worth, TX, 343
Fourteenth Annual Dallas Blue Book, 151
Fower, Dr. Peter, 267
France, 61
Freeman, Dr. Barbara, 357
Frey, Dr. Barbara, 359
Frieman, Dr. Barbara Grugan, 357
Funk, Dr. James, 267

G
"Gait and the Foot" (Mann), 268
Gallup, NM, 323
Gambrell, Herbert, 95
Garber, Dr. Nancy, 360
Gardner, Dr. Melinda, 352
Garland, TX, 286
Garner, Dr. Lynn Carole, 358
Garrett, Dr. Alice L., 350
Gatesville, TX, 160

Gavin, Dr. Kathleen Raggio, 357
Gelberman, Dr. Richard, 336
General Mining Corp, 171
General Motors, 160-161, 345
George W. Truett Memorial Hospital, 341
Georgia, 180, 267, 326
Georgopoulos, Dr. Gaia, 360
German Orthopaedic Association, 187
Germany, Germans, 44-47, 84, 187, 264, 300, 344
Gilles, Dr. Diane E., 331, 357
Girard, Dr. Percy, 134
Girl Scouts, 163
Glenden, Dr. Mike, 298
Glidewell, Dr. Maylene M., 364
Gloves, Stella, 162-163
Godesky, Dr. Maria T., 147, 351
Godzik, Dr. Cathleen A., 362
Goff, Dr. Charles W., 232, 235-236
Good Samaritan Hospital (Baltimore), 269
Goodfried, Dr. Paul, 13-14, 276-277, 295
Goodwin, Occo, 109
Gorai, Dr. Patricia A., 359
Gordon, Dr. Carole, 300-304
Gorsuch, Dr. Wanda Lee, 359
Grapevine, TX, 289
Great Depression, 124, 130, 152
"The Great Withdrawal" (Bernard), 89
Greene, John, 5
Greene County, IA, 4-5, 33
Greenhill School, 101
Guise, Dr. Edwin, 330
Gulf of Mexico, 32, 44

H
Hachigian, Dr. Aimee V., 358

Hall, Dr. Ed, 271-273
Hall, Dr. Suzanne E., 365
Hall, William, 13
Handley, Lawrence K., 253
Hannah, Dr. C. R., 102-103
Hargroves, Dr., 120
Harold Austin and his New Yorkers, 122
Harris, Dr. Charlotte J., 357, 360
Harris, Patricia, 147
Harrison, John F., 252-253, 294
Harvard University Medical School, 82, 92, 248
Hawthorne, Dr. Catherine, 322, 352
Hebbronville, TX, 41-42, 44
Hedin, Dr. Hanne, 331
Henderson, Laura, 94
Hidalgo County, TX, 51, 282
Hieb, Dr. Lee D., 364
Hill, Jeani, 167-170, 172-173
Hill, Tom, 168, 170-172
Hilliard, Dr. G. M., 87
Hillsman, Dr. Regina O., 360
Hirsch, Dr. Ilona Ruth, 358
Hixson, Dr. Marcia Lynn, 357
Hobart College Herald, 74
Hoffman, Dr. Janaleigh, 352
Holiday magazine, 70
Holmes, Dr. Cherie A., 362
Holmes, Dr. Denise O., 355, 360
Holmes, Oliver Wendell, 82
Home Owner's Loan Corp., 152
Homestead laws, 64
Honolulu County Medical Center, 177
Hood, Dr. Marianna, 253-254, 293, 316
Hopper, Helen, 164
Horses, 11-12, 18-20, 27, 120-121, 193, 319

Horstmann, Dr. Helen, 148, 333-334
Hospital for Joint Disease, 264
Hot Springs, AR, 151, 287
Houston, TX, 267, 290
Howard, Dr. Rex, 100
Hu, Dr. Serena S., 365
Hudson, Earl, 59-61
Hudson, Roscoe, 61
Huges, Judge Sarah, 157, 283
Hughes, Dr. Wendy Michelle, 356
Hulett, Dr. Carol L., 354
Hungerford, Dr. David, 269
Hunt, Dave F., 277, 293, 316
Hunt, Harriet, 82
Hunter-Griffin, Dr. Letha, 148, 352
Hunting, 49, 128, 140-141, 182, 191-192, 280, 300

I
Idlewild Club, 151
Illinois, 28, 117, 122-123, 126, 136, 139, 146, 178, 232, 251-253, 267, 335, 337
Indech, Dr. Christine, 360
Industrialization, 85
International College of Surgeons, 187, 300, 345
Iowa
  early days in, 3, 4-6, 10, 16, 23-25, 30, 33-37, 42, 57-60, 116-11, 123, 126
  studies in, 116-11, 123, 126, 264
  and Texas move, 33-37, 42, 57-60
Iowa City, IA, 116-117, 119, 123, 264, 341
Iowa River, 122
Irani, Dr. Roshen N., 350
Ireland, Dr. Mary Lloyd, 337, 353, 355

Ires, Dr. Caren R., 362
Isaacson, Dr. Julie, 356
Israel, 331

J
Jackson, Barney, 37, 39-40, 142
Jackson, Belle (nee Caroline Arabelle Babb)
 death of, 25
 influence of, 8-9, 15-18, 21, 28, 79
 marriage of, 5-7
 needlework of, 25
 physical attributes of, 5-6
 pregnancies of, 9
 and Ruth, 2, 111, 152
 Texas move, 33-35, 37, 44, 46
Jackson, Cindy, 58
Jackson, Darrell, 8, 75-76, 111, 128-130, 142-143, 314, 342
Jackson, Donald, 58
Jackson, Dr. Douglas W., 267
Jackson, Edythe "Babe"
 birth of, 10
 as child, 12, 14-16, 21-22, 27
 marriage of, 104
 phobia of, 22
 poetry of, 136-137
 and Ruth, 59, 73-74, 136, 191, 250, 296-297, 299
 schooling of, 51
 Texas move, 37-38, 41-43, 51
 at University of Texas, 71-73, 75
Jackson, Fern, 18
Jackson, Frances, 170
Jackson, Harley
 as first born, 9

  as older brother, 10-11, 16, 128
  on parents, 7
  Texas move, 35
Jackson, Irvin Riley (I. R.)
  fiancée of, 18
  on parents, 7
  on Ruth, 19-21
  Texas move, 37-43
Jackson, Jane, 128
Jackson, Kathryn Ruth, 170-171
Jackson, Kieth
  on Edythe, 16
  on grandparents, 8-9
  on Paul, 52
  on Ruth, 17, 142
Jackson, Mabel Mundy, 6, 11, 24, 35, 47-48, 60,
    203
Jackson, Marion, 128-129
Jackson, MS, 185
Jackson, O. N. "Tip," 125, 142, 170
Jackson, Paul Jr., 125, 191, 343, 347
Jackson, Paul Oliver
  as child, 9, 11-12, 17, 21, 24, 26-27
  and family business, 29
  schooling of, 51-54, 58
  temperament of, 51-52, 57
  Texas move, 38-43, 51, 75
  visits with Ruth, 125
Jackson, Ruth (nee Mary Ruth)
  at Baylor University Medical school, 72-73,
    90, 93, 95-100, 103-106, 112, 236
  birth of, 10
  business enterprises of, 170-172, 178-180,
    187-191, 193-200, 280-286, 288-289, 293-
    295, 299-300, 315-317

as card player, 39-40, 156
on cervical syndrome, 231-235
and Cervipillo, 165, 174-190, 193-200
and charity work, 76-78, 162-163
as Chief of Orthopaedic Surgery, 145, 155, 264, 266, 270
childhood of, 12, 14-15, 21, 23-28
and dancing, 25, 56-58, 74, 122, 156, 170
and driving, 29, 106-108
as expert witness, 244-249
and farm chores, 11, 13
and fashion, 73-74, 77, 115
and First Aid classes, 158
and foreign language requirements, 78-79, 89
as fraternity member, 100, 105
graduation from medical school, 111
honors for, 242
and horses, 11-12, 18-19, 121
and hunting, 49, 121, 140-141, 182, 191-192, 280, 300
illnesses of, 13, 53, 122, 174, 299
innovations of, 138-141
as intern, 112, 114-117
as inventor, 159, 165, 174-190, 193-200
lectures of, 141, 177, 187, 190, 230, 250-251, 253, 343
on love, 64-65
marriages of, 63-64, 148-157, 295, 296-299
as maverick, 7
medical aspirations of, 28, 67-69, 78, 80, 89-90, 93, 118-119
medical practices of, 134-135
and memories of father, 7-8
and oil leases, 50
and orthopaedics, 88, 108-109

patents obtained, 159-161
physical attributes of, 1-2, 30, 301-302
and physical pain, 12-13
and plastic surgery, 88-89
poem about, 136-138
residency of, 123, 126, 128, 131
schooling of, 24, 51-55, 58-60
suitors of, 58-59, 62, 63
as surgeon, 101, 114, 136, 138-139, 301-302, 307
temperament of, 17-18
Texas move, 37-39, 41-44, 48-49, 51
at University of Texas, 62, 63, 65, 67-73, 76, 89-90, 96, 106
works by
  "Automotive Injuries to the Neck", 187
  "Cervical Pain Non-Surgical Treatment", 190
  The Cervical Syndrome, 165, 230, 232
  "The Cervical Syndrome as a Cause of Headache, 177
  "Medicolegal Aspects of Injuries of Upper Extremity and of Neck", 250
  "Painful Feet", 141
  Treatment of the Cervical Spine, Shoulder, Arm Syndrome, 230, 235-236
and World War II, 87-88
Jackson, Velma, 125
Jackson, Walter, 9, 11, 24, 35, 48, 57, 60
Jackson, William Riley (W. R.)
 as business man, 5, 28-34, 47-51, 75, 124, 134
 as family man, 7-8, 18-19, 21, 25, 52-53, 59
 marriage of, 4, 6-7
 and Ruth, 2, 73-74, 79, 111, 128, 152
 Texas move, 35
Jackson, Winnie Ethel, 9

Jackson Road, 34-35, 47
James, Dr. Michelle A., 335, 362
James, Dr. Preston, 335
Japan, Japanese, 87, 233, 331, 344
Jefferson, IA, 4, 10, 33
Jennings, Dr. Candace, 364
Johansson, Dr. Joyce E., 353
Johns Hopkins University, 269, 322
Johnson, Lyndon B., 157, 341
Jolly, Dr. Susan L., 365
Joplin, Dr. Robert J., 230, 232
Journal of the American Medical Women's Association, 177
Juhasz, Dr. Annabelle, 364
Julliasson, Dr. Rigmor, 331

K
Kaga Dr. Kristine, 358
Kaiser, The Beast of Berlin, The, 61
Kalen, Dr. Vicki, 331, 354
Kane, Dr. Rosamond, 147, 351
Kaufman, TX, 71, 182, 271, 273-275, 278, 282, 288, 291-292, 299-300, 309-311, 317, 319-320
Kaufman Community Hospital, 270-271
Keenan, Dr. Mary Ann, 330, 333, 354
Kelley, Dr. Dorsey, 172
Kenebel, Moses, 70-71
Kennedy, Dr. Colleen A., 360
Kentucky, 331
Keyes, Don, 63, 120-123, 126, 145, 150, 167
King, Dr. Lucie M., 354
King Ranch, 41
Kirilenko, Dr. Linda T., 365
Kirkpatrick, Dr. Delores, 361
Kleberg, TX, 282-283, 286

Klepak, Henry, 294, 316
Knauer, Dr. Sally A., 357
Knowles, Lois, 312-313
Kolowich, Dr. Patricia A., 361
Kopach, Dr. Kathleen, 355
Kruse, Dr. Diana Lynn, 353
Kulowski, Jacob "Jake," 120-122, 145
Kyropoulos, Peter, 160

L
Ladd, Dr. Amy, 335-336, 364
Ladies Home Journal, 66
Lake Campacuas, 55
Lake Michigan, 126
Lake Texoma, 186
Lakrewaska, Marie, 83
Lamantia, Maria, 342
Lamb, Lake Texoma, 186
Fred A, 194
Land holdings, 9
Landy, Dr. Margaret A., 356, 362
Lane-Stanford Hospital, 104
Langa, Dr. Victoria M., 358
Larzalere, Christopher, 310-313, 317, 319, 343, 347
Larzalere, Sheri, 164, 310-313, 316-17, 347-48
Las Norias flag station, 45-46
Las Vegas, NV, 171, 329
Law Science Academy, 249-251
Lawhon, Mrs., 77
Lawyers' Medical Journal, 235
"Leadership Roles for Women in Orthopaedics" (Perry), 334
Lenk, Norma, 164
Leo, Dr. Jan Elizabeth, 355

Leslie, Dr. Eleanor, 252-253, 263, 299
Lester, Dr. Berisse, 365
Levine, Dr. Judith J., 358
Lewin, Dr. Phillip, 139, 146, 230
Little Rock, AR, 176
Livingston, Dr., 120
Llano, Constantino de ("Kiki"), 255-256, 258
Lone Star Gas Co., 285
Looney, Dr. William W., 100
Lopate, Carol, 84, 114-115
Lorenz, Dr. Adolf, 117
Louis Yellin, Inc., 179
Louisiana, 90, 193, 300, 327, 333
Love, Dr. Shelia, 359
Lozano, Dr. Francisco, 254

M
M. R. Properties, Inc., 284, 288, 293-294
Maffett, Dr. Minnie Lee, 110
Maffett, Dr. Minnie, 132, 148
MacIntosh, Dr. David, 267
Magnolia Building, 96
Maitin, Dr. Ellen C., 361
Majewski, Priscilla, 338
The Making of a Woman Surgeon (Morgan), 92
Malloy, Mrs. R. E., 172
Mankin, Dr. Henry, 330
Mann, Dr. Roger A., 268, 330
Maples, Dr. Dale L., 359
Marshall, Pat, 164
Marshalltown, IA, 35
Martinez, Dr. Elena R., 147, 351
Martinson, Dr. Alice M., 147, 351
Martinson, James, 290
Maryland, 269, 322, 324

Masear, Dr. Victoria, 357
Massachusetts, 5, 82, 110-113, 116-117, 119, 121, 123, 154, 322, 324
Matejczyk, Dr. Mary Blair, 353
Mayer, Dr. Leo, 264
Mayes, Vale, 193
Mayfield, Raleigh Regley, 295, 296-299
Mayo Clinic, 101, 116
McAllen, TX
  move to, 6, 34, 35, 38, 40, 44-45, 49, 51
  as Texas home, 53, 55-59, 61, 69, 75, 104, 129, 136, 296, 342
  visiting, 191
McAllen School Board, 56
McClung, Dan, 64, 148-157
McClung, Hugh (H. C.), 133, 152
McColl Road, 75
McHale, Dr. Kathleen A., 356
McNeil, Don, 136
McVay, Dr. Mary R., 147, 351
Medford, OR, 118
Medical Arts Building Pacific Avenue, 96, 134
Medical College of Pennsylvania, 83
The Medical Post, 324
Medical Reserve Corps, 87
Medicine
 as goal, 3
"Medicolegal Aspects of Injuries of Upper Extremity and of Neck" (Jackson), 250
Medicolegal Trial Technique, 251
Medi-Scan Computer, Inc., 198
Memorial Hospital Worcester Massachusetts, 110-112, 115, 123-124
Mendez, Mario, 46
Menkveld Dr. Sharon, 359

Mercedes, TX, 55
Mesquite, TX, 285
Methodist Church, 6, 22-23, 72, 109, 172
Methodist Hospital, 109-110, 164-165
Mexico, Mexican, 32, 34, 44-47, 168, 192, 253-258, 261, 345
Mexico City, 168-169, 254-256
Meyerdierks, Dr. Elizabeth, 359
Miami, FL, 196, 293, 343
Michels, Dr. Jeane, 147, 350
Michigan, 160
Middle East, 195
Millard, Dr. Amarilis Durieux, 359
Miller, Dr. Nancy A., 364
Miller-Breslow, Dr. Anne J., 362
Milwaukee, WI, 252
Mineral Wells, TX, 281, 283, 288, 292
Minneapolis, MN, 324
Minnesota, 104, 116, 267, 324
Mission, TX, 43-44, 48, 62
Missionary, 23, 79
Mississippi, 185
Missouri, 37, 243-244, 247
Mitchell, Dr. Laura A., 362
"Modern Miracle" (Edythe Jackson), 136-137
Molloy, Dr. Maureen K., 147, 350
Moore, Howard E., 160
Morden, Dr. Mary Louise, 322-325, 327, 330, 352
Morgan, Dr. Elizabeth, 92-93
Morton, Celeste, 72-73
Morwessel, Dr. Rosemarie, 336-337, 358
Mote, Fred, 132
Munich, Germany, 187
Murname, Dr. Alice M., 147, 350
Murray, Dr. David, 266-267, 268

Murray, Dr. John A., 267
Myers, Dr. Magda, 148
Myrtillocactus Schenkii Purpus (cereus schenkii), 256

N
Naas, Dr. Peggy, 333-334, 361
Narcotic Treatment Administration, 287
Nash, Ed, 310
National Congress of Orthopaedic Traumatology, 253
National Eclectic Medical Association, 83
National Fraternal organization, 105
National Guard, 59
National Institute of Health, 337
Nauts, Dr. Ruth Barrington, 357
Nebraska, 11, 331
Neck support headrest, 159-160
Necklash. *See* Whiplash
Neer, Dr. Charles, 267
Neiman-Marcus, 183, 189
Nevada, 329
New Mexico, 47, 267, 323
New Orleans, 90, 193, 300, 333
New York City, 125, 154-155, 162, 177, 186-187, 193, 267, 300
New York Infirmary for Women and Children, 83-84
New York State Supreme Court, 92
New York 7th Regiment (National Guard), 59
New Zealand, 331
Newman, Edith, 343
Newman, Stuart, 343
Newport, Dr. Mary Lynn, 363
Niagara, 123

Nicholas, Noreen, 135
Nickel, Dr. Vernon, 329
Nijus, Dr. Nina M., 358
Noll, Lois, 164
Norman, OK, 251
Norman Art Museum, 251
Northwestern University, 122, 126
Norway, 331
Nurses, 115

O
Oak Lawn Avenue, 109-110
Obstetrics-gynecology, 98
, 193-194
Ochsner Clinic, 194
O'Donnell, Dr. Christine S., 363
Office of Defense, 162
Ohio, 145
Oil, 49-51, 70
O'Keefe, Dr. Ruth Anne, 352, 353
Oklahoma, 37-38, 126, 172, 251
Oklahoma City, OK, 172
Olestad, Dr. Marie S., 358
Olsen, Dr. Evelyn, 120, 126
Omaha, 28
Omer, Dr. George, 267
Oppenheim, Dr. Judith R., 359
Ophthalmology, 104
Orchards, 47
Oregon, 118
Organo macho cactus, 256-257
Orlando, FL, 196
Orthopaedics, orthopaedists
certification, 147
Ochsner, Dr.

lectures, 141, 177, 187, 190, 230, 250-251, 253, 265-269
organization of surgeons, 145, 180
requirements of, 118
residency, 123
as selected field, 88, 108-109, 118-119
Orthopods, 118
Osborne, George, 55
Oschner Foundation Hospital, 300, 345
Osler, Sir William, 81
Otto, Dr. Nancy, 355
Ouellette, Dr. Elizabeth A., 360
Outward Bound, 318
Owens, Lela Mae, 163

P
Painful Feet" (Jackson), 141
Palmer, Captain, 55
Palmer House, 139
Palo Pinto County, 292
Pamilla, Dr. Jeanne, 351
Pancho Villa, 34
Paris, France, 187
Parkland Hospital, 18, 98, 109, 141, 145, 151, 155, 242, 264-265, 345
Parkland Memorial Hospital, 88
Paseo de la Reforma, 168-169, 254
Passion of Ayn Rand, The (Branden), 133
Patients
 and cervical issues, 99, 101-102, 114, 118, 131, 135-136, 186, 194. 196, 251-252, 259
 and neck pain, 232, 234-237, 340
 relationship with, 240-241, 248, 274, 280, 293, 302-303, 306, 314, 342-343, 346

surgery, 138, 140-141, 153-154, 158, 166-167, 175-179
treatment of, 12, 28, 88, 98-99, 124-125, 186, 194, 196, 298-99
women, 98-99
Payne, Corry III, 276
Peachtree Orthopaedic Clinic, 267
Pearl Harbor, HI, 87
Pease, Dr. Charles N., 232
Pecan Lake Mobile Village, 282, 285, 291, 293
Peking, 104
Pennsylvania, 80, 179, 184, 267, 330, 333
Perkins, Frances, 158
Perry, Dr. Jacquelin, 146, 324, 326, 330, 334, 350
Peters, Dr. Myra A., 146, 349
Pharr, TX, 33, 51
Phi Chi medical fraternity, 107
Phi Kappa Alpha fraternity, 152
Philadelphia, PA, 80, 179, 184-185, 197, 267, 330, 333
Philippines, 341
Phillips, Dr. Donna P., 361
Phipps, P. E., 55
Physicians
neurosurgeons, 136
student training of, 1-2, 80-82
women as, 1-2, 80-87, 90-93, 110, 132, 145-148, 251, 301, 323-325, 328-338
Physiotherapy Review, 141
Pioneer times, 85
Pittsburgh, 123
Pleasant Hill, IA, 6
Poetry, poems, 54-55
Polio, 117, 119

Popa, Dr. Anca, 351
Powell, Boone, 241, 270, 278, 340, 346
Powell, Dr. Mary M., 350
Prchal, Dr. Carol L., 365
Presbyterian Church, 55
Presbyterian Hospital, 271, 275
Preston Hollow, 143
Preston, Ann, 82-83
Price Neeley Medical Plastic Corp., 160
Priest, D., 292
"Problems of the Elbow, Wrist, and Hand" (Omer), 267
Prohibition, 106-107
Propst-Proctor, Dr. Sandra, 354
Pueblo, Mexico, 253-254
Puls Dr. Susan, 354

Q
Queen of Sheba Mine, 171
Quinlan, Dr. Elizabeth, 353
Quonochotaug Beach, 124

R
Raccoon River, 5
Railroad, 33, 40, 48, 51
Rangaswamy, Dr. Leela, 352
Ray, Dr. Suzanne, 355
Rea, Margaret, 88
Red Cross, 162-163
Red River, 38
Reflecto Sign Co., 159
Regan, Dr. Elizabeth, 357
Republic National Bank, 134
Reynosa, Mexico, 192
Rhode Island, 124

Rich, Dr. Margaret Mary, 354
Richter, Dr. Geraldine, 148, 352
Rio Grande City, TX, 32
Rio Grande River, 192
Rio Grande Valley, TX, 32-34, 36, 45-47, 50-51, 61, 75-76, 108, 128, 182, 191
Ripley, Dr. Margaret Jane, 356
Rivera, Diego, 169
Robbins, Martha, 337
Roberts Hospital, 344
Rochester, MN, 104, 267
Rochester, NY, 336
Rockefeller Medical College, 104
Rockwood, Dr. Charles A., 266
Rodin, Dr. Margaretha, 331
Rogers, Janis, 347
Rogers, Oakie, 243
Roosevelt, Eleanor, 158
Roosevelt, Franklin D., 86, 135-136
Rose, Dr. Roberta E., 353
Rothman, Dr. Diane M., 358
Roundy, "Let," 35
Roundy, Mattie, 35
Royal Opera, 190
Rubin, Dr. Cheryl, 364
Rudicel, Dr. Sally, 357
Russia, 331
Ruth Jackson Conference Center, 339
Ruth Jackson Library Fund, 277, 346
Ruth Jackson Orthopaedic Education Center, 277
Ruth Jackson Orthopaedic Society (RJOS), 321, 323-329, 331-338, 347
Ruth Jackson Research Foundation, 251-255, 262, 265, 269, 276-279, 284, 288, 294-295, 299, 327

Ruth Jackson Seminar in Orthopaedic Surgery, 341

S
S. H. Camp and Company, 185, 189
Sabanas, Dr. Alvina O., 147, 350
Sam Fordyce, TX, 48-50
San Antonio, TX, 39-40, 44, 151
San Diego, CA, 298, 329
San Francisco, CA, 13, 104, 335, 347
San Juan-Alamo school district, 51
Sanders, Dr. Melanie, 327
Sanders, Judy, 191, 193, 280-291
Sanders, Lorraine, 130-131, 133
Sanders Construction Co., 284, 287-289, 291
Sandruth Company, 281-285, 288, 294
Sanford, Dr. Brenda L., 356
Sarmiento, Dr. Augusto, 330
Scerpella, Dr. Tamara A., 365
Schafer, Dr. Michael, 330
Schlesinger, Dr. Iris E., 363
Schneider, Dr. Cynthia Ann, 356
Scopes trial, 69
Scottish Rite Hospital for Crippled Children, 120, 126-128, 130-131, 265, 342
Scottish Rites dormitory (SRD), 71, 77-78, 96
Scott's Drug Store, 271-272
Scovazzo, Dr. Mary L., 361
Scranton, IA, 6, 23-24, 27, 30, 35, 57, 59, 75
Scully, Dr. Thomas J., 330
Seaboard Air Line Railway Association, 180
Seale, Dr. Karen Sue, 354
Selective Service Act, 61
Shadowland Ballroom, 122
Shannon, Dr. Mary Ann, 324, 360

Sharp, Ralph, 186
Sharp, Ruth, 186
Sharpe, Ralph E., 253
She Came to the Valley, 48
Sherman, Dr. Mary, 300, 349
Sherwood, Dr. Penelope, 146, 349
Shields, Dr. Naomi N., 363
Shodding, Kate, 148
Shosone, CA, 171
Shreveport, LA, 327
Signoid Steel Strapping Corporation, 252, 278
Singleton, Virginia, 75
Sirna, Dr. Elizabeth, 361
Silverstein, Lewis, 184
Smallpox, 12
Smith, Alan, 251
Smith, Catherine, 251
Smith, Charles, 251
Smith, Dr. Angela Dorman, 358
Smith, Dr. Hubert Winston, 248-249, 251
Smith, Dr. Hugh, 230
Smith, Dr. Judith W., 364
Smith, James, 251
Smith, Stephen, 251
Smith-Hoefer, Dr. Elise, 357
Smoking, 7, 16-17, 39
Snow, C. P., 251
Solca, Dr. Patricia M., 365
South Africa, 4, 331
South Padre Island, TX, 347
Southern Medical Association, 134-135, 345
Southern Methodist University (SMU), 96, 142-143, 148, 152, 257

Southwestern Medical School. *See Also* University of Texas Medical School, 258, 260, 263-265, 275
Spain, 256
Specht, Dr. Linda H., 364
Sprague, Dr. Charles C., 260
St. Louis, MO, 90, 243-244
St. Paul's Hospital, 138, 141
Staiger, Dr. Linda F., 356
Stark, Dr. Liz A. Z., 363
Starr County, TX, 48, 50
State Fair Musicals, 170
State Medical Society (PA), 82
Stauffer, Dr. E. Shannon, 267
Stein, Dr. Ann C., 363
Steindler, Dr. Arthur, 116-117, 119-122, 232-234, 236, 264, 341
Stephens, Dr. H. D., 192
Stephens, Dr. Susan, 335
Stevens, Bobby "Governor," 62, 76
Stevens, Dr. Victoria, 358
Stockholm, Sweden, 190
Stone, Dr. Marvin, 267
Story, Jan, 164
Stovall, Roberta, 104
Suffrage, 65-66
Suffrage Association, 86
Sullivan, Dr. Joan, 365
Sullivan City, TX, 47-50
"Surgery for the Arthritic Knee: Pitfalls and Pratfalls" (Murray), 268
"Surgical Rehabilitation of the Hip and Knee" (Hungerford), 269
Sussman, Dr. Sharron, 360
Swank, Dr. Susan, 334

Sweden, 190, 193, 331, 344
Swiss Avenue, 105
Switzerland, 84
Syracuse, NY, 266, 268
Szalay, Dr. Elizabeth Ann, 356

T
Tanglewood Resort, 186
Tefft, Dr. Melvin, 267
Teitz, Dr. Carol Claire, 352
Tennessee, 230, 273, 330
Texas A&M University, 62
Texas Baptist Memorial Sanitarium, 94-95
Texas County Day School, 166
Texas Medical Association, 134
Texas Orthopaedic Association, 151, 242
Texas Power and Light Company, 292
Texas Scottish Rite Masonic Order, 109, 117
Texas Society for Crippled Children, 151, 158
Texas State Medical Association, 151
Texas Woman Magazine, 93
Thomas, Charles C., 230, 232
Thomas, Dr. Ruth Lourdes, 364
Thompson, Dr. Francesca, 334, 355
Thompson, Dr. Linda, 356
Thompson, Dr. Sandra J., 147, 324, 351
Three Point Two Ranch, 192
Tosi, Dr. Laura, 331, 338, 356
Trademark, 180-181, 183, 190
Treatment of Shoulder Problems" (Rockwood), 266
Treatment of the Cervical Spine, Shoulder, Arm Syndrome (Jackson), 230, 235-236
A Tribute to Ruth Jackson, 337
Triple C (Custom, Contract and Commercial), 170
Trojan Oil Company, 171

Trombino, Dr. Laura J., 365
Tru-Eze Manufacturing Company, Inc., 186-187, 194-98
Truman, Harry, 341
Tulane University, 90
Tullos, Dr. Hugh, 267
Tune, Melody, 143
Turtle Creek, 1, 40, 163, 168, 170, 251, 281, 289-291, 295, 297, 314, 320
"Twelve Outstanding Women in Texas" (1948), 70
"The Two Cultures " (Snow), 251

U
United Charities, 78
United States Army, 87
United States Children's Bureau, 158
United States Commissioner of Patents, 181
United States Congress, 44, 66
United States Constitution 19th Amendment, 65
United States Navy, 156, 271
United States Secretary of Labor, 158
University Hospitals, University of Iowa Department of Orthopaedic Surgery, 116, 119, 233
University of Arizona, 341
University of Chicago, 104, 122
University of Iowa, 63, 116, 233
University of Massachusetts, 322
University of Pennsylvania, 81
University of Rochester, 336
University of Texas at Austin, 2, 62, 63, 65, 67-73, 75-76, 78, 89-90, 96, 106, 248
University of Texas Health Scientist Center, 275

University of Texas Medical School. *See also* Southwestern Medical School, 253, 260, 263, 265, 275.
University of Vienna School of Medicine, 117
University Park City Hall, 143
University of Texas at Galveston, 90
Upsilon chapter. *See* Alpha Epsilon Iota
Upstate Medical Center, 268
USO, 163

V
Vaccination, 12
Van Geloven Lytle Dr. Francisca, 361
Van Hoosen, Bertha, 110-111
Van Winkle, Dr. Barbara, 361
Vandalia, TX, 282
Vanderbilt, Cornelius, 59
Venereal disease, 99
Vera Cruz, Mexico, 257
Victory B funds, 162
Victory Gardens, 163
Vienna, Austria, 117
Villagran, Alfonso Hernandez, Sr., 254-261
Villonodular synovitis, 253
Virginia, 327
Vitamin E, 193-194
Von Bernstorff, Johann Heinrich, 46
Von Stein, Dr. Diane, 358
Voytek, Dr. Anna, 361

W
Waco, TX, 39, 94, 300-301
Waldorf Astoria, 187
Walker, Dr. Carol A., 363
Walker, Dr. Janet, 331, 337, 361

Walton, R. O., 159
Walt Disney, 187
War, 4, 85
War Service Committee, 162
Ware, Dr. Leon, 295, 339-40, 343-346
Waring, Dr. Ruth M., 349
Warren, MI, 160
Washington, D. C., 46, 80, 158, 287, 331, 338, 347
Washington Township, IA, 5
Wasson, Pauline Bellcock, 10
Watkins, Butch, 174-75
Watkins, Dr. Margaret "Peg," 18, 100, 146, 154-156, 174, 271, 349
Watkins, Royal, 174
Watson, Jim, 290
Watson, Paulanna Jackson, 348
Watts, Dr. Hugh G., 267
Webb, Dr. Ernest, 68
Wells, Dr. Denise J., 363
Werner-Gren Center International Symposium, 190
Werntz, Dr. Joanne R., 360
Weslaco, TX, 258
West Texas, 140
Western Farm Land Company, 33
Western Orthopaedics Society, 167, 276-277, 298, 306
Westley, Dr. Elsie, 148, 151
Whiplash, 179-180
White House, 158
White Rock Lake, 144
White Rock Park, 143
White Wing doves, 49, 128, 182, 191, 296
White-Spunner, Dr. Susanne, 363
Who' Who in American Women, 283

Wichita Falls, TX, 289
Wild Horse Desert, 34
Wilhelm, Brett, 190, 199
Wilhelm, Enid, 190, 298
Wilhelm, Tru, 186-187, 189-190, 193-195, 198, 298, 306
Wilhelm, Brad, 190
Williams, Mattie, 163-164
Wilson, Woodrow, 44, 46
Winans, Dr. Henry M., 87
Winona Gardens, 282
Wintersteen, Dr. Virginia, 361
Wisconsin, 252
Wiss, Dr. Donald, 330
Witkin, Dr. Evelyn Davis, 355
Women
  at Baylor Medical College, 97-99
  and double standards, 97-99
  in early twentieth century, 6
  escorts for, 151
  faculty, 56
  fraternal organization for, 100, 105
  and homestead laws, 64
  and industrialization, 85
  liberation, 4, 65-66, 162
  loans available to, 134
  in media, 67
  network, 322
  as patients, 98-99
  and Ph.D. studies, 89, 146
  as physicians, 1-2, 80-87, 90-93, 110, 132, 145-148, 251, 301, 323-325, 328-338
  in pioneer times, 85
  as professionals, 147
  Steindler on, 118, 120

as surgeons, 109, 111
Women in Medicine (Lopate), 84, 114-115
"Women in Orthopaedics" (Horstmann), 333
Women in Service, 162
Women Medical College of Pennsylvania. *See* Female Medical College of Pennsylvania
Woods, Otto, 50
Worcester, MA, 110-113, 115-117, 119, 121, 123, 134, 322, 327
Works Progress Administration (WPA), 135-136
World War I, 44, 61, 85-86, 252
World War II, 86-89, 110, 162, 254
Wren Brace Shop, 178
Wright, Dr. John, 335
Wright, Dr. Judy, 335
Wynn, Dr. Audrea H., 363

X
Xalapa, Mexico, 257

Y
Yale University, 68, 235, 275
Yeakey, Mr., 185
Yellin, Adam, 198
Yellin, Arthur, 182, 185, 191-192, 196-197, 199
Yellin, Beatrice, 182, 185
Yellin, Louis, 179, 181-189, 191
"The Yellow Rose of Texas", 57
Young-Nguyen, Dr. Serena, 365
YWCA, 124

Z
Zembo, Dr. Michele M., 361
Zillmer, Dr. Debra A., 365

Zimmerman, Dr. Alfred, 46
Zonta Club, 148, 151, 162-163
Zuelzer, Dr. Wilhelm, 264-265

Made in the USA
San Bernardino, CA
26 November 2014